Pepys
AND THE
Navy

C.S. KNIGHTON

SUTTON PUBLISHING

First published in the United Kingdom in 2003 by
Sutton Publishing Limited · Phoenix Mill
Thrupp · Stroud · Gloucestershire · GL5 2BU

British Library Cataloguing in Publication Data
A catalogue record for this book is available from the British Library.

ISBN 0-7509-2972-3

Typeset in 11/14.5 pt Sabon.
Typesetting and origination by
Sutton Publishing Limited.
Printed and bound in England by
J.H. Haynes & Co. Ltd, Sparkford.

Contents

Preface

Pepys has been well served by his biographers, though in truth he did a good deal of their work for them. Seventy years ago, when the 300th anniversary of his birth was celebrated, there was still a feeling that his professional achievements were inadequately represented in the mass of writing about him. Now that we mark the 300th year of his death, his serious side is much more widely appreciated. The raffish *bon viveur* of the Diary will always have more appeal than the industrious naval administrator, but at least there are now several balanced accounts of his life. This, therefore, is an unbalanced one, leaving most of his personal history aside, and concentrating on his work for the Navy. All books about him deal with that, of course, but none has done so exclusively since 1920, when J.R. Tanner published four lectures on aspects of Pepys's administration. Tanner's writing was based primarily on the naval papers which Pepys left, along with the rest of his library, to Magdalene College, Cambridge. He edited a great many of these MSS (though but a fraction of those which survive there and elsewhere), and was principally responsible for establishing Pepys's place in the modern historiography of the Navy. More recent scholars have been sceptical of relying so heavily on Pepys's own archive for an understanding of the Restoration Navy. Account is taken of these reservations here, though this is again a view from the Pepys Library, and deliberately so. Some of it has been written there at Pepys's own desk, surrounded by the books which are themselves a part of the story.

In the general narrative of Pepys's life I make no claim to novelty in fact or interpretation, and sources are not cited for what is well established. My debt to the work of Tanner, Sir Arthur Bryant,

Richard Ollard, and now Claire Tomalin, is considerable, and is here acknowledged *passim*. I follow a broadly chronological sequence, but this is not a biography. For some, no doubt, it will seem to be all the dull bits of Pepys gummed together. The intention is, rather, to give those whose primary interest is Pepys himself a more concentrated view of his professional inheritance and activities, and to allow naval historians to follow his career undiluted.

Dates are given in Old Style, though reckoning the Year of Grace from 1 January.

I am indebted primarily to the Master and Fellows of Magdalene College, Cambridge, for having long enjoyed the privilege of working in and for the Pepys Library. More particularly I am grateful for the hospitality which has enabled me to complete this book in the most appropriate surroundings. At Magdalene I have special reasons to thank the President, Professor E. Duffy, the Pepys Librarian, Dr R. Luckett, and the Assistant Librarian, Mrs J.T. Fitzsimons. I am also obliged to the staff at the Public Record Office, the British Library, the Ashmolean Museum and the Bodleian Library at Oxford, and Cambridge University Library, who have assisted my research. Mr Ollard has kindly encouraged my work, and I am grateful to him for sending me a copy of his biography of Sandwich. Mrs Tomalin has helped me from much error, and I particularly thank her for giving me an advance copy of her biography of Pepys. Professor N.A.M. Rodger kindly read my text and usefully corrected some errors; he and Dr S.L. Adams were good enough to send me drafts of forthcoming publications. Professor D.M. Loades and Mr T.H. Wilson have been valued colleagues in previous Pepysian ventures. Above all, my work is sustained by the memory of the late Robert Latham, who introduced me to Pepys's world.

Needless to say, the imperfections of the book are my own special contribution.

Cambridge, Michaelmas 2002

ONE

The Calling

'Have sight of Proteus rising from the sea
Or hear old Triton blow his wreathed horn.'
Wordsworth, 'The World is too much with us'

At about noon on 26 May 1659, within sight of the battlements of Elsinore, Pepys enters British naval history. He was arriving aboard the ketch *Hind* with letters for his cousin Edward Montagu, commander of the Baltic fleet. For Pepys this was no more than an extension of the work he had been doing since he came down from Cambridge four years earlier, as one of Montagu's household officials. On this occasion he was a messenger only, returning the next day with packets for England. It was undoubtedly the first time he had been afloat in anything larger than a river boat, and we can be sure that the experience interested and excited him. He would have picked up a smattering of naval terminology; it was not until the following year that he had serious occasion to do so. For the present he was probably more interested in the complex political requirements of Montagu's mission: to prevent a war between Swedes and Danes which would imperil England's naval supplies, co-operating to that end with the recent and probable future enemy the Dutch, but with the possibility of conflict among any permutation of those four powers. What he did not know was that Montagu was beginning those secret contacts with the exiled royalists from which would develop his key role in the restoration of the monarchy.[1] There, rather than in the immediate round of Baltic diplomacy, lay the seeds of Pepys's naval career.

There was nothing in Pepys's ancestry or upbringing to suggest that the sea would be his professional concern for the next thirty

1

years, and an abiding interest for the whole of his remaining life. The Pepyses were countrymen, long settled in the Fenland north-west of Cambridge; several had made good livings through administration and the law, and Pepys's uncle owned a small estate at Brampton in Huntingdonshire. Pepys's father, a younger son, had moved to London and set up as a tailor in Salisbury Court off Fleet Street, where Samuel had been born in 1633. These modest circumstances were easily offset by his natural intelligence, sharpened at the great city school of St Paul's and then at Magdalene College, Cambridge. He had also spent some time at Huntingdon Grammar School, and it was probably there that he first befriended his cousin Edward, the son of his great-aunt Paulina's marriage to Sir Sidney Montagu in 1618. The Montagus were local magnates, and the connexion had been a considerable social achievement for the Pepys family. Sidney's son Edward, like his cousin and namesake the Earl of Manchester, became a commander of the parliamentary forces during the Civil War; he had kept out of public life during the King's trial and execution, but accepted political office under the republic. Cromwell made him a Councillor of State and, in January 1656, joint General-at-Sea with Blake for an expedition against Spain. Although he had even less experience of naval affairs than did Pepys at the start of his career, he contrived to return home laden with plunder in the high Elizabethan fashion. The mission to the Baltic in 1659 was his first major independent command, undertaken in the name of the Protectorate as continued by Cromwell's son Richard, to whom Montagu was loyal. Richard's fall and the return of the Rump regime in May hastened, if it did not initiate, his conversion to royalism. The new government placed the Admiralty in the hands of those who had run it in the early days of the republic, with whom Montagu had little sympathy. He managed to retain control of his force and bring it home in September, adroitly avoiding involvement in a premature royalist rising, and then retired to his seat at Hinchingbrooke.

Pepys meanwhile had been managing Montagu's London household, from where on 20 October he sent word of the latest turn of events; the Rump having tried to dismiss the principal army commanders, had itself been ousted and replaced by a new Committee of Safety; five civil and five military commissioners had just been nominated. This was simply a military coup, and deeply unpopular; Lucy Hutchinson would recall it as an 'insolent usurpation' as a result of which 'the whole nation began to set their eyes upon the king beyond the sea'. Pepys reported to the same effect on 22 October, though he referred to Charles II more prosaically as 'King of Scotts'. Opposition to the regime was strong in the Navy; the commander in the Downs, John Lawson, was among those who signed a remonstrance against the military government; the garrison at Portsmouth revolted, and made common cause with a part of Lawson's fleet. Pepys had all this from the Navy Treasurer, Richard Hutchinson, by 8 December, and could tell Montagu that the greatest worry in Whitehall was what Lawson might do next.[2]

What he did was stage the only naval coup in modern British history; on 14 December he left station and brought his fleet into the Thames. On the following day Pepys heard that proclamation was made for the return of parliamentary government. Lawson's ships successfully intimidated the City and the army command, and the Rump returned to its chamber on Boxing Day. Such, then, was the condition of the state on 1 January 1660 when Pepys began the Diary which he would keep for the next nine and a half years, and which would ensure his posthumous celebrity. Lawson was still, as he says, in the River; but General Monck, whom Pepys supposed still to be in Scotland with his army, had on that same New Year's Day crossed the Tweed. Pepys shared the general hope that Monck's arrival in the south would result in a more representative parliamentary regime. He had an informed interest in these political developments, because in addition to his work for Montagu, he served an Exchequer official, and was therefore an indirect employee of the successive regimes. He could not know how closely his own advancement hinged on developments he now began to chronicle.[3]

Lawson, naturally enough, had been high in favour with the restored Rump, but was distrusted by the larger number of members whom Monck brought back into the House in February. Montagu, however, now had friends there, and on 23 February was elected to the Council of State. By the 29th it was known that Lawson was to be outranked in the naval hierarchy by the commissioning of Generals-at-Sea for the summer guard: Monck and Montagu, whose appointments were confirmed on 2 March. Pepys was summoned to meet Montagu in Westminster Hall on the following day, along with some others who had been in the Baltic in 1659. It was three days later, in the garden of his Whitehall lodgings, that Montagu asked Pepys if he 'could without too much inconvenience go to sea as his Secretary' and invited him to think it over. At the same time Montagu cautiously began to talk about the return of the King; something to which he was now committed, but which he could not yet openly acknowledge. He said he needed a secretary whom he could trust; so perhaps he was now doubtful of John Creed, who served him in this capacity in 1659 and who was (at this time) a committed Puritan. What Pepys was now offered was not a permanent post, and acceptance might jeopardize his Exchequer place; it would certainly disrupt his domestic life. So think about it he did. The very next day he heard he was to inherit his uncle's country estate; the world seemed to be opening up for him. He ran into a naval acquaintance, Captain Philip Holland, at a tavern in New Palace Yard; the captain explained that Pepys should take half a dozen servants aboard, pay them a pittance and pocket the difference. This sordid consideration (which in any case remained a fantasy) was not the deciding factor; nevertheless, the following day Pepys accepted Montagu's invitation. Ever careful, he arranged a locum at the Exchequer and a safe house for his young wife. The only annoyance was learning that Montagu was, after all, taking Creed as deputy treasurer (the post normally combined with secretary).[4]

Pepys and Creed were of an age, and shared many accomplishments and intellectual or aesthetic interests; naturally they disliked each other a great deal. Creed was more polished socially and academically, but Pepys would surpass him as an administrator and in their master's favour. Their paths intertwined professionally for many years, and they sustained an uneasy friendship. Pepys had wanted the deputy treasurership for himself in 1660 (not merely that Creed should not have it), but his frustration was soon forgotten in the preparations for his voyage, and with the exciting discovery that money would be pressed into his hands by those seeking appointments in the fleet. The first he received was 'half a piece' on behalf of an aspirant chaplain; this kind of thing Pepys would come to deprecate as bribery (for future favour), and quite different from gold and silver he received for issuing Captain Robert Williamson with his commission, which was a gratuity (for services performed). With some of this ready cash Pepys was able to smarten his wardrobe, and to buy a sword; charmingly he also bought a telescope as a present for Montagu. Then on 23 March he took a barge from Tower wharf, and went aboard the *Swiftsure* anchored at Long Reach. This was temporary accommodation until Montagu's former and favoured flagship, *Naseby*, was made ready. After seeing Montagu come aboard to a salute from the assembled ships, Pepys went down to his cabin, and began writing. At first there were orders for immediate business to be drafted, but after a couple of days he was making out a list of all the ships in the fleet, their numbers of men and guns. He had found his billet.[5]

Both Generals now wanted the return of the monarchy; Montagu had been so disposed since the beginning of the year, but Monck had only committed himself in the previous week. They were, however, far from certain of support in the rest of the fleet. Lawson, now their Vice-Admiral, again played a key part. He had also been turned by royalist agents, but he had a following whose opinions remained hostile to the restoration. Pepys, who was getting to know the sea officers, heard of 'a great whispering of some of the Vice-admiralls captains' on the evening of March 29. Lawson defused the potential mutiny, and Montagu then proceeded to replace a number of Lawson's more extreme adherents with men of his own persuasion. His care, Pepys noted (1 April), was 'to put by as much of the Anabaptists as he can'. Most prominent of these was George Dakins (Pepys calls him 'Dekings') of the *Worcester*, whom Montagu first thought to send on a minor posting to the Mediterranean; when that mission was upgraded, Montagu manoeuvred Dakins out of his command altogether. By the time the Council had approved this (17 April), Montagu had already told Pepys to make out a commission for Robert Blake to captain the *Worcester*. Another key appointment was of Roger Cuttance to be flag captain of the *Naseby*, to which Montagu had transferred on 30 March. Pepys and Cuttance quickly struck up a friendship, lubricated by wine and oysters, and more usefully spent in a little nautical education. Cuttance would remain a favourite of Montagu's, and therefore of Pepys's, until the scandal over prize goods which touched them all in 1665. On this voyage Pepys first met many of those with whom he would shortly have considerable dealings. Others were at least glimpsed; while the fleet was still in the River two of the new Admiralty Commissioners came aboard, William Penn and George Thomson – the one to be Pepys's close colleague and neighbour for a decade, the other a formidable opponent in the enquiry which Pepys and Penn would face after the Second Dutch War.[6]

Political developments were now awaited. While Pepys had still been in Westminster the Long Parliament had finally agreed to scuttle itself, and in its place a Convention was to assemble on 25 April. Montagu would be elected, though in the event he needed no seat in Commons. On 9 April the fleet sailed round the North Foreland and came to anchor in the Downs, giving Pepys his first sight of the French coast. Montagu immediately contacted the King, now at Breda; over the next weeks the comings and goings proliferated, but discretion and subterfuge remained necessary. When one royalist agent, Henry Norwood, was given passage back to Holland on 21 April, Montagu told Pepys to keep the matter out of the log. A week later 'all the world knew' who Montagu's visitors were. On the 29th Pepys heard that the King had sent the newly assembled Convention the conciliatory terms (the Declaration of Breda), on the basis of which the Convention voted for the return of the King on 2 May. Charles had sent a copy of the Declaration to the Generals, asking for it to be published throughout the fleet, which he called 'the Wall of the Kingdom'.

A council of war was duly held aboard *Naseby* next day, at which Pepys read out the Declaration and the King's covering letter. He repeated this performance on the quarter deck and then on the other ships, to resounding cheers. None of the officers had spoken against the Declaration, but Pepys rightly suspected that many remained disaffected. The seamen he thought loyal to a man; in fact their enthusiasm had much to do with the promise that their unpaid wages would be met by the incoming regime. Diplomatically, the wraps were off, and Montagu could show Pepys letters he had received from the King and the Duke of York. Only now did Pepys fully understand the extent of the negotiations since the fleet had been in the Downs, in the logistics of which he had been involved. The King's letter to the Generals and the resolution of the council of war were published over Pepys's counter-signature, and the government newsletters also borrowed from one of Pepys's despatches.[7]

The fleet in the Downs had become the Royal Navy, and royal banners and other trappings were required to mark the fact. Pepys drafted the Generals' reply to the King on 9 May, the day after Charles had been proclaimed in London. It was obvious that the fleet would now sail to Holland to fetch the King home, but there was continuing debate about protocol. Monck wanted Charles to be brought in before the political mood changed, and Montagu (perhaps keen to take centre stage) decided to sail for Holland without waiting for instructions from London. Lawson and the Rear Admiral, Richard Stayner, had disagreed, but rank prevailed, and on the morning of 12 May the fleet, thirty ships in all, weighed anchor and set course for Scheveningen. Pepys went ashore at The Hague on the 14th, wanting to pay his respects to the nine-year-old Prince of Orange. This he did late that evening, and found Prince William 'a very pretty boy'. William would lose his looks, but he would gain three kingdoms and, among other consequences, destroy Pepys's career.[8]

There was disappointment when the King failed to visit the fleet as expected on 16 May (Montagu was reduced to spending the afternoon playing ninepins on deck with Pepys). But the next evening Pepys wheedled his way into the Mauritzhuis, where the Court was staying, and kissed the hands of the King and the Duke of York, their sister the Princess Dowager of Orange, and their aunt

Queen Elizabeth of Bohemia. The Duke had just been confirmed as Lord High Admiral of England, a post he had notionally held since childhood. This rather deflated Montagu, and Pepys found himself with little to do. However, a visit from the Duke and his brother Henry (Duke of Gloucester) aboard the flagship on 22 May made work for everyone; Pepys was allowed to fire one of the guns, and nearly lost an eye in the process. The next day the King and the Royal Family came aboard *Naseby*, promptly made the *Royal Charles*. The other ships which embarrassingly recalled the Civil War and republic were renamed at the same time; this might more tactfully have been done when the royal insignia was furnished, but possibly the tradition of the sea had discouraged the move. As they sailed for home, Pepys heard the King speak of his wartime adventures, much of which could only now be revealed. Twenty years later, when the stories had grown a little, Charles gave Pepys the authorised version with a view to publication. On the present voyage Pepys's only business with the King was to draft and present a document for his signature. He had some talk with the Duke, who addressed him by name and made what can only have been a conventional promise of future favour. In fact it was the start of a remarkable working relationship between prince and commoner, tarnished only in its final moment.[9]

Dover was reached on 26 May. A brigantine had been prepared to bring the King ashore, but he and his brothers chose to go with Montagu in his barge. Pepys also landed in royal company, having shared a boat with one of Charles's famous dogs (whose incontinence prompted a tortuous reflection on the humanity of kings). Pepys's account of the Restoration voyage vividly demonstrates that the King had already developed that easy manner and accessibility which would become legendary. He had to a large measure the special royal talent for focusing his full attention on a slight encounter. It is sometimes thought that the royal 'walkabout' was a modern invention, but no monarch walked about more than Charles II. Unfortunately, aboard the *Royal Charles* he walked into a beam, and Pepys arranged for the place to be marked in gold with the royal cipher. This apart, there were no accidents, and Montagu was 'almost transported with joy' that it was so. A more tangible joy was the Garter, which he received after the King had left for London. Another royal bounty was the promise of a month's pay to the thirty ships which had brought the King back; Pepys reckoned this at £6,538 ('I wish we had the money'). £8,000 was in fact at once provided, and though this was only a fraction of the arrears then due, it bought the seamen's loyalty. Pepys's personal finances were also gratifyingly buoyant; he had been given an advance of £30, and he now found himself worth £100. Even better, Montagu had promised to carry him along: 'We must have a little patience and we will rise together.' For neither was their patience strained.[10]

Once back in Westminster, the business of paying off the fleet brought Pepys frequently to Whitehall Palace, where the Admiralty Office was newly established. Montagu, who had been appointed Great Master of the Wardrobe, also now lodged in the palace. It was there on 18 June that Montagu first told Pepys that he was looking to get him the Clerkship of the Acts, that being the secretaryship to the Navy Board. As yet neither the Board nor the Clerkship existed, having been displaced by other administrative arrangements during the Commonwealth, but the King intended to restore the previous system. A few days later Montagu said he could promise Pepys the job, but it was not yet settled. Among other contenders was Thomas Turner, who as Clerk-General of the Navy Office for the past fourteen years was to some extent the in-post official. He had the backing of Monck, but Montagu politely observed that he would not meddle in army appointments, so Monck should allow him to make those he wanted in the Navy. On his own Turner lacked the drive and means to advance his candidacy; he would offer Pepys £150 for a share in the office, but someone else had already promised Pepys £500 to stand down altogether. Another bidder tempted Pepys with £1,000, though this was still short of his asking price of four years' purchase (£1,400). In the end he bought Turner off with £50 and a minor place in the new administration, and would help him in other ways in the future. It was from Turner that Pepys acquired one of the most notable naval MSS which now adorn his library.[11]

A technically more awkward rival was the surviving previous holder of the office, Thomas Barlow, who Pepys learned to his dismay was still alive and, worse, 'coming up to town to look after his place' (29 June). Barlow's job had been swept aside when Parliament abolished the Navy Board in September 1642; but now that institution was to be revived, might not his 1639 patent hold good? Here, with the contending claims of the incumbent Turner and the dispossessed Barlow, the State's servant and the King's, was the problem of the Restoration settlement in microcosm. Those who had sided with Charles I in war and Charles II in exile now expected their recompense, but the King could not hope to repay all their services. He had in any case not been restored by the Cavaliers, but by his erstwhile enemies. A balance had to be exercised in the distribution of offices and honours, though it was weighted heavily in favour of the Restoration's chief architects and their clients. Neither Pepys's brief service with the fleet nor his duties in the Exchequer gave him any large claim to promotion. It was simply his good fortune to be associated at this moment with Montagu, who was himself created Earl of Sandwich. On 4 July an Order in Council revoked the authority of the existing Admiralty Commissioners, and nominated the members of the new Navy Board. Pepys was there designated Clerk of the Acts, and instructed to take possession of all books, papers and other effects of the former Commissioners. When Pepys joined his colleagues on the following day, he was still worried about Barlow. He was reassured that even if the old man established a financial interest, he would not exercise the office in person. Pepys eventually agreed to pay Barlow a pension of £100 a year out of the £350 salary which was assigned to him by a further order of 4 July. All the Navy Board salaries were increased handsomely from the former rates (the Clerk's had been £180), so Pepys could well afford to be generous. He did not actually learn what his salary was to be until 7 July; characteristically he went off at once and bought a couple of fine engravings (after Rubens), then returned to the Office to begin listing the documents which were now his responsibility.[12]

The post to which Pepys was formally appointed by letters patent of 13 July was still officially known as Clerk of the King's Ships, and as such Pepys could claim succession to the oldest administrative job in the Navy. At first he seems to have had no interest in the position except as a source of income and advancement. Even later, when he planned to write a history of the Navy, he knew little of his distant predecessors. He would surely have been delighted by the suggestion that he might trace his office to William de Wrotham, Archdeacon of Taunton, who was styled *custos galliarum* in the reign of King John. However, it is now thought that naval administration properly derives from the Lord Admiral's secretaries, and that the first Clerks of the King's Ships can be identified in the mid-fourteenth century. The medieval Clerk was a rather lowly figure, whose responsibilities and status fluctuated according to the requirements of individual kings. He remained a financial officer, receiving funds from the Exchequer for the material requirements of the ships in dock. In times of high naval activity he might find himself fitting out an invasion force, but he was always a civilian. There was little for Henry IV's Clerk John Elmerton to do, since the Royal Navy was down to two ships. Even when the fleet expanded to thirty-six under Henry V, and the Clerk, William Soper, was a man of substance, only one additional official was needed. In Henry VI's reign the Navy and its administration were wound down completely, and the Clerkship became a sinecure. A new era opened with the appointment of Thomas Rogers by Edward IV in 1480. Rogers had been at sea as purser and master, and would have far wider remit than previous Clerks, hiring ships and appointing officers in addition to custody of *matériel*. He managed to retain office through the reigns of Edward V and Richard III, and into that of Henry VII. He also seems to have been the first Clerk of the Ships whom Pepys could have named, though not until many years later when one of his own clerks transcribed a document of 1482 into Pepys's collection of naval history.[13]

Pepys was confident that the 'first establishment of the Royal Navy' was owed to Henry VIII, but was hazy about the details. These are a good deal clearer to us, although the interpretation is sharply divided. David Loades has argued that with the Clerkship of Robert Brigandyne (1495–1523) 'the story of Tudor naval administration really begins'. According to N.A.M. Rodger, Henry failed to establish 'any sort of administrative structure for the fleet he rapidly built up' and matters 'remained rudimentary for the great part of his reign'. Brigandyne's duties were largely confined to Portsmouth, and marine affairs were handled on an *ad hoc* basis by officers of the royal household and others. Professor Rodger finds more significance in the building of storehouses at Erith and Deptford in 1512–13, which for the first time gave the Navy a roof over its head. A new post of Comptroller was created in 1512, but it was the keeper of the storehouses, William Gonson, who had become the leading naval official at the time of his death in 1544. By then four further offices had come into being: Master of Naval Ordnance, Lieutenant (or Vice-Admiral), Treasurer, Surveyor and Rigger. The French war of Henry VIII's last years occasioned the more formal tenure of these offices. On 24 April 1546 individual patents were delivered to the Master of Ordnance, Lieutenant, Treasurer, Comptroller, Surveyor, and Clerk, and to another unspecified official for 'marine causes'. Although no corporate body was specifically erected, these instruments are held to mark the emergence of what was already spoken of as 'the Admiralty' or 'the Council for Marine Causes'. Various other names came into use before the institution was finally dissolved in 1832: in full dress 'the Principal Officers and Commissioners of His (or Her) Majesty's Navy'; more simply though confusingly 'the Navy Office' or 'the Officers of the Navy', but usually 'the Navy Board'. The several patents of April 1546 are therefore the 'establishment' which Pepys wished to identify.[14]

Two important developments quickly followed. On 18 June 1550 further letters patent, now in the name of Edward VI, appointed Edward Baeshe as 'Surveyor General of Victuals for the King's Ships and Marine Affairs', to work under the direction of the Lord Admiral or the Navy Officers. It was a post which Pepys would reinvent for himself in 1665. Baeshe's thirty-seven years tenure has left ample records, some of which would be copied into Pepys's own collection. The Navy Board's overall functions were defined by an order of Queen Mary's Privy Council on 8 January 1557, which decreed an annual £14,000 to support the building and repairing of ships, material provisions of all kind, and the wages and food of the seamen. Mary is not usually regarded as one of the Navy's founders, but in the long term the establishment of this regular funding (the 'ordinary') was more important than anything her father had done.[15]

Despite all this burgeoning bureaucracy, the Navy Officers of the latter sixteenth century were often active sea commanders, and it was generally in this capacity that Pepys would know of them. While he recalled approvingly the appointment of Hawkins and Drake ('two plain tarpaulins') to flag commands in 1588, he probably never knew that Hawkins might have been one of his own predecessors. Hawkins had obtained a reversionary grant of the Clerkship in 1567; he never took it up, but sat on the Navy Board as Treasurer from 1578 to his death. His colleague there as Clerk of the Acts from 1580–8, William Borough, was the author of a popular textbook on navigation. Though Pepys acquired this and read it, he may not have realised that 'Burrows' the author was the same man as 'William Burrough' or 'Borrows' associated with Hawkins in the administration, and also the 'Mr Burroughs' whom Drake condemned to death in 1587. Borough was Vice-Admiral in the fleet which famously sabotaged the preparing Armada at Cadiz. Borough, aboard the *Golden Lion*, became detached from the fleet in circumstances which Drake interpreted as mutiny. Borough survived, albeit losing (as a modern commentator nicely expresses it) 'the dignity expected of a member of the Navy Board and Clerk of the Ships'.[16]

With the Gonson dynasty, prominent in naval administration through three generations, Pepys would have a surer link. William Gonson's son Benjamin had been named Clerk of the Ships in 1545, but did not actually join the Board until appointed Treasurer in 1549, as which he served until 1577. His great-granddaughter married Pepys's friend and colleague John Evelyn, who inherited many of Gonson's office records. Pepys was shown one such 'Lieger' in 1665, and (in the predatory manner perfected by the late Queen Mary) admired it so much that Evelyn had to give it to him. Pepys later acquired, seemingly by the same means, many other volumes of Elizabethan naval accounts. Although Pepys's primary interest in these papers was antiquarian, they could serve a contemporary purpose. When the Navy Treasurer's accounts were under parliamentary scrutiny in 1670, Pepys was able to score a point by citing one of the Elizabethan ledgers he had acquired.[17]

It was not until Pepys had been Clerk of the Acts for half a year that he heard something of his predecessors from the then Comptroller, Robert Slingsby. It pleased him to learn of Sir Peter Buck, who had succeeded Benjamin Gonson's son (also Benjamin) as Clerk of the Acts in 1600. Pepys was 'not a little proud' to hold a post which had been occupied by a knight, and he persuaded himself that the same honour might soon be his. It was indeed true that most of his colleagues at the Board had titles, but the Clerk was always the junior member; Buck had benefited from James I's lavish way with honours, and he would be the only Clerk of the Acts ever knighted. In other respects he was not a good role-model. A better one was Sir John Coke, whose prominence in Jacobean naval administration has won him praise as 'the Samuel Pepys of his day'. On seeing some of Coke's papers, Pepys was impressed that 'the order that was observed in the Navy then, above what it is now, is very observable'. Coke was the leading figure in the Commission appointed in 1618, which not only made immediate reforms, but superseded the normal Navy Board for a decade. This second Jacobean Commision would be Pepys's precedent and pattern for the Special Commission which he introduced in 1686–8 at the high point of his career.[18]

The specific functions of the Navy Officers were defined in the early years of Elizabeth I's reign, and again in a state paper of 1617. A more substantial set of instructions was issued by Lord Admiral Buckingham, of which the Pepys Library holds one of the two MS texts. From Buckingham's death until the appointment of the Earl of Northumberland in 1638, the Admiralty was in commission. Northumberland issued his own instructions in 1640, which would be the model for those which the Duke of York published in 1662, by which the Navy Board would be governed until its dissolution by William IV. The pre-Civil War routine was also set out by Sir William Monson, who described the Navy Officers as 'the conduit pipes' through whom the Lord High Admiral's commands descend 'to all other inferior officers and ministers'. To Pepys, Northumberland's regulations had already acquired the solemn authority of age; they were the 'ancient Instructions', to which the Navy had happily returned after two decades of alternative management.[19]

During the Civil War and Commonwealth naval administration operated through a number of agencies appointed by Parliament and the successive republican regimes. The process began with the creation of a parliamentary naval finance committee in August 1641. In the summer of 1642 the King lost physical control of his entire fleet, and Parliament appointed its own Navy and Admiralty Commissions. The former comprised six professional and six civilian members, and did not sustain the old Board's separation of duties. William Batten, who had been Surveyor in the old Board, was continued in that part (though in fact he was too busy at sea); and, since someone had to keep the records, one of the Commissioners acted as Clerk. No Comptroller was appointed, and after 1652 the Surveyorship lapsed. Although formal distinction between Admiralty and Navy continued, several individuals belonged to both Commissions; some also sat on various related committees. Secretarial resources, too, were shared, and the archives became inter-mingled. Understandably the separate functions of these several bodies were and have been confused.[20]

Pepys was not overmuch concerned with these distinctions; he commonly referred to the naval management of 'the late times', embracing all the administrative devices of Commonwealth and Protectorate. 'Late times' was itself no whimsical understatement, but a careful euphemism for the whole unsettling period from the breakdown of royal government in 1641 to its recovery in 1660. The war itself did not yet have a name: when in 1669 Pepys submitted a background paper which referred cautiously to 'the rupture between the King and the Parliament', the Duke of York asked him to change it to 'the beginning of the late Rebellion'. This, as James accurately observed, was when the Navy 'was put out of its old good course into that of a Commission'. Pepys would be irritated by those who viewed the naval administration of those days with nostalgic reverence ('as historians do of the primitive times in reference to the church'). In general terms he conceded that his predecessors left 'many things worthy imitation', and acknowledged the obligations personal and professional which he owed to them. Robert Blackborne, who had been Secretary to the Admiralty and Navy Commissions, and who but for his Puritan leanings might well have been made Clerk of the Acts, was generous with advice when the post went to Pepys. In retirement Pepys judged that under Richard Hutchinson, the Navy Treasury was 'never . . . better managed, or with more credit or satisfaction to the service'. But in particulars he would always defend the record of the restored Navy Board against that of the preceding commissions. The need to do so became acute after the Second Dutch War (1664–7), when the incumbent naval administration was compared unfavourably with its predecessor in the militarily more successful war of 1652–4.[21]

Pepys made detailed investigation of the records. Figures he compiled for the overall costs of the First Dutch War retain their value in modern analysis, and show much the same proportion of national expenditure as in the Second War. To Pepys's more immediate purpose he was able to demonstrate his generation's better economy – to the tune of £171,185 in the first year of the respective wars. He showed that several practices for which he and his colleagues were criticised – the issuing of credit notes to suppliers and of promissory tickets to seamen – were resorted to in the First War. Even so there had then been more money about; in consequence the republic had been able to raise seamen's pay in 1653, and impressment had been less necessary (or at least less complained of) than in the 1660s. The reliability of their payments gave the Commonwealth Commissioners a credit rating which their Restoration successors lacked, obliging them to 'hunt . . . abroad' in making contracts. Conversely, where some duties (such as auditing storekeepers' accounts) were indeed overlooked in the heat of the Second War, it was shown that similar corners had been cut in the First War without impeding the satisfactory operation of the fleet. Pepys does not trouble to make the elementary point that the republican government had the more money because it took more. The princes he served from 1660 to 1689 were paupers by comparison, and Pepys's whole career in the Navy was conditioned by the fact.[22]

TWO

Colleagues and Commodities

'Some really startling decision by the Board to reorganise the shore side of the Navy . . . would have an electrical effect on everyone.'
Admiral Sir Guy Grantham, 11 October 1955
[*Br. Naval Documents*, p. 1014]

The Navy Board as reconstituted on 4 July 1660 comprised the four main officials (Treasurer, Comptroller, Surveyor and Clerk of the Acts), together with three Extra Commissioners (Lord Berkeley, Sir William Penn, and Peter Pett). Pett was resident at Chatham dockyard, and other Out-Commissioners would later be appointed for Harwich and Portsmouth. The number of Commissioners without portfolio, as Penn and Berkeley were at the outset, would vary from time to time. In order to appreciate the junior status Pepys initially held, and his achievement in rising very rapidly from it, it is helpful to look in some detail at the careers of his original colleagues.

John, Lord Berkeley of Stratton, from the Somerset branch of the prominent West Country family, had commanded royalist forces in the Civil War. From 1648 he was in the service of the Duke of York, whose own military service in the armies of France then Spain he encouraged and shared. He annoyed the rest of the émigré court, but retained the Duke's friendship, and his appointment to the Navy Board is adequately explained by that. He was among those whom Pepys sourly classified as 'Brought into the Navy for want of other ways of gratification', and it is fair to say that of the newly appointed Commissioners he had the least acquaintance with naval affairs, Pepys not excepted. In fact Berkeley received much additional gratification, as Steward of the Duke's household and an

18

associate in his master's commercial interests. His public career would take him to Ireland as Lord Lieutenant (1670–2). He had played little part in the Navy Board, and by January 1665 had sold his place there to Sir Thomas Harvey for £3,000. He had not endeared himself much to Pepys, because of hostility to Sandwich and to Thomas Hayter, Pepys's Quaker clerk. Once Berkeley had left the Navy Board he was among those who drew unfavourable comparisons with the Commonwealth administration (of which he can have had no personal experience); more predictably he supported the appointment of gentlemen as commanders. Pepys concurred in Sandwich's view that Berkeley was 'very ordinary . . . as to parts and experience', and voiced a common suspicion that not all of his martial anecdotes were authentic. He later acquired a copy of Berkeley's posthumously published *Memoirs*, and several papers documenting his early career.[1]

Sir George Carteret was another Cavalier of impeccable credentials, from a family which had long been the foremost on the island of Jersey. His was, however, a junior branch, and he had to find his own living in the Navy. He was Vice-Admiral in the expedition which briefly triumphed over the corsairs of Salé in 1637. This was described by John Dunton in a book which Pepys admired enough to buy twice, though it has since been found 'artless and misleading'. Carteret returned to the North African coast in the following year, and has left a journal of his proceedings. His years afloat scarcely justify Clarendon's friendly lay opinion that Carteret was 'as good, if not the best seaman of England', but they usefully prepared him the administrative posts he subsequently held. In 1639 he was given reversion to the Comptrollership, to which he succeeded in 1641. During the tussle over naval commands in the summer of 1642, Carteret was invited to serve as deputy to the designated *de facto* admiral, the Earl of Warwick. The King, in forbidding Carteret to accept, further weakened his own control of the fleet, and so contributed to his altogether losing it. At the start of the Civil War Carteret served the King on land, returning to Jersey in 1643. He liberated the island from English occupation, and held it until 1651. He received the Prince of Wales there in 1646, and sheltered him again, as King, in 1649–50. These events and Carteret's part in them are featured in MSS which Pepys acquired. Carteret had been given a knighthood and a baronetcy for his services, and also an island in Chesapeake Bay, Virginia, which he called it after his existing territory. He failed to establish his title there, and it would be to another, larger, access of North American real estate that in 1664 he gave the enduring name of New Jersey. From 1651 to 1660 he shared the royalist exile in a variety of diplomatic and military functions. Charles I had designated him Vice-Chamberlain of the Household, a post which Charles II made substantive on the day after he returned to his capital in 1660. His appointment to the Treasurership of the Navy (4 July 1660) was quickly followed by admission to the Privy Council (11 July), and reflects the high personal esteem with which he was held by the King. Carteret's accent amused smarter people, and his imperfect education upset Pepys. He had no special capability for the complexities of public finance, from which he would eventually be obliged to withdraw. Pepys was not alone in thinking that Carteret's accounting revealed 'perverse ignorance'. Even so, he believed him capable of colluding in a complicated scam run by the Navy paymaster and the London bankers to defraud suppliers. Pepys also condemned Carteret for embezzling the naval chaplains' pay. This apart, Pepys's comments on Carteret are free from the abuse which he dispensed elsewhere. He retained his original impression that Carteret was 'very good-natured', and found Carteret and his wife 'most extraordinary people . . . to continue friendship with'.[2]

Sir William Batten (Surveyor 1660–7) had a similarly substantial *curriculum vitae*, intersecting with that of Carteret, but of a very different nature. He had been bred to the sea, and sailed with a whaler out of Great Yarmouth. He went on to command, as Carteret had done, one of Charles I's 'whelps' (fast patrol vessels); he then bought himself into the Navy Board, paying £1,500 for the Surveyorship in 1638. He had meanwhile aligned himself with the London shipping interest, whose religious leanings he also shared; and when in 1642 Parliament assumed control of the fleet, Batten was made Vice-Admiral and a Navy Commissioner. He featured prominently and controversially in the chief naval events of the war. His firing on the Queen at Bridlington in February 1643 was considered ungentlemanly by the neutral Dutch, and damned him for ever in the eyes of the Cavaliers. By 1648 he had become disenchanted with his political masters, and helped foment the mutiny in which a detachment of Parliament's ships 'revolted' to the King's cause. He was made Rear Admiral of the fleet which put itself at the Prince of Wales's disposal, but there were doubts about his sincerity. These were intensified when Batten advised against engaging Parliament's ships when this at last became a possibility. Pepys records Charles II's memory of Batten pacing the deck, mopping his sweat with a handkerchief; and of Prince Rupert itching to shoot him for seeming to signal to the enemy. After the stand-off the royal ships had returned to Holland, where Rupert took control. Batten was then allowed to return to England, but had now lost credibility with both sides. When the Restoration was imminent he offered the King his services, which were accepted. The return to the Surveyorship was his principal accomplishment; he was elected to Parliament in 1661, and in 1664 was licensed to build lighthouses at Harwich, the dues from which usefully increased his income.[3]

Batten's financial status was of considerable interest to Pepys. At first he gaped admiringly at the princely style in which Batten contrived to live at Walthamstow. Soon he came to suspect that the Surveyor's fortune was supported by embezzlement and outright corruption. Not all Pepys's instances are very damning; no doubt it was improper for the Surveyor to build himself a garden ornament with the Navy's ironwork, and to keep a chest of drawers after sacking the ropemaker who had given it to him. But then the Clerk of the Acts had his fine bookcases made by a dockyard carpenter, and accepted a pair of silver candlesticks from a purser he had discredited. Batten had a long acquaintance with the merchants, and Pepys believed him to be in collusion with suppliers of defective tar, hemp and flags. More importantly, Pepys objected to the favour which Batten showed to his son-in-law, the shipbuilder William Castle. Castle and his business partner William Wood were awarded timber contracts which Pepys thought could be better served by their

21

rival Sir William Warren. A part of Batten's 'cunning' was to come into the Navy Office on a Saturday morning or at other quiet moments to settle his deals. Soon, though, Pepys learned to ambush him. One time he managed to stop a Dutch auction into which the inexpert Berkeley had been unwittingly drawn. On another occasion he prevented a bill favourable to Castle being slipped through in a pile of other business. The most serious financial accusation against Batten is of embezzling the funds of the Chatham Chest, the fund for relief of distressed seaman, whose governing body Batten chaired. An enquiry begun in 1662, of which Pepys was a member, made him 'ashamed to see Sir W. Batten possess himself so long of so much money as he hath done'. At one stage Batten admitted having £6,000 of the Chest's cash in his own hands. It was a tempting pot, and Batten's thoroughly honest successor once borrowed the entire contents for a couple of days to pay off a ship. Batten was incorrigible, and died in the expectation that he was still owed £500 for his management of the Chest.[4]

Pepys also accused Batten of inefficiency, though this might seem incompatible with the charge of skilful peculation. In this respect Pepys's own comments are less significant than those of others which (though to support his own argument) he reports. Thomas Middleton, the next Surveyor, was fond of saying that, one book apart, he could find no evidence 'that there had ever been such a man as Sir William Batten Surveyor of the Navy'. Sir William Coventry, the shrewdest of Pepys's colleagues and informants, thought it was simply Batten's 'heaviness and unaptness for business' which made him act rashly to be done with it, and to gratify his friends. Coventry had a less kindly verdict after the Second Dutch War, when illness had increased Batten's inattention; it would have been better for the King to have given Batten (and Sir John Mennes) £1,000 a year 'to have sat still'. None of this prevented Pepys from going into partnership with Batten and Sir William Penn as owners of a privateer, the *Flying Greyhound*; astonishingly, Pepys let Batten keep the accounts of the enterprise. Outside office hours Pepys found Batten an amiable companion, and enjoyed his nautical reminiscences.[5]

The 'Sir Williams both', Batten and Penn, are frequently vilified by Pepys in a single swipe. Batten may have deserved some of this; Penn's reputation, on the other hand, is poorly served by being channelled through Pepys's pages. He has a distinguished place in British naval and imperial history, although overshadowed in celebrity by his son, the founder of Pennsylvania. Of those appointed to the Navy Board in the 1660s Sir William Penn had had the most prominent service afloat, and his active career would continue. He was, like Carteret, a junior member of a gentry family; and although he acquired an estate in Ireland through marriage, he had to make his way as a merchant seaman. Pepys gleefully recorded gossip about the modest circumstances of Penn's early life, and would scoff at the unappetising food which was still served at his table. More significantly Pepys heard how Penn had first supported Charles I, and then sided with Parliament. Penn acknowledged Batten as his mentor. He commanded parliamentary ships at sea almost continuously from 1642 to 1652, at first chiefly in Ireland, and latterly in pursuit of Prince Rupert's squadron in the Mediterranean. At the start of the First Dutch War he was made Vice-Admiral. At the first main engagement, Kentish Knock (September 1652), Penn's ships ran aground and looked to be sitting prey for the advancing Dutch. With great skill Penn refloated his ships and turned the contest to his own advantage. His seamanship was further demonstrated at Portland (February 1653) when he led his squadron through the Dutch line. Penn was decorated and promoted General. When the Dutch War had been satisfactorily concluded, and Cromwell launched a major assault on the Spanish empire in the Caribbean, Penn was chosen to lead the naval forces. The main target, Hispaniola, proved unassailable, and the expedition had to be content with annexing Jamaica. The usefulness of this was not immediately apparent, and on his return Penn was briefly put in the Tower for failing to accomplish the Protector's 'Western Design'. Penn gave no further service to the Protectorate, and from his Irish retreat began contacts with the royalists. Monck secured his return to public life as an Admiralty Commissioner in March 1660. It was in this capacity that, observed by Pepys, he joined Montagu's fleet. He had been knighted soon after the King's return.[6]

Penn had a major place in the Restoration Navy. Ashore he advised the Duke of York, who though he had 'shadowed' the post of Lord High Admiral, and had done a good deal of military staff-work, was necessarily inexperienced in naval administration. Penn revised the Lord High Admiral's Instructions for Fighting and Sailing; to this end he compiled a volume of precedents, of which Pepys obtained a copy. At the Navy Board Penn was in 1667 given the specific portfolio of Comptroller of Victualling Accounts, taking up some of the work which the Comptroller, Mennes, was failing to do. Two years later, when Navy victualling was put out to contract, Penn became a shareholder and resigned his Commissionership. He was by this time facing criticism for his part in the Second Dutch War , when he had been given the special rank of 'Captain Great Commander' as chief of staff to the Duke. He was accused over the controversial failure to pursue the Dutch after the battle of Lowestoft (June 1665), for involvement in the breaking bulk of prizes taken by Sandwich later that year, and (as Commissioner) for the defective sea defences exploited by the Dutch in 1667. He was severely censured by Parliament, though he escaped actual punishment.[7]

Pepys thought Penn able but lazy and corrupt. At the Board they argued over the appointment of masters, and about the purchase of stores. He accused Penn of cursory attention to pursers' accounts ('slubbering over and easy allowing' them), and other negligence. He took particular exception to what he regarded as a fraudulent pay claim which Penn put in for his service in the Second Dutch War. When Penn started taking over the victualling business, there was a row when he wanted a private area in the open-plan office. The common Pepysian label of 'rogue' was freely pasted on him, not least when he was suspected of cheating on his share in the *Flying Greyhound* partnership. By 1667 Pepys imagined that he and Penn hated one another, though he provides a good deal of evidence for Penn's continuing friendship towards *him*. Pepys's more considered view of Penn was 'though I do not love him . . . I think it discretion, great and necessary discretion, to keep in with him'.[8]

At the time of the re-establishment of the Board in on 4 July the Comptrollership was left vacant, to be filled on 31 August by Robert Slingsby, whose father Sir Guilford had held the same post from 1611 to his death in 1632. Robert Slingsby had been another to captain one of the 'whelps' in the 1630s, and to continue his service to the crown on land during the Civil War. At the Restoration he claimed the Navy Treasurership by grant from Charles I, and unsuccessfully disputed Carteret's appointment. The delayed award of the Comptrollership was therefore a consolation prize. He was created a baronet in March 1661. Earlier that year he had submitted to the Duke of York a 'Discourse' on the past history of the Navy Office and proposing its further regulation. Pepys was shown a copy by Slingsby in January, and later had one of his own bound up with a more substantial work by John Holland (a Navy Commissioner 1642–53). When the writs went out for Charles II's first Parliament in February 1661, Slingsby told Pepys it would be appropriate for all the Navy Officers to seek election. At the time Pepys was dissuaded by the expense, and Slingsby set a poor example by losing his own contest at Newcastle. Another failed scheme of Slingsby's was a naval order of knighthood, an idea toyed with years later by Pepys, and to no better effect. Slingsby died in October 1661, having had little time to make an impression on the naval administration. Pepys's comments about him are generally friendly, but so they were of his other colleagues when he was a respectful newcomer.[9]

Slingsby's successor was Sir John Mennes, whose experience was the longest of any of Pepys's colleagues, stretching back to the Navy of James I. In Charles I's service he had been noted as an unusually literate sea officer, a true *virtuoso*, with artistic, literary and scientific interests, and the correct social accomplishments. In July 1642, when the King had withdrawn Lord Admiral Northumberland's patent, Mennes (then Rear Admiral) attempted to take control of the fleet, but was out-manoeuvred by Warwick and Batten. During the war he had a cavalry command and held North Wales for the King. From 1648–50 he was Rear Admiral in the miniature Royal Navy led by Prince Rupert. Thereafter he rendered diplomatic and medical assistance to the exiled court. Though he was past sixty at the Restoration, he was appointed captain of the *Henry* and, in May 1661, Vice-Admiral of the Channel fleet; he still held active command when appointed the Comptrollership in November. Within a couple of years Pepys had formed a low view of his competence. When Mennes told him of his venture in 1642, Pepys affected to believe the King's cause was irredeemably doomed by entrusting so great a charge to 'such a knave'. Derisory epithets about Mennes abound in the Diary and the Navy White Book, and it is true enough that he could not exercise the high level of administrative oversight which the Comptrollership demanded. Nor was it only Pepys who complained: there was a concerted effort to move him out, or at least sideways, and in 1667 he was eventually made to delegate part of his duties. Nevertheless Pepys's criticisms must be taken in context, a part of which being his own hope of promotion in Mennes's place.[10]

Alone of Pepys's original colleagues, Peter Pett gave consecutive service to the Commonwealth and the restored monarchy as resident Commissioner at Chatham. He had been one of the original Navy Commissioners appointed by Parliament in 1648, retaining his place and exchanging it for one in the Navy Board of 1660. His family had run the dockyard at Chatham for generations, and had been under investigation for corruption before the First Dutch War. Peter Pett was primarily a shipwright, and, in addition to the yard Commissionership, he held the post of Master Shipwright at Chatham from 1664. As the Second Dutch War had progressed Pett came under increasing pressure for refitting damaged ships and building new ones. Pepys concluded that Pett had 'no authority in that place where he is', and would best be removed to another less vital one. The opportunity to be rid of him entirely came in the aftermath of the 1667 Medway raid, when everyone (Pepys included) found it convenient to put the main blame on the Chatham Commissioner. Ironically the *Royal Charles*, whose capture was the most humiliating part of the disaster, had been Pett's own building.[11]

On Pett as shipbuilder, Pepys was of course not an expert commentator. He was sceptical of Pett's intention to build a better yacht than the *Mary*, which the Dutch had given the King. When he saw Pett's *Catherine* on the stocks, he conceded that it would be 'much beyond the Duchman's'. Pepys was not convinced by Pett's disparagement of the catamaran designed by Sir William Petty; he thought Pett was prejudiced because Petty was not a professional seaman, and would therefore 'stop all encouragement to be given to her'. It was a project which Pepys continued to champion, though sea trials eventually vindicated Pett's judgment. Pett took Pepys into his confidence by showing him sectional drawings for his own design. The gesture was wasted: Pepys was quite unable to understand the 'great mystery' being shown him. A little later Pepys expresses astonishment that Pett cannot supply him with standard dimensions for a 5th-rate ship. He does not, however, presume to tell the shipwright his business.[12]

What is extraordinary is how soon Pepys was prepared to do just that to the rest of his colleagues. In technical knowledge and practical experience they dwarfed him. Even though their loyalties had been divided, they shared a good deal more with one another than Pepys did with any of them. This would have been of no great significance had Pepys been content with a secretarial role. The Clerk of the Acts was essentially that. He prepared the agenda for meetings of the Board, and kept its minutes. He also had custody incoming correspondence and other papers, and kept file copies of outgoing warrants and letters. The other three dedicated officers had much wider remits. The Treasurer's duty was greatest, receiving money from the Exchequer and paying it out for the Navy's manning and material requirements. He had his own separate office (in Leadenhall Street until 1664, and then in Broad Street), and rarely attended the ordinary meetings at the Navy Board's main premises in Seething Lane. The Surveyor's particular concern was the physical state of the ships, docks and stores, and he was required to inspect them annually. The Comptroller was there to check up on the Treasurer and Surveyor, keeping duplicates of their records. These, however, were only the specific duties of the four main officers. Corporately the Board attended the Lord High Admiral, usually every week, and passed on his directions to the dockyards and, in non-operational matters, to the ships. At their own meetings – weekly if not more frequent – their main business was contracting with merchants for supplies of all kinds. They had oversight of the dockyard officers, who were required to make annual accounts to the Board. When ships came in, one or more of the Commissioners generally went down to issue the pay. This was their most high-profile duty, and an irksome one. If they did have all the necessary cash with them, there was a security risk. Often they had nothing more to discharge the seamen with than paper tickets, cashable only at a special office in London. The issuing Commissioners might face violent discontent in consequence. The Board also had general oversight of victualling, for which various administrative structures were tried. At first this was a distinct department under Sir Denis Gauden, himself not a member of the Board. During the Second Dutch War the operation was, at Pepys's suggestion, directly managed; afterwards it was handed over to a syndicate of private investors.[13]

Pepys's success in this early stage of his career consisted in doing his own particular job extremely well, and encroaching as much as he dared on those of his colleagues. He exemplified the Churchillian dictum 'be there'; as he put it: 'nothing passes without me'. The Clerkship rooted him in the Office, and he made himself the master of its records and practices. The Treasurer had, as said, a separate establishment. Batten's surveying duties took him away a good deal, and in the course of the war, with his health failing, he was seen less frequently at the Office. Penn had his sea commands, and Pett was in theory permanently at Chatham. Mennes, who should have been exercising overall control, lacked the necessary enthusiasm for book-keeping; that left a vacuum which Pepys naturally abhorred and in practice filled. He had a keen sense of the power which information brings, and set himself to learn every facet of the job. But information's power can only be harnessed through analysis and calibration. Here was Pepys's greatest talent: the ability to store and retrieve the knowledge he gathered. This he did through a series of inter-relating registers, which included the personal Diary he kept from 1660–9. What he liked best of all was making lists and tables, reducing the messy world with which he dealt to a pleasing symmetry of headings and columns. We have seen him set to work in this way as soon as he had joined the fleet as secretary in 1660. When searching questions were asked by Parliament about the costs of the Second Dutch War, Pepys was exasperated to find that none of his colleagues had sent in an exact list of the fleet. On calling for a list from the Surveyor (whose responsibility this most particularly was) and comparing it with his own, he found sixteen names missed from the 3rd- to 6th-rates, and twenty smaller vessels omitted altogether. The comprehensive registers which Pepys compiled of the ships and the sea officers for the years 1660–88 were the *Jane's Fighting Ships* and the Navy List of their time, and remain fundamental reference works.[14]

For Pepys himself the basic manual was the Lord High Admiral's set of Instructions for the Navy Board. Having been revised by Penn, this was re-issued under the Duke of York's authority on 28 January 1662. As the Duke himself conceded, they contained only minor alterations to Northumberland's Instructions of 1640. They laid greater stress than before on finding the best price for commodities, and prohibited the members of the Board from themselves acting as or in partnership with suppliers. Pepys breached this rule by trading in calico for flags, and then lied to the parliamentary enquiry about the profit he had made. It was sometimes supposed that Pepys had drafted the 1662 Instructions. At the time he was far too junior to have done so. The first he saw of them seems to have been on the morning of 5 February 1662 when he, Carteret, Batten and Penn had the Instructions before them at the Office. Even then they only read what directly concerned themselves, deferring the rest for another day. It was five months before Pepys made a detailed study of the instructions concerning the yard officers. He then went through the whole document and summarised each section. The dockyard officers were then notified of their re-codified duties. When Pepys came to defend the Board's conduct to the Commissioners of Accounts in 1669–70, he would cite article after article of the 1662 Instructions. When it suited him, he would treat them as Holy Writ; there were circumstances, however, which would not permit 'the nice attention to these rules', and then the Board had a discretion to interpret them by majority verdict. So, at any rate, Pepys argued, and his sophistry was underwritten by the King and the Duke.[15]

According to an anonymous writer on naval administration *c.* 1649, the Clerk of the Acts had been demoted from parity with the other Navy Commissioners to keep him at a distance, lest he should be too forward in discovering what private interest might conceal. On the contrary, it was argued, he was of equal consequence because his records were 'the ringleaders to all transactions'. If, as he ought to be, he was an able accountant, well versed in naval affairs and familiar with the inferior officers' duties, no man would see more of the Navy's business or be as able to speak on it with such authority. Pepys had this treatise bound immediately before his best copy of the 1662 Instructions. It made a most encouraging preface.[16]

The Instructions gave the Clerk of the Acts general oversight of the minor purchases ('petty emptions') which had once been his direct responsibility. Pepys was keen to exploit this extra sphere of activity. He won an argument with Batten and Penn over the right to sign for all such transactions and installed his old rival, Thomas Turner, as the actual purveyor. For his own part he began to learn about the multitude of goods which the Navy purchased, talking to the officers and workmen in the yards, and to the merchant suppliers. The findings were duly written up in one of his memoranda books or the Diary itself. Not all the advice he received was disinterested, and he sometimes discovered later that his informants had been crooks. For basic mathematics he engaged Richard Cooper, mate of the *Royal James*. It was only at their first session in July 1662 that Pepys learned the multiplication table. Cooper also taught Pepys a good deal about ships, demonstrating with a model in the Office. In return Pepys found Cooper a master's place, and stood up for him when his captain, the formidable Sir Robert Holmes, wanted to turn him out. Cooper was said to have a weak brain, addled by drink, and Pepys accepted that he should be dismissed. Nevertheless Pepys had learnt from him well, and was now competent to handle some of the complex accounting which his business involved. Calculating the charges of tar and pitch from the Baltic, he could begin in Swedish copper dollars, add in the commission on the Hamburg exchange, switch *en route* into Flemish dollars, and end up in sterling.[17]

The measurement of timber gave opportunities for a variety of malpractices, and Pepys was advised to take advanced lessons from a mathematician, Henry Bond. In the event he learned most from Anthony Deane, whom he first encountered as Assistant Shipwright at Woolwich in 1662, and who was to become one of his firmest friends. Deane took Pepys to see timber being felled in Waltham Forest and explained a particular type of fraud. After the practical came a written test, and by the end of their outing Pepys felt he had his mind round the subject. A year later, having acquired a slide-rule for the purpose, he could measure timber 'with great ease and perfection' and thought he understood it 'thoroughly'. He then found that there was more to be learned from the timber merchant Sir William Warren, though he could teach him something in return. Warren instructed Pepys more generally about his trade, the different varieties of Norwegian fir, seasonal fluctuations in cost, and the specific uses for different cuts of wood. Pepys now began to bring his knowledge to bear. On a visit to Chatham yard in August 1663 he put the official Timber Measurer through his paces, and publicly rebuked his failings. This soured his relations with Commissioner Pett, who did not care for Pepys's boast that he could do the job as well as anyone employed to do so. Still, he had not mastered quite every detail, having to admit to Pett that he could not resolve a dispute at Deptford as to the measuring of blocks by diameter or length. Down at Deptford in July 1664 Pepys challenged Assistant-Shipwright Jonas Shish to measure a piece of timber 32 ft × 20½ in × 6 in, which Shish reckoned at 37 cubic feet. Pepys and Richard Fletcher the Timber Measurer then did the calculation by logarithms and the slide-rule, and found 10 cubic feet less than Shish, which by Pepys's estimate represented £1 overpaid on that single timber. In 1668 Pepys brought a more serious instance of Shish's miscalculation to the Board, and was exasperated by their 'general indifference in all matters of this kind'.[18]

The preservation of timber once bought had also to be understood. Oak needed its sap dried out by the circulation of air before being worked. Mast timber, on the other hand, had to retain its gummy resin for flexibility, and the firs and pines suitable for this purpose were best kept submerged. Pepys learnt the scientific basis of this from Daniel Whistler, physician and mathematician, and the practicalities from Warren and Captain John Taylor, a shipbuilder who joined the Board as Commissioner at Harwich. By March 1664 he felt he had 'a thorough understanding in the business'. More insights came on a field trip later that year, when he found masts stored among thigh-high weeds, and rotting away as a result. The Woolwich shipbuilder Christopher Pett explained the effects of corrosion, and why, though merchants might cut away rotted matter, the resulting piece would not have the strength of a whole timber of the same dimension. Duly informed, Pepys was alert to the sharp practices of suppliers, and the more careful in making contracts with them.[19]

Pepys's determination to learn dull facts sometimes quite overcame the lighter and more familiar side of his character. So one afternoon in a Rotherhithe tavern: 'meeting Mr. Stacy with some company of pretty women – I took him aside to a room by ourselfs and there talked with him about the several sorts of Tarrs.' Pepys collated the information Stacey (a tar merchant) had given him with the opinions of a Wapping ropemaker, Joseph Stapeley. He docketed the relative merits of the supplies from Stockholm, Bergen and Archangel, and remembered to take into account the varying weights of the casks. He was therefore curious when the wife of a dockyard official casually asked him if a forthcoming supply of tar would come in thick barrels. Her husband, it emerged, gave her the empty casks, and for thick ones she could get 6*d* apiece. A quick calculation showed that she would make £30 on the next consignment. A New Englander told Pepys of the two types of North American tar: Plymouth ('thick and bad') and Connecticut (which Pepys heard as 'Kennedicutt': 'thin and good'). The merchants regularly tried to serve in bad tar mixed with good, and Pepys suspected Batten of collusion with a fraudulent supplier. A more inventive ruse was tried by William Cutler, who launched a rumour that the Stockholm tarhouse had been destroyed by fire, and so attempted to hike his own contract price.[20]

It may be that as a tailor's son, Pepys had some prior knowledge of cloth. He could certainly call on a neighbour of his father's, Jane Croxton (perhaps herself trading as a mercer), for advice about measuring silk for flags. He took samples of flag material home, and noted their dimensions and qualities. In measuring sailcloth his slide-rule was again useful, and he was soon able to hold his own in negotiations with suppliers. The Navy's sailmaker, John Harris, gave him helpful advice, recommending that each yard should have a sample of the different varieties of cloth, and warning against false measures. Pepys subsequently found occasion to note Harris's own 'falsities'. When these matters were discussed at the Board, Pepys could not match the seaboard experience of his colleagues. Mennes, for example, was able to give a very specific account of the way in which sailcloth wore in service. But such points were noted, and deployed in argument as necessary. Pepys was soon able to recognise a fraudulent bill, and to reduce the price accordingly.[21]

An iron merchant called Weston told Pepys about the relative qualities of Spanish, Swedish and English iron, recommending the Swedish. The Navy Board's most considerable and controversial purchase of ironwork was the chain which was placed across the Medway anchorage in 1667, and which the Dutch breached. Pepys noted that this had been of Swedish iron. Weston also told him that General Blake had such high regard for shot made from English iron that he would allow the merchants whatever price they asked. Pepys would not have been so indulgent; in any case armaments were not provided by his department but by the Ordnance Office. The Navy Board's requirements were for anchors, chains, tools and fittings of various kinds. Pepys was still learning about some of this merchandise in 1668, when he had arranged for his clerk Hayter to succeed Turner as Purveyor of Petty Emptions. He heard how hinges and suchlike were commonly sold in pairs, but without this being explicit in the bills; how hatchets fell apart after three or four blows; how the Navy ironmonger supplied the smallest versions of some commodities for the price of the largest. Another time Pepys strolled into the glazier's shop at Woolwich yard and started asking awkward questions about the working practices. He could find no proper accounts kept, and nobody seemed to know the right way of measuring lanterns. Much of the new glass had 'plain holes through it'.[22]

Of the ships themselves, the end product of all this industry, Pepys naturally wanted to learn as much as he could. In June 1661 he borrowed Sandwich's model of the *Royal James* and spent an afternoon assembling it for display in his chamber at home. A little later he moved it to his Office to have more opportunity for study, and it was there that Cooper taught him with it. The ship itself had been built by Christopher Pett in 1658 as the 2nd-rate *Richard* (for Richard Cromwell), and had been re-named and upgraded to 1st-rate in 1660. The model presumably reflected the original build, and so must have resembled one now in the US Naval Academy at Annapolis. Pepys was keen for a model of his own, and Anthony Deane obliged with one in September 1662. It would be the first of a prized collection, elegantly displayed and informatively labelled; none can now be located with certainty. Deane then began to teach Pepys to draw the lines of a ship ('well worth my spending some time in'). Deane might be a little conceited, but that was no matter; he was able to communicate his skills more lucidly than Commissioner Pett. As a further visual aid Deane made his pupil a draught of a ship; in return Pepys determined to promote his tutor's career. In 1664 he secured for him the Master Shipwright's place at Harwich, and in 1670 Deane would compose his 'Doctrine of Naval Architecture' at Pepys's request.[23]

The art of shipbuilding, Pepys discovered in 1664, was 'not hard', and he set himself to learn something of it. This sanguine resolution was prompted by the sight of a couple of ships on the stocks, and perhaps also because the day before he had been lent 'a manuscript of one Mr. Wells, writ long ago, teaching the method of building a ship'. The loan became a possession, and the manuscript, which Pepys catalogued as 'Fragments of Ancient English Shipwrightry', came to be recognised as originally the work of Matthew Baker, Master Shipwright to Elizabeth I and James I. John Wells had inherited the volume and added to it; it had then passed to Thomas Turner, from whom Pepys had borrowed it. Its numerous fine illustrations would have attracted Pepys's interest; it is doubtful if he had the mathematics to make any great use of the text. He was still at the naming-of-parts stage with Deane. The subject proved more complex that Pepys had supposed. In 1665 Christopher Pett had written to him giving his objections to a proposal for lowering the topmast abaft the mainmast; Pett thought this might work for merchantmen but not with men-of-war. When, a good while later, the issue was debated in the presence of the King, the Duke of York, and many commanders and shipwrights, Pepys for once was speechless: 'a business I understood not'.[24]

Casting of accounts was another matter. Pepys had the skill to keep his own books in order, and ruthlessly to audit those of others. Pursers, who ran a kind of private franchise in selling food and clothing to seamen, were almost proverbially corrupt. In 1662 Pepys began to learn about pursers' accounts from Thomas Lewis, a clerk in the Victualling Office. A couple of years later he concluded that Lewis was no better than the rest. Another informant, Thomas Hempson, was 'a cunning knave'; so Pepys listened to what he had to say. He found this issue much harder than the technicalities of shipbuilding, but all the more necessary because it was 'little understood' by his colleagues at the Board. The pursers themselves predictably regarded Mennes as a soft touch. It was not until Pepys took charge of victualling in 1665 that he was in a position to implement tougher controls which the Duke of York had recommended. Pepys was then greatly assisted by his clerk Richard Gibson, who had been a purser (though an honest one), and who knew how the system operated. Having compiled a dossier, he was at first 'at a perfect loss what to advise'; soon enough, though, he marshalled his thoughts into a set of cogent proposals which the Board adopted.[25]

In these and other spheres of activity Pepys built up a fund of technical knowledge and personal contacts which progressively offset the imbalance in naval experience between himself and his colleagues. As a result he was able to push his job specification to the limits, and then to encroach on the duties of the Surveyor and the Comptroller. It is, however, always necessary to remember that we continue to view Pepys's achievement mainly through sources which he created and shaped. It is, as Professor G.E. Aylmer concluded, 'intrinsically unlikely that he could have done it all single-handed'. One great advantage he enjoyed was the competence and loyalty of his office clerks. The two he started with in July 1660 were key figures. Thomas Hayter was an established official whom Pepys took over; Pepys stood by him when he was in trouble for religious nonconformity, and secured his promotion to the chief clerkship of the Office in 1664 and the purveyorship of Petty Emptions. When Pepys moved up to the Admiralty in 1673, Hayter took over as Clerk of the Acts in partnership with Pepys's brother John; he again succeeded Pepys at the Admiralty in 1679, then returning to the Navy Board as Comptroller from 1680–3. William Hewer's association with Pepys began at the age of eighteen, when he was employed as a domestic servant as well as in the Office. After some uneasy moments the relationship solidified, and Pepys took Hewer with him as his career advanced. Hewer had the means and competence to prosper on his own account, becoming prominent in the East India Company and other commercial ventures. His riches were not dissipated by matrimony; instead, he and Pepys (by that time long a widower) set up house together. Pepys's other cherished clerk was Richard Gibson, who served him from 1667 until he was appointed Purser General in 1670; he returned to the Navy Office two years later, and moved to the Admiralty on the eve of the Revolution. Hayter, Hewer and Gibson all shared their master's passion for administrative order, evidenced in a considerable amount of the documentation of Pepys's career.[26]

One further vital component in Pepys's apprenticeship was the appointment to the Navy Board of William Coventry, son of Charles I's Lord Keeper. During the Civil War he had held an infantry command, and then served the exile court. From the Restoration he was secretary to the Duke of York and therefore a key figure in naval affairs. He joined the Navy Board in 1662 as an Extra Commissioner, and never involved himself much in the daily business there. His special value was as liaison between the high command and the civil administration; he also had significant commercial and colonial interests. He was knighted and made a

Privy Councillor in 1665. On becoming a Treasury Commissioner in 1667, he left the Duke's service, where many thought Pepys should succeed him. Pepys admired him for his intelligence and careful judgement, and above all for his high regard for the dignity of public service. Pepys cultivated his company and recorded their conversations in detail. It was awkward that he was hostile to Sandwich; but Pepys was outgrowing his original mentor, and in a sense Coventry replaced him. Coventry spoke at length about the relative merits of 'gentlemen' and 'tarpaulin' captains, and sided with the latter. Pepys would do the same. Pepys was similarly receptive to his views about the orgins of the Second Dutch War.[27]

THREE

Contracting and Expanding

'We might have kept a larger Navy if we had agreed to its being a second-rate Navy.'

Admiral the Earl Mountbatten of Burma, 6 April 1959
[*Br. Naval Documents*, p. 818]

The sword with which Pepys equipped himself for his first service in the Navy never drew blood. Some training with the militia in his younger days would be his only active service. He was always a civilian 'Officer of the Navy', except briefly in 1669 when he was commissioned captain of the *Jersey* to enable him to sit on a Court Martial. He saw nothing of the fighting in the two naval wars fought with the Dutch in Charles II's reign. His career nevertheless was significantly advanced because of them and the expansion of the service which they entailed.[1]

When Pepys first entered the Navy, the policy was contraction not expansion. On his return the King assumed control of an ostensibly impressive fleet of 109 ships. Some of these, including eleven of the fifteen 1st- and 2nd-rates, were survivors from the old Royal Navy, but the majority represented the Commonwealth's successful determination to compete with the Dutch. Though the war of 1652–4 had been militarily and commercially successful, the subsequent campaigns in the Caribbean and Flanders had drained the Exchequer. The government had been unable to sustain its previous reliability on forces' pay, thereby weakening its best hold on the loyalty of the soldiers and seamen. In the fleet which Pepys joined in March 1660, every ship's company was in arrears for pay, many of them for two or three years. Charles II therefore inherited not only the grand fleet of the Commonwealth, but also a formidable naval debt. This would require lengthy assessment, and Pepys began the process on 31 July. Two days later the House of Commons, on being told that the debt would rise by £16,000 a month if ships were not paid off, appointed a committee to examine the problem. The following week the House was warned of discontent in the fleet 'ready to break into a Flame'. This business brought Pepys his first experience of the parliamentary process, and, in the person of the committee chairman John Birch, his first brush with an argumentative MP. Pepys reported to Birch's committee on 13 August that the accumulated debt to 27 June was £678,000, with a further £273,255 5s 4d liable by the end of August for ships remaining in pay.

The King had already decided to cut the active fleet back to a winter guard of thirty-six, and on 15 September the Board had selected the first twenty-five ships to be paid off. Those twenty-five alone, Pepys estimated, would cost £161,132 10s, which was more than the sum Parliament had just voted for disbanding the whole of the army and 'some part' of the Navy. The job was nevertheless done, but slowly. Seventeen of the twenty-five remained in pay at 5 December, together with a further forty-eight above the number designated for the winter guard. The soldiers had been given priority, and the frustration in the fleet grew. Parliament's commissioners, frightened of meeting angry seamen on their home territory, began to conduct pays in the relative safety of Guildhall, beginning with the 4th-rate *Hampshire* on 27 February 1661. The Navy Board, to whom this duty normally belonged, were glad to have no part in it, though Pepys went along one time as a spectator. By the end of July the process was complete.[2]

At the start of Charles II's effective reign his kingdoms faced no significant foreign threat. The war with Spain which Cromwell had begun was notionally still open. The King, however, had latterly been Spain's pensioner, and the Duke of York, with many of the other exiles, had fought for Spain against France. Charles was minded to sustain that alliance when he was restored, and a truce was signed in July 1660. Charles's retention of the Cromwellian conquests of Jamaica and Dunkirk hindered the making of a permanent treaty, and for a time seemed likely to offer a new *casus belli*. England's existing alliance with France was complicated by its being of Cromwell's making, and having involved the expulsion of Charles and his Court from their previous place of exile. Relations were further soured by the efforts of the Cardinal Mazarin and Charles's mother, a daughter of France, to make trouble for the Hispanophiles by whom the King was surrounded. Charles was offended because Mazarin's government offered no congratulations on his restoration, and he sent the French envoy home without the usual courtesy of passage aboard a ship of the Royal Navy. A complete breakdown with France was perhaps only prevented because closer ties with the Spanish and Dutch would have been commercially unacceptable.[3]

With the Dutch republic there had been peace for six years, although the economic and diplomatic issues which had caused the war of 1652–4 remained alive, and would soon enough bring a second war and a third. For the moment the English and the Dutch had reverted to their more natural condition of concord. It had been to Dutch territory that Charles had moved for the last few weeks of his exile, and from which Sandwich's fleet had fetched him. This was more for domestic political consumption than any practical convenience: Charles did not want to be seen emerging from the protection of one of the major Catholic powers. The Dutch authorities had entertained him handsomely, as Pepys discovered, and then (in marked contrast to the discourtesy of the French) celebrated his return with two splendid gifts. The first to arrive was a yacht *Mary* given by the city of Amsterdam; Pepys records the King's inspection of her early on the morning of 15 August 1660; when he went aboard himself later in the year he admired her neat lines. The States-General then presented the King with a collection of works of art, including pictures by Tintoretto, Schiavone, Veronese and Titian, all displayed in the Banqueting House in November. Charles's delight in these gifts was undoubtedly genuine, as was his gratitude to the Dutch government for their hospitality. These feelings may have contributed to his reluctance to reopen the Anglo-Dutch conflict. At the same time he was bound by family loyalty to the House of Orange. In the early years of his exile he had been aided by his brother-in-law William II, who then ruled in the Netherlands. After William's death in 1650 his son had not been given any constitutional position, and so in 1660 the fortunes of the Stuart and Orange dynasties were reversed. Charles wanted to see his nephew William Henry attain the collection of offices by which the Princes of Orange had formerly exercised quasi-monarchical power in the Dutch state. The death in 1661 of Charles's sister Mary, the Dowager Princess of Orange, disposed him the more strongly to promote his nephew's cause. In the Baltic, too, a moment of peace had arrived following the sudden death of Charles X of Sweden in February 1660. This meant that England and the Netherlands would have surer access to the marine supplies they needed for a resumption their own mutual hostilities.[4]

The one continuing conflict on the continent was between Spain and Portugal. Portugal had maintained its independence from the Spanish crown since 1640; now the ending of Franco-Spanish hostilities allowed Spain to concentrate force against what she regarded as an internal rebellion. The Portuguese had negotiated a military-aid treaty with Monck in the last weeks of the republic, but Charles II's government had been wary of risking immediate war with Spain. The Portuguese therefore upped their bid by offering a massive dowry if Charles would marry Afonso VI's sister Catherine. The dynastic alliance would chiefly benefit the House of Bragança in their assertion of sovereignty; in return the English would get possession of Tangier and Bombay, and more than £¼ million in cash. Though the matrimony itself would be unfruitful, the issue for British and imperial and naval history was to be considerable. By chance it would provide Pepys with an influential and lucrative place in the committee which ran the Tangier colony until its surrender in 1684. Back in February and March 1661, Pepys could only speculate about 'two great Secrets . . . known to very few': whom the King was to marry, and why a fleet was being prepared. He did not connect the two. Although he was himself involved in setting out ships, and rightly supposed that Sandwich would command them, he was unsure if they were going to fight 'the

Turke' at Algiers (which was part of the plan), or the Dutch in the East Indies (which was not). When Sandwich casually asked him on 9 March what was being said about the King's marriage, Pepys answered 'as one that knew nothing', and Sandwich did not enlighten him. In fact there was to be a multi-purpose expedition: to negotiate (or failing that, make war) with Algiers and the other corsair bases in North Africa, to take possession of Tangier, and to bring back Catherine and the cash. Actually, the Portuguese proposal was temporarily on hold while a counter-dowry was considered: the Spanish were offering a larger sum and a choice of more gynaecologically promising ladies. The Dutch, who had their own conflict with the Portuguese in the East Indies, and had no wish to see an English settlement in India either, also tried to bribe Charles II to think again, as Pepys correctly reported (3 April).[5]

The decisive factor may have been the death of Mazarin, which Pepys (correctly again) recognised as 'very great news'. It resulted in better Anglo-French relations; the French wanted to see Spanish forces tied up in the Portuguese campaign, and so supported the Anglo-Portuguese alliance. On 20 April the Duke of York revealed to the Navy Board that the ships they had been preparing for some months were indeed for Algiers. A few days later the Privy Council finally agreed to the Portuguese marriage, which the King announced to Parliament on 8 May. Sandwich was then given command of the fleet, and ambassadorial rank. A month later Pepys at last heard about the whole mission from Sandwich himself, who delegated large responsibilities to him. Pepys was gladdened by the confidence, by the enhancement to his patron's honour, and (he hoped) by some prospect of his own profit.[6]

This ebullience was dimmed within twenty-four hours, following a depressing meeting of the Navy Board to discuss the current cash shortfall. Afterwards, Pepys drafted a submission to the Duke of York, noting that in complying with his orders for fitting out seventy ships over the past year, the Board had run up a debt of £67,000 for provisions alone. The stores could not meet demands for a further six ships. The King's return had temporarily restored the Office's credit, but now it was 'so far fallen as it will scarce pass for anything without some of our personal engagements'; and it would be impossible to contract for further supplies without reverting to the old practice of credits assigned from the Exchequer to the Navy Treasury. This became again the regular course; there was an oasis of solvency in 1663/4, and at other times the Board might have cash in hand for its purchases. In general it bought on credit, and was obliged to do so at inflated prices in consequence. For suppliers a main concern was negotiating a satisfactory security against which to advance goods to the King.[7]

Sandwich sailed with his fleet on 13 June. Pepys saw them off, honoured with a salute of five guns (though he was entitled to seven). The first part of the mission was to renegotiate a treaty with Algiers, as part of the intermittent attempt by the European powers to curtail the piracy operated from the Barbary States. Of these the principal were Algiers, Tunis and Tripoli, notionally regencies of the Ottoman Empire, and Salé (known to the English as 'Sally' or 'Sallee'), part of the independent kingdom of Fez. Corsairs based on these ports habitually attacked shipping in the Mediterranean and the Atlantic, seizing their goods and taking their crews into slavery. From time to time they had reached into the English Channel, raiding fishing villages and abducting their inhabitants. Charles I's government had responded to this threat, and the expedition of 1637 in which Carteret had sailed redeemed a large number of hostages. But since the ransom payments and other profits of plunder were crucial to their economy, the States had no interest in a permanent peace. Instead, the cycle of commercial piracy continued, conditioned largely by the States' wish to avoid war (or peace) simultaneously with the English, Dutch and French. In 1661 these three powers were in amity, which made it a propitious time for Sandwich's fleet to pay a call at Algiers.[8]

Horror stories about the treatment of Christian prisoners in North Africa naturally abounded. Pepys heard some of them from sea captains earlier in 1661, and later enjoyed a book on the subject. The rescue of hostages, and stern measures against their abductors, were prime duties of the Royal Navy. So when the Algerines declined to treat, Sandwich bombarded them heavily but ineffectually until unfavourable winds persuaded him to withdraw his main force. Pepys heard of all this when a packet of letters sent from Lisbon reached him on 24 September. John Creed, still serving Sandwich as Deputy Treasurer, addressed Pepys in polished Latin, as if he were chronicling the battle of Actium. He followed this up with a letter in French, descending into English for its deadpan *reportage* ('there was 15 that conspired against the King of Algiers and cut him in peeces, whereupon hath followed a change of government'). Pepys was presumably more impressed by the succinct personal despatch from Sandwich himself. A longer account came from Sandwich's steward, Edward Shipley, together with a request for (among more prosaic items) anchovies, pickled oysters, and Cheshire cheese. Pepys feared for his own pocket, but was assured that the King would pay for all. And his own first dividend had already arrived: a hamper of melons. Pepys was unnecessarily worried that the Algiers action would be to Sandwich's discredit, 'because [he] hath not done what he went for'. It was true enough that a more successful action was fought by Lawson in the following year, forcing the Algerines to a new treaty. But even Lord Exmouth, who in 1816 repeated the operation to the most devastating effect, did not quite eradicate the problem.[9]

Sandwich's failure before Algiers was soon forgotten in the excitement of annexing Tangier, where his fleet arrived on 10 October. Since they were taking over an existing Portuguese base, they did not have to fight their way ashore. Nevertheless England was now going to have Moorish neighbours. That they would be unfriendly was taken for granted; their hostility was a main reason for wanting a Mediterranean base in the first place. The leading Moroccan warlord, Abd Allāh al-Ghailān (whom the English called Guyland) at once announced himself as the subject of Spain. Back in London Pepys and his colleagues were busy arranging the transport of the 1,000 infantry and 100 cavalry to defend the new colony. On 26 October they met all morning with the newly appointed governor, the Earl of Peterborough, 'completing of the affairs and preparacions for that place'. England was learning how to rule in Africa, and Pepys had joined the kindergarten.[10]

In these early stages Tangier was for Pepys just an extension of the business of the Navy Board. Creed continued to send him colourful résumés of local politics, as well as official accounts of his payments to the fleet. Sandwich reported his reinforcement of the garrison following Portuguese losses in a raid up country. At the same time he entrusted Pepys with a map of Tangier, to be delivered personally and unopened to the Duke of York. Sandwich had himself executed a competent scale plan of the harbour shortly after his arrival there. What he now sent was done by a Swedish artillery officer, Martin Beckmann, who had joined Charles II's service and became Engineer-General at Tangier. Pepys came to known him in 1683 when the fortifications were dismantled. Beckmann's original map had been handed over, as instructed, to the Duke on 28 February 1662, and Pepys was allowed to examine it. His own first map of the colony seems to have been Hollar's 1664 engraving from the work of Jonas Moore, which he had a part in commissioning.[11]

A month before Beckmann's map was opened and evaluated in Whitehall, on 29 January 1662 Governor-designate Peterborough arrived in Tangier Bay with a squadron of twenty-seven ships commanded by Sir John Mennes. When Mennes had joined the Navy Board as Comptroller in the previous November, Pepys had welcomed the appointment of this seemingly 'good fair-condition[ed] man'. Before the month was out he was dismayed to hear it said that his new colleague was deeply suspicious of the uses to which Sandwich and the other old republican commanders might put the ships now in the Straits. Mennes feared the King 'would not be master of the fleet at its coming home again'. In time the Tangier station would indeed nurture a measure of disaffection, but in 1662 Mennes's anxieties were unnecessary. Sandwich had already purged the most radical elements. If Mennes's warnings were seriously entertained, then his mission may have been more than honorific. His rendezvous with Sandwich began badly, with Mennes grumpily hauling down the flag at his main. But Sandwich, who had read the instructions properly, composed matters by telling Mennes he should wear his flag in the foretop. Thereafter amity prevailed, and they sailed together to Lisbon to execute the final part of the mission.[12]

Meanwhile the *Royal Charles* had been sent from the Downs to convey the Queen. Pepys and his colleagues were setting out other ships to serve the sharp end of the marriage alliance, taking English troops to fight for the Braganças. Two regiments of foot, 2,000 men in all, were redeployed from the residual elements of Monck's army in Scotland, and a cavalry regiment of 1,000 was formed from the Dunkirk garrison and volunteers. Four merchantmen were hired to carry the infantry, others for the cavalry, and the transports could not sail without naval escort. Pepys was heavily involved in these complex logistics, though not always informed of the larger purposes they served. At the end of April he spent three days at Portsmouth with Carteret and Penn, paying off ships which had come in and despatching others. He saw the lodgings prepared for Catherine's arrival, and the mayor, John Timbrell (who was also the dockyard anchorsmith) showed him the fine silver salt which the town would present to her. Pepys also heard a sermon aboard the ketch *Swallow* from the dockyard chaplain, forgiving the preacher his 'nonsense and false Latin' when he prayed for the Navy Board as 'Right Honourable'. Meanwhile the return of the fleet from Portugal was anxiously awaited, as Dutch and Spanish ships were thought to lie in wait off the Tagus. A false report of the Queen's arrival had set the bells ringing pointlessly in Westminster before Pepys left, and he was back there when the fleet actually reached Portsmouth on 14 May.[13]

Sandwich was for the moment credited and rewarded for the completion of the triangular mission though some untidiness remained; the Queen's dowry was not fully paid, Sandwich was still in debt, and it had been Lawson, left behind when Sandwich moved on to Tangier, who had enforced a treaty on the Algerines. Sandwich was at pains to tell Pepys that the latter was of his own devising, and he tried to have this spelt out when the terms were published. He thought the Duke spiteful in disallowing this, and suspected his advisers (especially Berkeley and Coventry) of plotting against him. Nevertheless he was disposed to humour them, and he had not risen to the Duke's bait when he suggested it was 'the old Captains that must do the business, and . . . the new ones would spoil all'. On the contrary, Sandwich had said, the 'King's new Captaines' (the code for Court nominees of proven loyalty) 'ought to be borne with a little and encouraged'. This was a valuable lesson in political manners for Pepys, whose prospects seemed threatened by a falling out between the Duke and Sandwich, with his new friend Coventry lining up against his old patron. It was a relief to see Sandwich and Coventry conversing amiably together a few day later, and Pepys did his best to promote good relations between them.[14]

Pepys's long-term prospects would depend on an enlargement of his influence within the Navy Office and without. He was already acquiring other functions. From July 1660 to August 1662 he had an additional position as Sandwich's deputy in the Privy Seal Office. Pepys himself exercised this Clerkship by deputy, and although at first the little extra it brought him was welcome, he was soon able to dispense with it. Since September 1660 he had been a JP for the counties of Middlesex, Essex, Kent and Hampshire: this was an *ex-officio* appointment held by Officers of the Navy for the counties in which the naval dockyards lay. In 1663 Pepys drafted a proposal which led to their being given similar status within the City of London. First to come before him as a magistrate was a seaman suspected of making off with his captain's money and clothes; there was no evidence, so Pepys let him go. It was a different matter when he confronted Robert Annis, a plumber's mate found walking away with ¼ cwt of the King's lead. Pepys remained on the same four county benches until his public career ended in 1689, and latterly was nominated for Huntingdonshire (from 1681), Suffolk, Surrey, Sussex and Westminster (from 1687).[15]

Pepys was sworn a Younger Brother of Trinity House on 15 February 1662. Sandwich, the incumbent Master was represented by his deputy, Sir William Rider, a prominent merchant whom Pepys already knew. Pepys had previously enjoyed the hospitality of the Corporation as a guest: with Sandwich at the Election dinner in 1660, and more recently with Penn. He had dined with some of the Trinity House men when they came to lobby Parliament for confirmation of their privileges, and had 'lent' a shin of beef to a dinner (to which he was not himself invited) to mark the granting of their new charter. All this doubtless helped his election. He interested himself in the politics of the Corporation, and regularly attended its dinners and the annual service at Deptford church. In 1672 he was advanced to the rank of Elder Brother, was elected Younger Warden in 1675, and had two terms as Master (1676–7 and 1685–6). At times he found his colleagues 'corrupt and useless', as neglectful of their protocol as of their larger duties. He was driven 'almost mad' by their failure to supply pilots as required, while defending the Corporation's monopoly in licensing them. He also upheld their privileges against erectors of private lighthouses. The Pepys Library contains a substantial amount of material relating to the Corporation, including a 360-page collection documenting its history from the foundation by Henry VIII in 1514.[16]

Most important of all Pepys's ancillary appointments was membership of the committee set up to administer Tangier. Once again this was owed to Sandwich, though Pepys only heard of his nomination from a chance conversation with Creed on 19 August 1662. He had confirmation from Sandwich himself next day, and was gratified to find that he would be in distinguished company. Coventry, also to be a member, happened to be there, and complimented Pepys as 'the life of this office'. The commission was formally issued on 20 November, and included the Duke of York, Prince Rupert, Albemarle, Sandwich, Carteret and Rider. There were other lower-ranking members (including Creed as secretary), but Pepys was perfectly right in his initial assumption that it was both a great honour and a likely source of profit. Although quite separate from his Navy Office function, it necessarily meshed with it at all levels. It involved more hiring and fitting out of ships, and dealings with merchants and captains already known to him. One such (whom he met just a few days before learning of his appointment to the committee) was John Bland, a merchant experienced in Spain. He had talked to Pepys a good deal, and had sent him a selection of his own publications on trade in general and that of Tangier in particular. Bland gave Pepys further advice, ranging from mathematics to the practicalities of mooring a ship in the icy River. After a couple of years Pepys found the business of hiring Tangier ships a bore; more congenial was his appointment (in March 1663) to a sub-committee for framing a civil constitution for the colony.[17]

When the committee was established, Thomas Povey, the Treasurer of the Duke of York's Household, was made Treasurer for Tangier. At first the Treasurer was not meant to be on the committee (which Pepys allowed Coventry to persuade him was always a good rule). In fact this separation of powers was not practised. Povey had married well and lived in a grand manner; Pepys soon recognised him as 'most excellent in anything but business'. By March 1665 the whole Committee was incensed by the disorder of Povey's accounts. Two meetings on 17 March broke up with sharp words and threats of disgrace. The following day Creed (as ever) passed on the Duke's suggestion that Pepys should take on the Treasurership. Pepys was hesitant; the Dutch war had begun, and he would be fully stretched in his Navy work. He suspected, though, that Creed coveted the post, and did not mind disobliging him. Three days of intense negotiation (in the course of which Povey was savaged by Creed's parrot) concluded with Pepys's appointment on 20 March. He agreed to give his predecessor half his profits, which would be considerable, though disputes between them would nevertheless occur. He enthusiastically took up the new task, soon finding that he was indeed neglecting the Navy.[18]

On receipt of the Duke's instructions to the Board in February 1662, Pepys had resolved to observe his particular duties to the letter and to the limit. He had already taken advantage of the Clerk's revived responsibility for petty emptions, which enabled him to initiate business rather than merely to record it. He began to make his mark in other areas. No satisfactory record was kept of hours worked in the dockyards, and Pepys determined to introduce one. He put the idea to two of the officers at Deptford, Thomas Cowley (Clerk of the Cheque) and John Davies (Storekeeper), who could muster no realistic objections. Cowley himself was keen to improve matters, though Pepys found fault with both men's books. Pepys therefore designed a new form of 'call book', sending a sample down to Deptford just before Christmas 1662. Cowley was asked to use it for the next quarter, and to mention any useful refinements before Pepys ordered a batch to be printed.[19]

Within his own office Pepys improved the record-keeping in countless ways. One register or commonplace book, unimaginatively described as his 'Manuscript of the Navy', is frequently mentioned from 1663 onwards, and was once lent to Coventry. This does not survive. The Navy White Book, which does, is a purposeful collection of instances, calculations and reported conversations, covering all aspects of the Board's business between 1664 and 1672. The first part of this was kept in the same shorthand as Pepys's personal Diary, and although he alludes to it in writing to Coventry, the volume itself was for his eyes only. Pepys not only assiduously recorded everything he did, but every day he made out a 'list of particulars remaining undone'.[20]

The crucial business of the Navy Board was the negotiating and drafting of contracts. When pressure on the royal dockyards was extreme, the entire building of a ship might be put out to contract. More commonly it was a matter of contracting for the supply of specific goods. The Duke's Instructions required the Clerk to keep a record of all contracts, and in April 1662 Pepys and Hayter set about compiling an alphabetical index to those made since the Restoration. The Instructions also said the Clerk was to 'present' contracts (and other business) to the Board, and Pepys understood this to mean he should 'draw the heads thereof'. At a meeting in June 1662 Penn accused Pepys of thereby poaching the Comptroller's business. Recent precedent was marshalled in Pepys's favour, and it was agreed that he might continue. The absence of the Comptroller himself (Mennes) made this decision easier. Mennes's imperfect exercise of his duties was a continuing problem. He was keen enough for some low-grade assistance, but when it was proposed to make Penn his formal coadjutor he flatly refused; only in January 1667 did he agree to delegation.[21]

From 1662 onwards Pepys is seen to take an increasing part in contract business. Often merchants would come to Pepys directly with their tenders. He responded favourably to those he already trusted, or who were likely to favour him. He contested bids from those he considered rogues, especially if they were supported by Batten. Since the evidence for these negotiations comes largely from Pepys's own records, and was often written up when the issues were still live, its partiality is never in doubt. In June 1662 he drew up a major contract for 500 tons of hemp from the consortium of Rider, Capt. George Cocke and William Cutler; because it remained 'secret', the final version had to be written out in full by Pepys himself. This deal ended in recriminations, and fears that Cocke's Russia hemp, mixed with Riga, would produce a lethally weak compound. Cocke came, quite literally, knocking on Pepys's door with an offer of tar in November 1663; his product was currently being evaluated in the ropeyard at Woolwich. A while after that Pepys was sitting up late, negotiating terms with a glazier, Thomas Steine, who had been awarded a contract on promising to inform against his fellow-tradesmen. Another time he helped a merchant on the Royal Exchange to put in a successful tender for hammocks.[22]

Sometimes the argument goes round in circles: Pepys secures a contract with Robert Waith for 150 bolts of canvas, whereas Batten had favoured the previous supplier, Potter. When Waith's goods come in, Batten has them rejected as defective, even though they come from the same supplier as Potter's, and then contracts for a smaller consignment from Potter at Waith's price. On another occasion Edward Dering, who was 'King's Merchant' for naval supplies from the Baltic, offered 100 bales of a canvas at a fixed price, and 400 more at whatever might be the current price on delivery. When Batten objected to buying 'a pig in a poke', Pepys pointed out that they had done just that for Edward Harbin; Batten acknowledged this, but said he would not agree to it again. Dering was dismissed and Harbin (who, as Pepys knew, was waiting outside) was brought in. Batten then allowed Harbin to name his own price for goods unseen.[23]

In February 1663 Pepys had a meeting with Sir William Warren about a prospective 'bargain' for New England masts. This developed into a more complex deal comprising 150 masts from Göteborg, 300 from Norway, and three shiploads from New England, the whole worth £3,000. This was, in the older sense of the word, Pepys's 'masterpiece', the work with which he concluded his apprenticeship and rose above his seniors at the Board. Warren's tender was submitted on 6 August, and on 10 September Pepys spent all morning pushing through this 'great contract':

> the whole business, from beginning to end, being done by me out of the office, and signed to by them [his colleagues] upon but once reading of it to them, without the least care or consultation either of quality, price, number, or need of them . . . But I hope my pains was such as the King hath the best bargain of Masts hath been bought these 27 years in this office.

In Pepys's view the key benefit of the deal was its advantage to the King over the counter-bid of New England masts from Warren's arch-rival, William Wood – 5 per cent for the Swedish masts and 7 per cent for the Norwegian. Wood was supported by Batten, but Batten had been away on 10 September. When he returned he was furious that Pepys had triumphed in his absence. Penn and Mennes affected not to recall the details of what they had signed; Pepys, who had been pleased enough by their passivity on the day, was illogically annoyed not to have their firm endorsement now. The arguments rumbled on for several months, and when Warren's masts were delivered, Batten did his utmost to disparage them. In November Pepys explained at length to the Treasurer that his preference for Warren's offer had not been just about the price; Wood's masts were already in the river, and the best had already been taken up. They were buying for stock, and so could afford to wait to take the pick of Warren's delivery. A third of the quantity was intended for Portsmouth; extra freightage would be payable in transferring Wood's masts, whereas Warren could ship a consignment direct at no additional charge. Any immediate needs could be bought from Wood, who would have to lower his prices to match Warren's. Pepys then moved on to the offensive to show that Wood's masts, when measured by the same system as those from Sweden, were less serviceable. Pepys did not succeed absolutely, because when the Second Dutch War came a year later, the Board needed to buy all the masts Wood had left.[24]

Pepys' motives in all this were undoubtedly mixed. He had an authentic desire to secure the best deal for the King, and took pleasure in conducting a large transaction for its own sake. Batten's discomfiture was certainly intended, and Pepys's pained reaction to it was pure cant. Naturally Pepys expected a sweetener, and in February 1664 Warren duly slipped him £40 – a modest 1.3 per cent commission which was a trivial expense for Warren. Pepys, however, was so pleased that he could scarcely eat; even so, it was not the best bonus he had so far received. Just a few days before Dering had given him £50, and during the whole of 1664 he netted £444 'other gain' beyond official fees of £305. And to come there would be more Navy contracts for Warren, more bounty for Pepys: in total Warren provided £990 out of the £2,566 'other gain' Pepys acknowledged between 1660 and 1669.[25]

Another position came Pepys's way in March 1664 when he was nominated to the Corporation of the Royal Fishery. Once more this was Sandwich's doing, and as usual Pepys was pleased by the distinction of his fellows and the expectation of gain. In this instance his hopes were disappointed. The new Corporation, although launched with the Duke of York's encouragement, attracted little backing in the City. Pepys found himself on a fund-raising sub-committee, which considered a lottery and other doubtful schemes. He had a large hand in the committee's report (25 October), and worried that this, like Tangier, was taking up time he owed to the Navy. The Fishery was for Pepys just another quango in which he could make himself useful. It was of course intended to stimulate the general health of the fishing industry; but more particularly it came into being as part of the commercial rivalry which was now leading towards the Second Dutch War.[26]

The Anglo-Dutch reconciliation seemingly expressed in the Restoration voyage had not lasted long. The Navigation Act of 1651, designed to exclude Dutch carriers from trading into England and her colonies, had been a contributory cause of the war of 1652–4. Dutch hopes of a more *laissez-faire* policy from Charles II were disappointed: the King accepted legislation sent up by the

Convention Parliament in 1660, closing loopholes through which the Dutchmen had previously managed to sail. The new Act was promoted by Pepys's Exchequer superior, Sir George Downing, who had been the republic's last ambassador to the Netherlands, and who was virulently anti-Dutch. Charles II sent him back to The Hague to maintain a firm line. Although the principal concern of the 1660 Act was to protect English trade in the Baltic and Mediterranean, conflict with the Dutch focused in West Africa and the Indies. A new company was formed to 'venture to some parts of affrica to dig for gold-ore there' as Pepys artlessly understood it. The Duke of York, Rupert, Coventry, and Carteret were subscribers, and the King was guaranteed two-thirds of all the gold they found. Early in 1661 this Royal African Company sent out an expedition to Guinea, hiring five warships and Robert Holmes to command. Holmes annexed two islands at the mouth of the Gambia and attacked Dutch settlements. The Dutch replied by capturing six English ships and destroying the English factory at Cape Coast. War was expected in June 1662, and twenty ships were ordered to sea: Pepys hoped this was 'but a scarecrow to the world' because the Board lacked the stores, cash and credit to fit out five. Relations with the Dutch were patched up in September 1662. In this new treaty they undertook to cede Pulo Run, in the Moluccas, as originally agreed in 1654; they still failed to do so, and the quarrel resumed. With the English acquisition of Bombay a new sphere of discord was opened up, the Dutch preventing the East Indiamen *Leopard* and *Hopewell* from trading at Cochin and Porakad on the Malabar coast.[27]

Just when the Fishery Corporation was being created, bellicose noises were coming out of the existing chartered companies and the mercantile community generally. On 8 March 1664 the African Company made formal complaint to the King about Dutch 'abuses', and its members were the greatest enthusiasts for a war. The Duke of York, as governor, took the lead, supported by his deputy Lord Berkeley. Other leading figures in the Company included Pepys's contacts Captain Cocke, Sir William Rider and Sir Richard Ford. On 26 March a Commons trade committee, packed with courtiers, began to investigate allegations of obstruction by foreigners, and the London merchants were invited to submit their grievances. Cocke explained this to Pepys as a ruse by the King to get the merchants to ask for a war, so that they would be obliged to pay him to wage it. Pepys well understood the linkage between the government, the trade committee and the chartered companies. From contact with the Duke himself he realised that the merchants' agitation was being worked up from Whitehall. Nine of those on the Commons committee, including Coventry, were members of the African Company; six, again including Coventry, and Pepys's friend Bullen Reymes, had been appointed to the Fishery. Pepys found the Royal Exchange bustling with complainants, and news of Dutch diplomatic counter-protests. On the 21st he heard that the Commons, having received the trade committee's report, had formally asked the King to move against the Dutch, promising to 'stand by him with their lives and fortunes'.[28]

FOUR

The Ships do the Business

'It is highly dangerous to consider that our ships as a whole are superior or even equal fighting machines.'

Vice-Admiral Sir John Jellicoe, 14 July 1914

[C. Barnett, *The Swordbearers* (1963), p. 108]

The Second Dutch War has commonly been understood as a commercial venture, pressed on a reluctant King by a combination of merchants looking to capture Dutch trade, and courtiers, from the Duke of York downwards, seeking martial success. An alternative view sees it as merely an extension of Court faction, for which the quarrel with the Dutch was a convenient cover. It has more recently been suggested that the war was a crusade by 'Anglican royalists' against the Calvinist republic, an away fixture in a continuation of the British Civil Wars. That Pepys does not offer much in support of modern ideological interpretations is unsurprising; his comments have long been familiar, and helped to form the traditional historiography. His pithiest observation, that 'all the Court are mad for a Dutch war' (22 February 1664), was just the view of the King's brewer. Pepys, of course, did not rely on backstairs gossip; he had direct access to the Duke of York, whose role he understood well enough. What he heard from his other sources varied about the timescale but not about the issues. In October 1663 the tar merchant William Cutler spoke of the 'great likelihood of a war'. In the following month Carteret assured him 'there is no such thing likely yet', if only because neither side was ready. It would come eventually, 'our interests lying the same way'. In April 1664, a week before the Commons trade resolution, Coventry showed him Downing's opinion that there would be no war, and that although a Dutch fleet had just put to sea, it was not going to attack the African Company's ships (as actually it did). In July the Duke was expecting a war to begin in the winter. When the end of the year came, and a state of war virtually existed, Carteret repeated the view that trade was the only issue. The counter to all cleverer interpretations remains the Duke of Albemarle's simple manifesto: 'What matters this or that reason? What we want is more of the trade the Dutch now have.'[1]

As events unfolded, Coventry gave Pepys a more realistic political analysis. Coventry was by no means the hawk that his place in the Duke's household implied, and as which Clarendon's influential memoirs identified him. He agreed with Downing that when the Dutch saw that Parliament and King were united, and that therefore adequate supply would be voted for a war, they would back off. In other words, the whole parliamentary procedure was a charade, intended only to frighten the Dutch into negotiations. This intricate scenario was disrupted by reports from Guinea, where Holmes had again been despatched by the African Company with the Duke of York's licence to 'kill, take, sink or destroy' any opposition. Arguably he exceeded his overt instructions by seizing the island of Goree and a number of other Dutch possessions. Even so, Coventry continued to tell Pepys there were no real grounds for war. Holmes's raiding was an embarrassment which would oblige the King to conciliate the Dutch. He dismissed the other main arguments, albeit unconvincingly: he estimated trade lost to the East Indiamen off Malabar (for which the Company would later claim £53,560) at £3,000. The African Company's losses from Dutch interference could not, he supposed, be above £300. He thought it might be only false rumour that the Dutch were not evacuating Pulo Run.[2]

Pepys was certainly familiar with the political and economic theory which underlay the feuding over sea routes and spice islands. The global market, Captain Cocke told him, was 'too little for us two' – that is the Dutch and the English – 'therefore one must down'. He was quite wrong, but it was a common view. Pepys heard the merchants on the Exchange talk of Dutch claims to be 'lords of the Southern Seas'. The Governor of the East India Company, Sir

Thomas Chamberlain, told him how these self-proclaimed lords asserted sovereignty at Surat: thrashing Englishmen, and (worse) flying their flag above the cross of St George. Nevertheless the EIC was coolest of all the companies in agitating for war, and delayed its submission to the trade Committee so as not to appear among the more bellicose. Even for the African Company the war would bring commercial disaster in the short term, and this was reflected in a 45 per cent fall in its share price. Coventry put it plainly once hostilities had begun: 'our plantation trade will be in worse condition than before the war'. Which being so, it is argued, the war cannot have been genuinely caused by or for the commercial interest: hence the search for more intellectually convincing explanations. Particular significance is attached to the publication in early 1664 of Thomas Mun's *England's Treasure by Foreign Trade*, written in 1623. This contained propaganda material about Dutch commercial aggression which the government found useful to recycle. Mun's larger message was that world domination (what contemporaries called 'universal monarchy') was achieved through trade. In the 1620s it had been the Spanish who seemed to threaten in that way; in the 1660s some thought the Dutch entertained a similar ambition. Pepys bought Mun's book, probably on publication; unfortunately there is no record of his response to it.[3]

By contrast, the practical consequences of the drift to war are amply illustrated by Pepys's involvement in the intense naval preparations made during 1664. On 6 April he heard (wrongly, as it happens) that the Dutch had opened hostilities by granting letters of marque against English shipping. The Navy Board now needed extra workmen in the yards, whereas just a few months earlier men were said to be starving at Chatham for want of employment. The Board also began stockpile provisions, especially those which had to be imported, which in turn led to problems of storage. By 12 May Pepys was convinced that the Navy was being put on a war footing. On the 18th the Duke, receiving intelligence of a Dutch fleet in the Channel, ordered twelve ships to sea, and the Board set to work 'with all imaginable dispatch'. It proved to be a false alarm, which was as well, because stores were still so low that no one ship could be fitted out without borrowing from another, and men could not be had without press warrants. That process was put in hand on 7 June, despite doubts about its legality in what was still officially peacetime. 2,000 seamen were required, in addition to dockyard craftsmen and labourers The ships preparing at Chatham had been inspected on 23 May by the King, who was said to be satisfied that he could put a battlefleet to sea at eight days' notice. Pepys found Sandwich upset that, although he had daily and ostensibly friendly contact with the Duke, nothing had been said of his being given a command. Sandwich wryly suggested that only the lingering guilt of his republican past kept him from pressing his claim; instead, he asked Pepys to pass a message via Coventry. Pepys did so at once, but Coventry's guarded response made him uneasy. Was it really that the twelve ships did not need a commander of Sandwich's rank? Nevertheless, he was put in charge of them by the time they were ready in the River on 30 June. Amidst all his other concerns Pepys had to deal with the aesthetics of war: Sandwich was fussing about lanterns, and the King sent an urgent order for gilding the carved work of the *Henrietta*. The King and Queen inspected the ships at the Hope on 4 July, and Pepys took a private trip to see them two days later.[4]

Pepys gives support to the view that prolonged diplomatic posturing was leading to a conflict which neither side really intended. A diplomatic solution had remained a possibility while Dutch negotiators were in England from June to September. Pepys heard that at the end of their stay they were roughly handled by the Duke; even so he could still hope for 'a tolerable offer of accommodation'. The Dutch had kept their home fleet in port, not yet ready for open war in European waters. Instead, they secretly ordered De Ruyter out of the Mediterranean to confront Holmes's ships in Guinea. Sandwich advised that this threat should be countered with the strike force immediately available, without waiting for general mobilisation. Prince Rupert, as Pepys learned on 31 August, was therefore ordered to sail with six men-of-war escorting six of the African Company's own ships. Pepys was never dazzled by Rupert's heroic reputation, and when this squadron sailed on 5 October, he could only sneer 'God give him better success than he used to have'. Two days before, he had heard the Duke announce that he would pull rank on Sandwich by taking personal command of the home fleet, with Penn as his chief of staff. The Board was immediately charged with fitting out seventeen sail, including the 1st-rate *Royal James*. Preparing this one ship absorbed all the seamen at Chatham; Pepys was asked to draft in 300 Thames watermen, and promised 200. At least they would be better than the handful of countrymen ('millers, sawyers, and such like' some of whom 'never saw a shipp before') pressed to serve at Portsmouth. Meanwhile a new building programme had been hastily approved. James argued that firepower was more important than numbers; a few capital ships would have been a better investment than a quantity of lesser rates, in which the Dutch were always likely to be superior. A concentration of forces was nevertheless thought necessary, and on 16 October the decision was taken to halt Rupert before he passed Spithead; his ships were then redeployed in the enlarged Channel guard.[5]

It was in the midst of these preparations that Pepys made a private purchase of calico for flags, a shortcut in the emergency, by which he genuinely hoped 'to save the King money and to get a little by it to boot'; nevertheless it was an infringement of the 1662 Instructions, and would catch up with him years later. Also in October there was a celebratory launch for the 2nd-rate *Royal Catherine*, which Christopher Pett had been building at Woolwich since 1661. Pepys attended the King and Duke, and provided the gilt flagon which by custom was presented to the shipwright to drink the King's health: an altogether more pleasing ceremony than the smashing of a bottle. The King was greatly pleased with the ship and, as Pett later assured Pepys, retained his enthusiasm although she was found to be crank. Despite his walk-on part at the *Catherine*'s launch, Pepys knew well enough that his own service ended at the water's edge. He resented the deference being given to Penn because of his previous commands, and the favour he was receiving from the Duke. Still, he could take pleasure in the frequency with which the King now mentioned his own name. At this time the Board was strengthened by the appointment of further Extra Commissioners (Pepys having argued against their being designated 'Sub-Commissioners'). First, Captain John Taylor and Colonel Thomas Middleton were chosen to reside at Harwich and Portsmouth. When Batten objected to Taylor as a religious extremist, Pepys argued that his proven professional competence was what mattered; this view was underwritten by Coventry, and won the day. A proposal to bring Sir William Rider on to the Board failed; a merchant, even a very grand one, could not be trusted to serve the King impartially. Instead an additional seat was provided for Lord Brouncker, the incumbent President of the Royal Society. Pepys gave his appointment a grudging welcome ('if any more must be'); in the event he was to prove a competent if not always valued colleague.[6]

There was some uncertainty about the point at which the war was actually begun; a formal declaration was not made until 4 March 1665. For financial purposes Parliament subsequently calculated the start from 1 September 1664, though Pepys was to argue that it should be backdated to include all the preparations and skirmishes. As early as 14 July the King asked him for details of gratuities paid in the previous war, so that the relatives of those already killed might have similar compensation. It may be said that the war's most significant event happened before it began: the capture of New Amsterdam on 30 July. The acquisition was re-named New York in honour of the Duke, who had efficiently planned the operation along with Berkeley, Coventry and Carteret. Pepys was not involved, and paid little attention to his colleagues' triumph. He considered that the seizure of the Swedish ship *St Jacob*, bringing a load of Sir William Warren's masts, of which he heard on 12 November, was the first significant act of hostility. Reaction had been swift if fortuitous, as bad weather drove several Dutch ships towards the English coast. Captain Thomas Teddeman had intercepted a wine fleet from Bordeaux, and taken about twenty merchantmen and their two escorts into Portsmouth; three other merchantmen were taken at Dover, and their men treated as prisoners of war. With this, Pepys felt, the war had begun; nevertheless it was assumed correctly that there would be no battle in the North Sea until the winter was over. The Dutch fleet which had been standing off the Texel returned to port, and early in December the Duke of York and Sandwich came in to Portsmouth: 'so much like a victory', Pepys told Sandwich, 'your enemy fleeing'. He likewise congratulated Penn on his 'triumphant return'. Actually, the English had been sold a dummy; the real action was taking place in West Africa, where De Ruyter recovered everything the Dutch had lost to Holmes earlier in the year, and took more besides. Pepys heard the dire news at the Exchange on 22 December, and at once wrote to Sandwich lamenting the 'utter ruin' of the Royal African Company to the tune of £100,000, and the cowardice of the English in surrendering calmly. Jokes about Dutch courage went out of fashion, and the apprehensions which Pepys had consistently felt about Dutch naval superiority were now more widely expressed.[7]

It was all a matter of money. Parliament had called for a war, and now it was to be asked to put cash on the table. Immediately before the new session, Pepys worked long with the Lord Treasurer's secretary, Sir Philip Warwick, to concoct the largest claim they dared. At the State Opening on 24 November the King claimed £800,000 to defray naval charges already incurred in defence of trade. Coventry confided to Arlington that this was a deliberate exaggeration; the wages bill for the current emergency was not above £504,000. Nevertheless, a little tweaking by Pepys the next day brought the sum to £852,700, by way of 'a scare to the Parliament, to make them give the more'. Which is exactly what, a few hours later, they did: £2½ million over three years, the largest supply ever yet voted. Pepys was initially joyful at the news, especially as the whole amount was intended for the Navy. A few days and some further calculations later he was confidently warning that this grant (styled the Royal Aid) would not support the war for more than two and a half years. He was right, but even his estimate of £1 million a year was inadequate: the three years of war eventually cost around £5 million. For the moment there was a breathing space; the mobilisation of autumn 1664 had revealed much unpreparedness, but lessons had been learned without the test of a general action. Now there was money (or rather the promise of it) to prepare for the spring.[8]

For Pepys, the approach of war meant intensified work within the Navy Office, as well as collaboration with associated agencies which now became necessary. Before a formal state of war was acknowledged, the government authorised general reprisals against Dutch shipping and stipulated the rewards for officers and men. A commission was established to dispose of ships and cargoes which the Court of Admiralty adjudged to be lawfully prize. Pepys, Mennes and Batten petitioned the King for appointment to the Prize Commission, pointing out that their predecessors so served in the First Dutch War. Pepys and his two colleagues were acting unofficially, and managed to upset Berkeley by not involving him in their suit. The King and the Duke of York preferred to take the opportunity of paying some political debts, and the members of the naval Committee of the Privy Council were appointed *en bloc* as Prize Commissioners on 24 December. Disappointed of this additional function, Pepys was very soon finding occasion to chivvy along the 'Lords of the Prizes'. In the long term he had his revenge by taking apart the Prize Commission's submission to the post-war enquiry.[9]

By the same proclamation of 1 November which authorised and regulated pillage, the King promised relief and care to the sick and wounded, and compensation to the widows, children and needy parents of the dead. Following the precedent of the First Dutch War, a Commission to administer these charities had been nominated on 28 October. Pepys's friend, the merchant George Cocke, was appointed Treasurer. One of the original Commissioners, Bullen Reymes, was also already well known to him as a supplier to the Navy, and through this new association their mutual regard would be extended. Sir Thomas Clifford and Sir William Doyley, MPs, were only vaguely familiar to Pepys at the time; the other appointee, John Evelyn, seemingly not at all. It was an incidental but not insignificant outcome of the Commission's work to bring Pepys and Evelyn together, leading to a social and scholarly relationship in which the study of naval history featured prominently. During the Second Dutch War their correspondence remained chiefly professional, as it was to be when Evelyn served again as Commissioner during the Third War. It testifies to the deep concern felt by both men for the sufferings which the war brought, and their belief that proper record-keeping was essential for the effective deployment of the funds provided. Despite Evelyn's often harrowing and always plaintive letters to Pepys on the subject, the medical and charitable care provided in Charles II's Navy contrasts favourably with that of former times.[10]

In the early January 1665 Captain Holmes had returned from Guinea, and had been sent to the Tower for exceeding his orders. Pepys realised this was a 'matter of jest only', though musing that Holmes might just have to be sacrificed to mollify the Dutch, as Sir Walter Ralegh had been for the sake of peace with Spain. Back in 1663, following their spat over the dismissal of Holmes's master, Richard Cooper, Pepys had been terrified that Holmes would challenge him to a duel. That quarrel was long forgotten in March 1665 when Pepys attended the dinner with which, in the civilised fashion of the time, the Lieutenant of the Tower celebrated Holmes's release. By this time the war was official, and the legality of Holmes's actions in Guinea ceased to be an issue. In the event it was not Holmes but Captain Thomas Allin who executed the definitive *casus belli* by attacking the Dutch Smyrna fleet off Cadiz on 19 December. Unlike Holmes, Allin had no need for the masquerade of self-defence; he was acting on direct orders from London. Despite the advantage always attending unprovoked aggression, Allin's success was limited: only two Dutchmen were sunk and two captured. Pepys was with the Duke of York on 16 January 1665 when the first despatches were received, and welcomed the news. This was tempered by confirmation that two 4th-rates, *Nonsuch* and *Phoenix*, had earlier been wrecked after grounding off Gibraltar. The public identified *Nonsuch*'s captain, Robert Mohun as a Jonah, recalling that he had lost his previous ship in similar fashion. Pepys knew better, that there had been a corporate navigational failure by Allin's masters, young and old.[11]

The first weeks of 1665 were a phoney war, as reaction to the Cadiz attack was awaited. Rumours of the Dutch in the Channel were frequent; on 3 February they were reported 'on the back-side of the Goodwin'. Sandwich could not find them; before radar, whole fleets commonly failed to locate one another in quite limited areas of open sea. Meanwhile xenophobia was being primed by further stories of Dutch atrocities. On 22 February the Privy Council announced the issuing of letters of marque in response to a similar action by the Dutch. On 4 March the heralds read the declaration of war at Whitehall and at points in the City. Pepys reported the proclamation at the Royal Exchange: the war mongers were being given what they had asked for. Nemesis struck swiftly, blowing up the 2nd-rate *London* as she was being brought into the River on 7 March; all but a handful of the 351 aboard were killed. Carelessness in the magazine as a salute was being prepared seems to have been the cause. For Pepys this was the first major disaster within his professional domain; while acknowledging that there was little that an enquiry could establish, he was dismayed that the incident was as quickly forgotten as a minor accident to the *Royal Charles* a few weeks before.[12]

A final peace mission was sent by Louis XIV, who had no wish to see either the English or the Dutch emerge as a maritime superpower. Pepys knew that ambassadors had arrived, but was astray in assuming they intended an Anglo-French war against the Dutch. Their immediate purpose was to keep the English fleet at Harwich. In that they failed, and on 20 April the Duke of York put to sea with over 100 sail. As late as 8 April Pepys's prayers had still been for peace; now they were for victory. Accompanying the Duke in the *Royal Charles* was Coventry, whose absence from the Office Pepys regretted. With Penn also aboard the flagship, Batten's health failing, and Mennes often away, the management of naval supplies was concentrated in Pepys's hands. He thrived on the challenge, working late, and forsaking social pleasures. In the Duke of York's absence he was reporting to the Duke of Albemarle, for whose solid competence he was grateful. In turn Albemarle told Pepys he was 'the right hand of the Navy here' (the qualification needs to be remembered). Pepys also received a quite literal pat on the head from Lord Chancellor Clarendon for helping to keep the Thames watermen at work loading beer and water. Meanwhile the Duke of York took his ships to within six leagues of the Texel, from where Coventry wrote on 28 April. By despatch of the same day Pepys was first alerted to the possibility that plague from Holland had been brought into the quarantine port of Hole Haven in Essex. Two days later he makes first mention of the epidemic which had in fact been developing in London for a month.[13]

Early in May came news of the Duke's imminent return, which made Pepys yet busier. Even so he was unable to get the necessary supplies to Harwich, where the fleet anchored on the 15th. There was a shortage of men to crew the victuallers, beer could not be sent until casks (emptied at the rate of 812 a week) were returned from the fleet, and when supply ships were ready, they were kept in the River by contrary winds. This was understood at Harwich, but in London Pepys fretted that the Office would be blamed, and that he had been spending too much time on Tangier business. On 23 May he heard that the Dutch battlefleet of 100 sail was at sea, and found Albemarle 'mightily off the hooks' (as we might say 'unhinged') at the continuing detention of the victuallers. Aboard the *Charles* the Duke of York was also becoming impatient, and on 26 May decided to meet the Dutch as soon as a minimum of victuals was received. Before he could do so a convoy from Hamburg had mistaken the Dutch fleet for the English, and had sailed straight into the enemy; tar, timber, copper, iron and other provisions which Pepys estimated at £200,000 (though mostly the merchants' liability) were lost. Coventry was criticised on the Exchange for not telling the convoy that the English were back in port; Pepys countered that the correct intelligence had been sent, but the convoy had delayed its departure.[14]

At 1.30 p.m. on 1 June Coventry reported the appearance of the Dutch off Southwold. Pepys knew before he went to bed that night that the fleets were in sight of one another, and had confirmation from Batten (at Harwich) the next day. On 3 June the first general action of the war was fought off Lowestoft. Many people in London, the King included, persuaded themselves that they could hear the rumble of the guns 120 miles away; Pepys does not in so many words say that *he* did so, and it may be that what the

Londoners heard was mere thunder. It was some days before Pepys had certain news of a considerable success and the flight of the Dutch; it was a particular relief to hear that the Duke, Prince Rupert, Sandwich and Coventry were unharmed. He summarised the news reports in a special entry in his Diary, and understandably so. Lowestoft was the Restoration Navy's finest hour; arguably it was the best result for British forces between the Armada and Blenheim. The estimates were that of the 100 or so Dutch sail, 43 had found safety, 24 had been sunk or taken, and the rest were being pursued. Dutch casualties were put as high as 10,000, English not more than 700; this exaggerated the numbers but not the ratio.[15]

When the Duke and his staff arrived back in London on 16 June, Pepys had an authoritative report of the action from Coventry, including a better assessment of the losses in ships and men on both sides. The 250 or so English dead included the Earl of Falmouth (Berkeley's brother, a favourite of the King) and Rear Admiral Robert Sansum. Vice-Admiral Sir John Lawson died a few days later from an infected wound; a national tragedy, Pepys conceded, though not one for which he felt any personal grief ('for he was a man never kind to me at all'). Holmes was so disappointed at not being given the flag vacated by Sansum that he handed over his commission, and the Duke tore it up. A more serious concern was the extent of the English triumph, since the fleeing Dutch had not in fact been pursued, and were themselves claiming a victory. Coventry warned that they had ships and money enough, and would be out again as soon as they had the men. It eventually emerged that after the battle, one of the Duke of York's courtiers had presumed to order *Royal Charles* to slacken sail, allowing the Dutch to escape. Penn, as the Duke's senior aide, was to be caught up in this controversy. For the moment, he was among the heroes, and Pepys forgot their quarrels in welcoming him home. Sandwich, who gave his own account of the battle to Pepys on 23 June, had also done well, assisted by the heavy armament which his flagship carried. The superior firepower of the English 1st- and 2nd-rates was, Pepys concluded, a decisive factor: 'The great Shipps are the ships do the business, they quite deadening the enemy.'[16]

A public thanksgiving was held on 20 June, and when the King visited the fleet at the Buoy of the Nore he knighted several of the victorious commanders. The celebration was spoiled by news that the Dutch were at sea again, and another fight would be needed to finish the business. Coventry, who had also been knighted, and admitted to the Privy Council, kept Pepys abreast of debate in the royal household about the Duke of York's continuing command. They agreed between themselves that James had done all that should be asked of him, and ought not be exposed to further risk. The Duke's automatic precedence had inhibited rivalries which now emerged in the contest to succeed him. Coventry argued that Rupert, who was by social standing the next in line, was too disdainful of contrary advice; he thought Sandwich would do the job better. The King tried to persuade Sandwich and Rupert to share command. Sandwich was willing enough (and though no friend of the Prince, he had recently told Pepys that his conduct at Lowestoft deserved better recognition). Rupert at first proposed two independent fleets, but when the King rejected this idea, he too accepted joint-command. This was sabotaged by Coventry's insistence that Rupert and Sandwich would never agree; the King yielded, and invented a need to keep Rupert at Court. By the time that Pepys had learned some part of these manoeuvres, the fleet had sailed from Sole Bay with Sandwich in senior post as Admiral of the Red, Penn and Allin commanding the White and Blue squadrons. The Dutch home fleet was back in port, so the English proposed to intercept De Ruyter's return from West Africa, and to plunder the East India fleet sheltering in the Baltic. By early August it was known that De Ruyter was safely home, and Pepys feared that Sandwich's reputation would be dented as a result.[17]

Throughout this summer the plague took devastating effect in London and other parts of the country, complicating the war effort. On 27 July the Navy Office decided to hold its twice-weekly meetings at Deptford. Pepys had just evacuated his wife to Woolwich, but he stayed at the Office's London building until August, his functions increasingly impeded as his colleagues and contacts took refuge in the country. When eventually he found himself alone, he proposed that the whole naval administration be moved to Greenwich, which the King authorised on the 15th. Pepys moved his own lodgings to Woolwich on 28 August, transferring in October to Greenwich, where he stayed until January 1666. As he immediately discovered, the plague had already reached Woolwich and Greenwich, and was spreading to Chatham. There it compounded the problems of caring for the Lowestoft survivors and other casualties (including many Dutch prisoners). At Portsmouth there were fears that the infection would be brought from Southampton, and Commissioner Middleton prohibited commuting by his dockyard carpenters. He remained worried about seamen and their wives coming from London, some with open sores; like all his contemporaries he was unaware that the plague bacterium spread only by the bite of a flea, and so the suppurating buboes of London refugees did not in themselves threaten his workforce. Nevertheless his precautions were sensible enough, and Portsmouth remained free of plague during 1665. Penn saw the epidemic as a good opportunity to extend the use of tickets for paying seamen, since fewer would then congregate in the dockyards. In the King's ships themselves there seem to have been relatively few plague casualties. The worst case was the *Convertine*, aboard which forty-seven died from a complement of 190 (though possibly not all of plague). Three officers of one ship died at Yarmouth, and eight men aboard the *Essex* (which eventually brought plague into Portsmouth in 1666). Three or four men from the *Rupert* died after coming ashore at Harwich: 'but that' as Clifford put it, 'clears the ship well enough of it'.[18]

While Pepys was still in London on 16 August he heard the confusing rumours of events in the North Sea. Three days later he learned from Sandwich's despatch that Sir Thomas Teddeman had on 3 August attempted to seize the thirty Dutch East Indiamen as they lay in the neutral port of Bergen. The Danish governor was not party to his own King's collusion with the English, and had instead joined with the Dutch to repel Teddeman's squadron. Among the casualties was Sandwich's (and therefore Pepys's) kinsman Edward Montagu. Though no ships were lost, it was a bad humiliation. Pepys was philosophical, more concerned that the fleet had returned with virtually all its victuals spent, and had to be set out again in greater force. Sandwich was at sea again before the end of the month, though he still failed to prevent the main Dutch East Indies fleet reaching the safety of the Texel. When he did capture a few stragglers, he allowed a distribution of their cargoes without waiting for the Admiralty Court's declaration of prize, thereby committing the offence of 'breaking bulk'. The ensuing scandal temporarily ended Sandwich's naval career, and he was packed off to Spain as ambassador. Penn and many others were deeply implicated, and the issue was doggedly pursued in the post-war enquiries. Pepys had joined with George Cocke in buying £1,000 worth of spices from the plundered ships; he quickly sold his half-share to his partner when it became clear that a major row was developing. The incident continued to worry him, though its main consequence (Sandwich's absence in Spain) probably worked to his advantage, moving him more directly into the Duke of York's affinity.[19]

Pepys's anxieties over victualling the fleet before Lowestoft were increased by the further problems encountered in the autumn. Sandwich had told him that the provisions he had taken to the Baltic were the worst he had known. Sir Denis Gauden ran the whole victualling business as a kind of purser-general. Gauden was himself competent; but as Coventry pointed out, he could not be everywhere, and the whole system hinged precariously on his vitality. Pepys was asked by Albemarle and Carteret to consider alternative arrangements: inviting or compelling Gauden to take partners, or de-privatisation. His analysis defined the perennial problem of recruiting successful businessmen to run public concerns. He thought it would be even more difficult to bring in men of suitable standing during the continuing epidemic. Instead, he proposed that Crown surveyors be appointed in every victualling port, with powers to examine all paperwork, and reporting weekly to a Surveyor-General in London. Collation of this information from the localities was, Pepys believed, the key to the operation, and, writing to Coventry on 19 October, he coyly nominated himself for the post. Busy though he already was, he expected he would actually save paperwork and mental labour by processing this additional business through his own desk. In

Coventry's absence the Duke of York had himself opened Pepys's letter and approved it. On 27 October Albemarle invited Pepys to become Surveyor-General, which of course he accepted. The formal appointment was made on 4 November, bringing Pepys a further annual stipend of £300. He had already nominated the port officials, and set about devising instructions for them. One of the Office clerks, Thomas Pointer, was seconded to him for the victualling business, and another, Tom Wilson, was given the surveyorship of the port of London. Gauden retained his own position, and helped Pepys to understand his new responsibilities.[20]

He had more to learn about public finance. Parliament had voted a further £1¼ million for the war in October 1665, with new provisions allowing the government to accept loans and goods on its security, and for naval purchases to be made directly from the Exchequer. Pepys was at first sceptical. knowing that most potential investors were already owed more by the Navy than they could now advance. He was also influenced by Carteret, who stood to lose some of his poundage commission as Navy Treasurer. Downing (who with Coventry was chiefly responsible for the act) explained advantages in it which Pepys admitted he had not considered. Nobody, Downing assured him, would operate the system better than Pepys himself. The Duke of York invited him to see the new fiscal machinery as 'a cake in the oven' which might yield £200,000 down. By the end of the year Pepys had duly contracted with Warren for £2,000 worth of Norway masts, and with other suppliers for goods to almost the same amount. Eventually the Duke's cake rose well enough, and Pepys would help himself to a generous slice; but as the year turned he remained doubtful of its prospects. The war was going badly, and inadequate finance seemed to him the only explanation. Clearly the Dutch were not beaten, and were rebuilding their fleet. They had appeared menacingly off Southwold and Margate during October, although only managing to shoot a couple of sheep. Pepys knew they would be back, and that without adequate naval protection, the English were dead as mutton.[21]

FIVE

Question Time

'We are having shock after shock out here. The damage to the
battleships at this time is a disaster . . . The worst feature is that
we do not know how they penetrated the boom defences.'
Admiral Sir Andrew Cunningham, 28 December 1941
[*The Cunningham Papers*, I, ed. M.A. Simpson
(NRS CXL, 1999), p. 557]

While the fleet was laid up for the winter, Pepys had time to
appraise the victualling business he had wished upon himself.
He began with an analysis of the pursers' duties as variously defined
in the past, and concluded that the original method was best: to
make them fully answerable for wages, while allowing reasonable
trading margins in supply of victuals. His principle was simple: 'my
work is likeliest to be best done by him whose profit is increased by
the well doing of it without increase of charge to me that employs
him'. The exegesis, however, took ten hours to dictate, and occupies
eighteen printed pages. The proposal was despatched to Coventry
on 2 January 1666, and was substantially approved by the Duke of
York in April. Meanwhile Pepys set his wife and her companion to
work, ruling up new-style account books for the pursers.[1]

The overall financial problem was not to be resolved by market
economics or cottage industry. In March Pepys showed that against
book credit of £1,498,483 (chiefly represented by the £1¼ million
promised from the Additional Aid), the Navy debt stood at
£2,775,644. By Easter the tax had yielded some £798,727, but was
also having to subvent the Ordnance Office. In May the Board
petitioned the Duke of York for £167,000 to cover outstanding bills
and wages due in the dockyards, and £20,000 a week to sustain

72

current expenditure. Two months later they were obliged to point out that only £124,000 had been received.[2]

Against this background of insecurity the war entered its second year with a new enemy. Louis XIV, who had continued to mediate between the English and Dutch, had come to fear that an English victory would upset his own plans for the Netherlands. In particular he did not want to see the House of Orange restored to power under Charles II's protection. So in January he declared war. 'God knows', Pepys commented, 'how little fit we are for it'; he voiced the common expectation that the French and Dutch navies would combine to the destruction of the English. Actually, Louis was disinclined to venture his newly built fleet, and he did not need to. The mere threat of the French and Dutch fleets joining up induced a near-fatal division of the English. Charles had unwittingly contributed to this by deciding in November 1665 (and as Pepys belatedly discovered on 8 December) that Rupert and Albemarle should hold joint command in the following year. It was not until April that they went to sea. Pepys was unenthusiastic, because the new Admirals were taking the place of the disgraced and absent Sandwich. Nevertheless he recorded the general optimism which accompanied their departure. Once again his energies were stretched in supplying the fleet as it stood at the Buoy of the Nore.[3]

That Pepys was as yet some way from the centre of affairs is well shown by events on 14 May. Early that morning Coventry and Carteret were summoned down to the fleet, and Penn followed them. Pepys was left to play Cinderella, with nothing to do except tidy the Office. Unknown to him, Carteret and Coventry, as Privy Councillors, had been delegated to make a firm battle plan with the Admirals. It was agreed that Rupert should take twenty ships to intercept the French before they could join the Dutch. Rupert sailed westward on the morning of the 29th, expecting to encounter the Duc de Beaufort coming from La Rochelle. The same day Albemarle, who was in the Downs, had certain news that the Dutch were at sea. The Duke of York let him decide whether or not to face them with his residual fleet, but had advised moving to the Gunfleet, where he could more readily be reinforced by great ships still in the

River. For Pepys the first indication that the Dutch were out was the government's sudden proclamation on 28 May of a day of prayer. By the time the services were held on 31 May he knew where the two sections of the fleet had been sent: though just before midnight, the Duke of York had signed an order for Rupert's return. The Prince received it at 10 a.m. on 1 June, when Albemarle had already sighted the Dutch off the Kent coast, and was preparing to engage. It was not until the following morning that Pepys was officially informed that battle was joined, and the news put the whole Board 'into a Tosse'. In the afternoon he went down to Greenwich, and supposed he heard the guns clearly (though later accepted it was just thunder). He now knew of Rupert's recall, and optimistically thought he would have reached Albemarle by noon that day. In fact he did not do so until the afternoon of 3 June, and did not join the fight until its fourth and final day. There was, Pepys realised, 'great bad management in all this'. The delay in communicating with Rupert, and the Prince's seemingly tardy response, were already matters of public debate, and would feature prominently in the postwar recriminations about the division of the fleet. Pepys was immediately inclined to blame the secret service ('How bad we are at intelligence'), a line which would be pursued by the parliamentary critics. In reality the Secretaries of State were well informed on the Dutch movements; it was not their fault that the French threat never materialised, and Rupert's excursion was therefore unnecessary.[4]

Reliable news of the action of 1–4 June was slow in coming. On the 6th, when guns could no longer be heard, a victory was confidently presumed. This seemed to be confirmed by Captain John Hayward of the *Dunkirk*, who reported that at the end of the third day the Dutch had withdrawn with the loss of half their ships. Court and City celebrated. On the 7th came quite different news: great losses of ships and men; the famous old 1st-rate *Royal Prince* run on to the Galloper Sand and burned, with Admiral Sir George Ayscue taken prisoner. Pepys concluded that 'we are beaten in every respect'; he and Creed talked morosely of the failings of Albemarle and Rupert, and how much better things might have been had Sandwich still been in command. Pepys shortly had an eye-witness account from James Pearse the Surgeon-General, who told him how Albemarle was criticised in the fleet for his conduct of the battle, yet remained convinced of his having won a victory. Pepys was soon able to refute Albemarle's bogus statistics. The truth was that nobody had won, and it all had to start again. Pepys was at once busy with setting out more ships. Rupert was soon complaining that only the Navy Board's incompetence was keeping them back. More money was sought on the security of the Additional Aid; Pepys thought the City would not 'lend a farthing', though in fact the government heavyweights squeezed out another £100,000.[5]

The work of reconstruction paused on 13 June to bury Sir Christopher Myngs, the senior Vice-Admiral, who had died from wounds after the battle. Myngs had been a dashing and charismatic figure, perhaps the only one of Charles II's commanders cast in the Elizabethan mould. His irregular exploits on the Spanish Main had brought him official censure and public renown. The loyalty of his 'following', that special chemistry which bonded men to a respected commander, was vividly demonstrated to Pepys after the funeral. A group of Myngs's men came up to him and Coventry, begging to be posted to a fireship where they might serve the memory of their lost leader. Pepys thought it an 'extraordinary case – one of the most Romantique that I ever heard of'. Here 'romantic' has no emotional connotation; rather it means 'story-book' or even 'outlandish'. Even so, Pepys was moved to tears, and penned a glowing tribute to Myngs's heroics.[6]

The Dutch won the race to refit, and were out again by 25 June. One of Pepys's less welcome duties was transporting pressed men, who were being held in the London prisons, down to the fleet. He was upset by the spectacle, and angered by the illegality of taking up landsmen; at the same time he abhorred violence used against the press-masters. All he could do was to ensure that the men were delivered to the ships as efficiently as possible. Some of the conscripts nevertheless made their escape, and a number of men already aboard and in pay quite literally jumped ship. Morale throughout the fleet was understandably at rock bottom. Plans were discussed for building ten more ships (2nd- and 3rd-rates), for which

Pepys knew there was no money: 'but . . . the show must be made to the world'. New building, authorised before the war, was replacing losses, but losing ground against Dutch expansion. Over the whole war just ten ships (3rd-, 4th-, and 5th- rates) were built in the dockyards, against forty of 50 guns or more (equivalent to 4th-rates and above) built by the Dutch. During 1666 the Jacobean 2nd-rate *Victory* emerged after an expensive refit. A new 2nd-rate, *Loyal London*, was built at the City's expense to replace the *London* blown up in the previous year. She was not quite ready in time for the Four Days' Fight, and her launch on 10 June was all the more welcome in its aftermath. Then, when all twenty-two of her main 42-pdr guns shattered during trials, she appeared to be the largest white elephant afloat. Pepys feared this would depress confidence in the King's service yet further; fortunately he was soon assured that she had proved to be 'the best ship in the world'.[7]

The new *London* joined a fleet of 89 men-of-war and eighteen fireships assembled at the Buoy of the Nore. It was, Pepys believed, the greatest force of ships, guns and men the Royal Navy had ever set out. With justifiable pride he reported to the Duke on the successful provisioning of the second fleet within a year. A few hours after this was written, on the afternoon of 25 July, he stood on the leads above the palace of Whitehall to hear the gunfire as battle was again joined in the North Sea. It was two days later before he had the first news; that the 3rd-rate *Resolution* had been destroyed by a fireship, while four or five Dutchmen had been sunk. A firmer report from Coventry, arriving on the 29th, confirmed that no other English man-of-war had been lost, while two of the Dutch great ships had been taken and burnt. The enemy fleet had retreated to home waters. After the premature celebration in June, Pepys was understandably reluctant to believe in the victory which Coventry assured him had now been won, and which he heard proclaimed from the pulpits that Sunday; it seemed 'but a poor result after the fighting of two so great fleets'. The St James's Day Fight was certainly won by the English; the Dutch lost twenty ships and about 4,000 men, whereas the English casualties were numbered in hundreds. Yet, as at Lowestoft, there were accusations that the fleeing Dutch were not more strenuously pursued, and Pepys's perspective was realistic: 'we keep the sea . . . at least . . . we are not beaten'.[8]

The battle was followed up on 9–10 August when Holmes raided the Dutch coast, firing over 150 ships at anchor in the Fly channel. Pepys was cheered by this unplanned success, though regretting that it would consolidate the recovery of Albemarle's reputation. At the same time he was worried that he would be blamed for delays in victualling the fleet as it lay in Sole Bay. He was right: the Admirals wrote to the Duke of York and then directly to the King, complaining of shortages, of the quality of the beer they had received, and (worse) of the accuracy of Pepys's manifest. They articulated action man's age-old contempt for the backroom boy: 'when we send up our demands, instead of having them answered and complyed withall, we have accounts sent us from Mr Peppys of what hath been ship't for the fleet'. Pepys managed to talk himself out of trouble when summoned before the King and his advisers on 26 August, and was indignant at the second 'most scurvy letter' from Rupert and Monck. He remained genuinely convinced of the accuracy of his paperwork, while recognising that it needed to be backed up by solid performance. The incident also reminded him to prepare against the larger enquiry which would one day be made.[9]

That day came perhaps sooner than he anticipated, as when Parliament reassembled in September, the Commons asked to see the Navy's books. Pepys met Carteret and Coventry on the 23rd to discuss tactics, and they reckoned that the two years of war had cost the Board £3,200,516, towards which they had received £2,270,020. Their accounting, Pepys admitted, would not bear strict examination, and Coventry wondered where the full £4 million voted by Parliament had gone. (In fact the yield was less, and part went to the Ordnance Office.) When on the following day Pepys saw the accounts which Carteret was going to take over to the House, he was horrified to see that the second entry was a record of his own illicit traffic in calico. He had the presence of mind to scratch out his own name and insert another. Preparation of the audit took place in the aftermath of the Great Fire which had devastated London on 2–5 September; the Navy Office and Pepys's house were lucky survivors, but their temporary evacuation had understandably caused much disorder of books and papers. Otherwise the Fire had little immediate bearing on naval management; the stores were untouched, and were even able to supply Navy bread to the homeless (though they declined to eat it). George Cocke actually suggested to Pepys that the disaster would make Parliament docile, and the more willing to vote further supply; in similar vein, Coventry thought the members would soon tire of their enquiries, and give the King what he wanted. More realistically, when Pepys heard on 26 September that a select Committee was appointed to inspect the Navy and Ordnance accounts, he anticipated 'much trouble and blame', perhaps even a rolling of heads. The Committee immediately asked for a statement of the numbers of ships and men serving during the war, and the sums paid to them. Such lists were duly provided, and the Board then did some provisional calculations in case Parliament should question the rate of £4 per man per month on which their previously declared estimate of £3,200,516 was based. A rate of £3 16s per man per month, 'the least the Parliament in utmost severity can allow' would lower that sum by £235,031, but the Board then identified a further £345,323 paid out or written off, allowing them to claim an additional £110,292, even with the lower monthly rate per man. The Navy Officers appeared before a sub-Committee for naval accounts on 3 October. Pepys's fears were compounded when he found how unerringly his interrogators hit on the weak points in the Board's accounting (such as whether ships were really fully manned from the dates given). Parliament would not allow the Board's claim that fleet preparations before 1 September 1664 should be included in the war estimates, and deducted £150,000 which they judged to be saved by laying up the fleet that winter. They did, however, accept the £4 per man monthly rate, establishing a standard which stood for the rest of the century. On 12 October they voted a further £1,800,000 for the war, at which Pepys first shared Coventry's satisfaction. A few days later he was reflecting that this further grant was likely to be the last, and would serve only to encourage the King to make a quick and unsatisfactory peace.[10]

In the end Pepys coped well with parliamentary scrutiny in 1666, and his talents had been advantageously deployed before that discerning audience. It was again suggested that he might enter the House of Commons (particularly if Coventry should be elevated to the Lords). Pepys was flattered to be canvassed by so distinguished a parliamentarian as Sir Stephen Fox, but for the moment he was content to remain an administrator. The worry over the accounts nevertheless confirmed his view, endorsed by Coventry, that the system could never operate properly as long as Mennes remained Comptroller. They discussed the possibility of making him an honorific supernumerary on the Board, something which Coventry thought the Duke of York would implement. They reckoned without the old man's tenacity, and the reluctance of the royal brothers to demote him. Pepys was not keen that the vacated Comptrollership might go to Penn, though conceding that he was 'the only man fit for it'. This did not come about, and he welcomed the compromise arranged in January 1667, by which Brouncker and Penn were deputed to assist the Comptroller in, respectively, the pay and victualling accounts. Pepys continued to press for Mennes's further marginalisation, and two years later Brouncker was given additional responsibility for auditing one of Sir William Warren's major accounts.[11]

The campaigning season of 1666 had concluded without further large-scale encounters. On 1 September, when English and Dutch fleets had been in sight of one another off Calais, bad weather and uncharacteristic hesitation by Rupert had prevented engagement. The larger part of the English fleet was still fitting out at Portsmouth, and when Albemarle was called up to deal with the Fire crisis, sole naval command devolved on the Prince. Pepys was unhappy that the fleet was now in the charge of 'an unlucky man', though he was persuaded that the Dutch were only at sea for the benefit of their own people, lacking the men and *matériel* to sustain hostilities. Rather more was now feared from the French, as Beaufort's fleet eventually made its way into the Channel to link up with the Dutch. An intended interception failed, and Sir Thomas Allin merely caught a few stragglers. One of these, the *Rubis*, sailed up to her captors, having mistaken Allin's white command flag for the French standard. It was the only triumph Pepys could think of when reviewing matters at the end of October. He saw the military and administrative state of the Navy locked in stalemate, and was acutely aware of discontent among the seamen and in Parliament. All parties were looking for escape routes. The King noted that even his brother now wanted the war to end, 'beleeving it nether good for him, nor for me'. That was not, of course, what the Duke told the Navy Board, though he was unable to offer them any immediate solution of the financial impasse. Pepys was frustrated, telling Coventry that 'something should be done by us more than is', and the result was a typically massive report, the 'great letter' to the Duke. This was composed by Pepys during a twelve-hour session on 17 November, and signed by the Board on the following day. The 'great letter' reviewed their previous submissions and accumulated debts (£934,000), and itemised £179,793 10s worth of materials required for the next year's campaign, and to fit out ships then building.[12]

Although Pepys was gloomy about the war and its finances, he had a new personal interest in its prolongation. Along with Batten and Penn, he had become a shareholder in a privateer, the *Flying Greyhound*. This was a 20-gun Dutch prize, designated as a fireship, but for which there was no immediate service. She had therefore been handed over to the triumvirate, who undertook all the manning and operating costs. Letters of marque had been issued on 4 October, and some successes were achieved. Pepys soon surrendered a third of his share to Sir Richard Ford, though for a while he continued to enjoy the vicarious thrill of legalised robbery. Before long he was caught up in disputes with the Swedish diplomatic resident, Baron Leijonbergh, two of whose nation's ships had been seized by the *Flying Greyhound*. There were squabbles between the partners over instructions to the captain, Edward Hogg, who emerged as a 'most observable embezzler'. Then a disgruntled Navy Office clerk leaked the inconvenient truth that the ship's crew had been helped to the front of the pay queue. The Commissioners of Accounts made awkward enquiries, which Pepys was obliged to play with a dead bat. He eventually came to regret the whole venture. The ship had been due for return to the King in the spring of 1667, when the partners hoped the loan might be made into a gift. Batten and Pepys were furious when Penn secured such a grant for himself. In October 1667 Pepys was given another Dutch prize, the 108-ton *Maybolt*; an uneconomic acquisition, which he sold off as soon as he could. Meanwhile Batten had died, leaving his widow little except a claim on the proceeds of the *Flying Greyhound*'s plundering. She promptly married Leijonbergh, who took up the other side of the case, and in 1670 threatened to call Pepys out. Happily these differences were composed, and in 1687 Leijonbergh made a handsome present to Pepys's library, inscribed with a tribute to their long years of friendship.[13]

The £1,800,000 voted by Parliament to continue the war into 1667 would never have done more than soak up old debts; in any case the larger part (£1¼ million) would not be collected before 1668, and the supply was so hung about with conditions that in the end neither the donors nor the recipients were happy. The Navy Board continued to be asked to fit out ships; but they could not do so without men, and the men would not go without money. Pepys heard in mid-January that the Dutch had offered to negotiate once a location was agreed; he dismissed this at first, and so was genuinely surprised to learn a month later that the diplomacy had begun. While he knew that the war could not realistically be continued, he remained scornful of a cut-and-run peace. With Rupert temporarily out of action (actually having his head examined), it was unclear who was in command of the fleet, or indeed if there would be a fleet to be commanded. The decision, revealed by the Duke of York to the Navy Board on 6 March, was for 'altering the manner of the war this year'. Squadrons of small ships would be kept at sea, to annoy the Dutch where they could; but the great ships would remain laid up. In other words, no general action would be risked, even though this meant yielding control of the sea to the enemy. The prospect of the Dutch blockading the River was already anticipated, and resources would be concentrated on coastal defence. The King and the Duke made light of the fact that the Dutch were well aware that the English were cowering behind half-built fortifications. For his part Pepys did his best to cheer up the increasingly embattled Navy Treasurer by calling the port-based commanders the 'land-Admiralls'.[14]

The jokes had worn off by the end of April, when it was known that a Dutch battle group was operating in the North Sea. In fact this was no more than a diversionary force, and the main fleet of eighty sail appeared off Harwich in the first week of June. The war was no longer exclusively a naval affair, and the militia were called up to meet the expected invasion. Pepys helped out with some maps. He was unimpressed by the enthusiasm with which many Court gallants set off for East Anglia with 'pistols and fooleries'; he doubted if they would threaten anything except the virtue of the local women. The Navy put its best hope in fireships (so successful in dispersing the Spanish Armada), and the Privy Council authorised the impressing of merchantmen to serve this purpose. Their despatch was Pepys's more immediate concern, and on 10 June he went scouting down the River, which was now effectively a war zone. For once he had ready money, as £500 meant for Chatham yard was diverted to the emergency. At Gravesend, he 'heard distinctly great guns play below'; as he learned the following day, this was the Dutch taking Sheerness. Albemarle planned to block the River with a line of ships, but chief confidence rested in the iron chain stretched across the Medway at Chatham. Behind it were the laid-up 1st- and 2nd-rates, defended only by their skeleton crews of standing officers, and by the land forts. On the morning of 12 June Pepys had been cheered by Albemarle's report that 'all is safe as to the great ships'; but within hours he had heard that the Dutch were through the boom, and several ships had been fired. The *Royal Charles*, which Pepys had first understood to be among the casualties, was famously taken back to Holland, where all that remains of her may still be seen.[15]

The Medway raid was the first of two great humiliations inflicted on the Royal Navy during Pepys's professional career; arguably it remains the service's worst hour in a thousand years. Pepys's immediate concern appears to have been the security of his own employment and the safety of his gold. His fear of 'violence on this office, or perhaps some severity on our persons' was real enough, and moving cash out of London was a sensible precaution. A little more self-sacrifice might have been in order, but this was not Pepys's style. Even the King (as Pepys reported him) fell some way short of the heroic model, telling the assembled militia that they 'should venture themselves no further than he would himself'. Rather more commendable were those seamen who told Pepys they would risk their lives if only their existing tickets might first be paid. He did his best to oblige them. The disaster struck to the heart of Pepys's domain: not just in the obvious geographical sense, but because it could not be blamed on the sea officers. The Chatham chain was hardware, and for its failure the Navy Board would have to answer. Pepys's first understanding was that a combination of strong easterly winds and a spring tide had enabled the Dutch to break the links. At the end of June he went to look for himself, and found no evidence of fracture; he could only think that either the Dutch ships had dislodged the floats which held the chain below the water, or that the tension had been slackened by destruction of the pulley mechanisms ashore. This leaves out of account the skill and heroism of the Dutch captain who steered straight at the hazard and seemingly did breach it.[16]

The crisis did not end when the enemy withdrew from the Chatham anchorage, and the *Royal Charles* was on her way to the Rijksmuseum; the Dutch simply sat in the mouth of the Thames until the peace was concluded. They came up as far as the Hope on 23 July, again assisted by an easterly which prevented the deployment of fireships against them. Though they were beaten back on the following day (Pepys again hearing the guns 'mostly distinctly and loud'), their continuing presence enforced an economic blockade every bit as worrying to Londoners as the actual military threat. The Navy made one last and rather feeble effort, when Sir Joseph Jordan brought down a squadron from Harwich. This time the fireships mostly failed to ignite (being packed with combustible matter but no explosives), or self-destructed to no purpose. The Dutch once again demonstrated their superior seamanship by withdrawing their ships through unfamiliar channels 'better', as Pepys ruefully noted, 'then we could do ours in the main sea'. When, on 28 July, he was certain than peace would be concluded, he was only too happy to see an end to further misery, contrasting the 'industry and advantages of the enemy' with the 'abjection, indigence and supineness of our own'. Knowing that there would be calls for retrenchment, he resigned his Surveyorship of Victualling before being forced to it.[17]

Despite his anxieties at the time of the Medway raid and more generally through the war, Pepys's main job was secure in its aftermath. Indeed it was the more so by his own efforts, and because of various changes in the administration. Mennes had been persuaded to accept the assistance of Penn and Brouncker, who in January 1667 were designated respectively Comptrollers of Victualling and of Treasurer's Accounts, and were between them given seven additional clerks. As soon as the war was over Carteret had given up the Navy Treasureship to the Earl of Anglesey, taking Anglesey's place as Vice-Treasurer of Ireland. Carteret was principally and unsuccessfully concerned to evade further parliamentary enquiry into his Navy accounts. At least his new post was potentially more lucrative. The new Treasurer was an old political ally of Sandwich, and at first impressed Pepys with his readiness to listen to him. Anglesey remained in office just long enough for this relationship to turn sour. Batten's health began to fail in the course of the summer of 1667, though his death on 5 October took Pepys by surprise. He and Penn immediately recommended Middleton, the incumbent Commissioner at Portsmouth, as 'a most honest and understanding man' to be advanced to the Surveyorship. Middleton had run his yard with a firm hand and, allowing for the permanent shortage of money, with a good measure of efficiency. When he took his place at the Board on 19 December, Pepys was confident that he would be a great improvement on his predecessor, and for the most part he was not disappointed. Early on, Middleton was unwise enough to accuse Pepys's trusted clerk Will Hewer of corruption, and had to retract when Pepys came powerfully to his defence. Afterwards Middleton took greater care with his paperwork. He had been an assiduous informant in his Portsmouth days, and Pepys's respect for his expertise grew when they became closer colleagues.[18]

Coventry had opposed the laying up of the fleet, and had threatened to resign his Commissionership over the issue. In the first week of 1667 he actually did so, prompting Pepys to ponder the implications for his own position. Although Coventry (who transferred to the Treasury) co-ordinated efforts to blame Clarendon for the failure of the war, he was himself brought down by the Lord Chancellor's fall, and in September he resigned his place as the Duke of York's secretary. Many people thought Pepys would succeed him, and Pepys was of course alive to the possibility. In the event the post went to Matthew Wren, who had been Clarendon's secretary. Once this was announced, Batten and Penn rather cruelly assured Pepys that they 'had long cut [him] out' for the job. The appointment did not make Wren a member of the Navy Board, but he sat in on their meetings by way of training. Pepys knew him as an acquaintance of the merchant George Cocke, and as a fellow member of the Royal Fishery. He welcomed him as a colleague ('a very ingenious man'), but Wren did not have his predecessor's stature. He upset Pepys in a variety of ways; by incompetently presenting naval estimates before Parliament; by his firm persuasion that only the nobility and gentry were fit to command on land or sea; and by telling a mildly scurrilous story at a meeting of the Board when the Duke was present.[19]

Although Pepys did not advance upwards to the Surveyorship or the Comptrollership of the Navy, or sideways into the Duke's direct service, his profile was raised during the parliamentary enquiries into the conduct of the war.

On 17 October 1667 the Commons established a Committee for Miscarriages, whose fifty-six members would open every can they suspected of containing worms. This was itself a constitutional innovation of great importance, the forerunner of tribunals more fully developed now on Capitol Hill than at Westminster. This embryonic form was too large a body to focus its attention, and lacked power of subpoena; its ultimate sanction was impeachment, which the Crown could and did thwart by proroguing the session. Pepys nevertheless viewed it with apprehension. However, much of the MPs' attention was directed to operational mishaps, which were not the Navy Board's responsibility. Pepys was glad to find that the first item on the agenda was the division of the fleet in 1666, for which he simply had to supply lists of the relevant ships. The Committee then looked into failure to chase the Dutch after the battle of Lowestoft; it was alleged that Penn, as the Duke of York's senior aide, had given the order to slacken sail by way of shielding the Duke from further danger. Pepys thought Penn's explanation (complete ignorance of the issue) suspicious, but the MPs accepted that the culprit was Lord Brouncker's brother Henry, a member of the Duke's household. The Committee took a prolonged interest in the Bergen prize-goods scandal, in which Penn was again heavily implicated along with Sandwich. The matters in which Pepys and the Board as a whole were most scrutinised were victualling, the issuing of pay tickets, and of course the failure of the Medway defences. It was in this last connexion that the Navy Officers were first examined by the Committee, on 22 October. Pepys had time to observe the nuances of parliamentary protocol: Penn went straight in and sat with his fellow MPs, but Brouncker (a mere Irish peer) was shown no more deference than Pepys himself. Pepys thought the questions 'impertinent' (a favourite word, by which he meant simply 'irrelevant'), but felt he fielded them well enough. Commissioner Pett, however, floundered. He had already been hauled before the Privy Council; now the MPs were targeting him, and his colleagues were happy to expose his position further by pointing out that the Chatham defences were his specific and sole responsibility. By the same token Sheerness was shown to be the concern of the Ordnance Office. Pepys did coach Pett a little in the political arts, not wishing him to suffer undeservedly, 'there being enough of what he doth deserve'. On 13 November the Commons voted for Pett's impeachment; this was dropped, but he lost his job.[20]

Pepys was bemused that the Commons should commend Rupert and 'that blockhead Albemarle' for their direction of the war in 1666, unaware that this was coupled with an invitation to leak information to them. Otherwise he was quite pleased with the direction of parliamentary proceedings, until the Miscarriages Committee started to ask about tickets. At the time and much later Pepys dismissed their concern as folly, resenting the labour of rebutting allegations of particular abuses, and of explaining the general necessity of the practice. In November the Committee ordered all the relevant books to be produced, and Pepys responded with one of his magisterial submissions. While this was well received by the Committee chairman, Sir Robert Brookes, the issue would not go away. When the Committee reported in 1668, ticket irregularities were still alleged, and on 22 February were formally voted to be miscarriages. The Navy Board had to respond, and Pepys did so in a three-hour speech before the whole House on 5 March. It was his most considerable public performance to date, staunching all criticism, and was much commended. Despite its length, Pepys's explanation was so orderly that one country MP was able to set down his own lucid digest of the issues.[21]

There was still a further and more daunting parliamentary inquisition to face: the Brooke House Commission. This was a hybrid descendant of the original Commons Committee of Accounts, to which Pepys had given evidence in the autumn of 1666. For some time the King had successfully thwarted Parliament's efforts to develop an effective enquiry into finances of the war, but in its embarrassing aftermath he was obliged to yield. He therefore agreed to establish a statutory Commission, its nine members to be nominated by Parliament; they were to include peers but no sitting members of the Commons. They were provided with salaries, clerks, and premises (the Brooke House in Holborn, from which they took their name), and were empowered to call for State Papers, to examine witnesses under oath, and to sue in the Exchequer for recovery of debt. They began their work in January 1668, and therefore operated concurrently with the Committee for Miscarriages. The Commission's smaller membership, professional staffing, and wider powers made it a more effective instrument; and its focus on financial affairs meant that the Navy Treasury and Board, not the Admiralty and the sea officers, would attract its chief attention. Pepys's initial impression was that the Commissioners 'being few and not of the House, will hear reason'. This gave way to apprehension when he heard of the great powers the Commission would have, and it was a while before he could bring himself to read the details in the empowering statute. He made his first appearance before them on 31 January to answer questions about tickets, which he did with his usual confidence. He was less happy when examined under oath on 5 February over the Bergen prize-goods scandal; the Commissioners, already impressively well-informed, produced as witness a waterman whom Pepys had unwisely rebuked while he was fencing his loot. This particular issue was no real danger to Pepys (at worst he would have to refund his £500 profit), but it served to warn him that Brooke House would need handling with care.[22]

For almost two years the Commissioners gathered information, issuing interim reports. With equal diligence Pepys answered their particular requests, and compiled evidence towards answering their final report. During the same period he conducted his own personal inquisition into the naval management of the war, as something necessary in its own right, but also by way of anticipating Parliament's charges. He had long felt that responsibilities within the Office were too loosely defined, and recognised that the necessary restructuring had to be imposed from above. So he primed the Duke of York with a detailed analysis of the failings of his colleagues, which James accepted *verbatim* and issued on 26 August. Of the Clerk of the Acts himself, the Duke (or rather Pepys himself) wrote: 'there hath not as yet occurred to me any particulars wherewith to charge him with failure'. Everyone else had his job specification scrutinised, and lapses from the 1662 Instructions noted. Individual responses were required, to which the Duke (in fact again Pepys) added further 'Reflections'. Needless to say he awarded himself straight alphas. The audacity with which Pepys directed this in-house examination is astonishing and, in a horrible way, impressive. There followed a larger questioning of the whole function of the Board, involving much searching of precedent on Pepys's part; his conclusion (submitted on the Board's behalf in April 1669) was that the traditional system, if operated properly, had a professional competence superior to the alternatives which had been tried under the republic. All this industry took its toll on Pepys's health. Failing eyesight caused him to give up his personal Diary on 31 May 1669; though his eyes recovered, he never took it up again. He had asked the Duke for three or four months' leave (until the new parliamentary session had to be faced), citing his unstinting wartime service and his wrecked eyes. It was an unusual request at the time, but one to which the King and the Duke readily agreed. Pepys and his wife took a holiday in France and the Netherlands, which was coupled with a little naval espionage. Pepys recovered quickly, but was then devastated by his wife's sudden death.[23]

Before he had time to cope with his loss, on 20 October Pepys 'met with a parcel': Brooke House had reported. They made ten 'Observations' on Carteret's accounts as Navy Treasurer, and a further eighteen 'Observations' on the management of the Navy Board. They appended a sensational allegation that over £½ million of the parliamentary vote had been spent on 'other uses' (by which scurrilous folk understood the King's mistresses). Carteret's accounts were examined by separate Committees of the Lords and Commons in November. Pepys's evidence to the former helped to ensure that, although the accounts themselves were in disarray, Carteret was not blamed. By contrast the Commons found the Treasurer guilty on nine out of the ten counts, and would have voted for his dismissal had the King not prorogued the session. In the recess the King acted swiftly by moving the debate on Brooke House's report to the Privy Council, where he could chair proceedings, and where his people would be protected. Carteret's accounts and the 'other uses' issue were debated again in the new forum. Pepys first appeared there as a witness on 5 January 1670, after a two-day briefing at the Treasury. The King was understandably indignant at the insinuations of personal corruption, and in fact the Commissioners acknowledged that he had spent beyond £½ million of his ordinary revenue on naval preparations. The question turned on how much of this applied to events before 1 September 1664, the date from which by statute the war finances were calculated. Pepys disputed the relevance of the date, and when taken to task by the Commission chairman, he advanced the questionable theory that the statute was 'penned for . . . information', and therefore he had 'a right of delivering [his] sense of it'. That was good enough for the King, who afterwards called Pepys his advocate, and repeatedly expressed his satisfaction. This developed as the Council moved on to discuss the second part of Brooke House's report, in which Pepys was much more substantially concerned.[24]

Pepys had sent a written response to the 18 'Observations' on 27 November 1669, without waiting to consult his colleagues. He followed this up on 6 January with a more detailed 'General Defence' on the Board's behalf, and a 'Particular Defence' of his own, which he also copied to the King and Duke. Mennes, Penn and Brouncker submitted individual written responses, but again it was Pepys who led for the Board when the eighteen 'Observations' were debated (12 January – 21 February). At the outset he secured the King's agreement to a procedure which would follow the lines of his prepared defence. After each Observation was read, and 'instances' cited, Pepys gave an extended version of his general answer. The other Navy Officers then had an opportunity to answer for their particular responsibilities. We have only Pepys's record of these proceedings, and while this is undoubtedly shaped to his advantage, there can be no disputing the competence with which he defended himself and his department. The Commission's most distinguished member, Lord Halifax, had declined to sign its report, and seems only once to have attended the hearing. The chairman, Lord Brereton, was a minor figure, respected for his intellect and tact, though he soon upset the King with an insolent remark. Pepys had shared the general view of him ('a very sober and serious, able man') until the debate began, when they had a few altercations. He had rather more of a contest with Colonel George Thomson, the only Brooke House man with relevant experience. He had served in the republican Admiralty and Naval Commissions, and retained a firm belief in the superiority of their management. Pepys at first had good hopes of Thomson ('likely to mind our business more then any'), but in debate he proved an awkward opponent. In part this was because

Pepys privately admired aspects of the administration in which Thomson had served. Also, since Pepys needed to justify recent practices by citing precedents in the First Dutch War, he found himself appealing to Thomson to support his own case.[25]

The 'Observations' touched three areas. Numbers 1, 2, 15, and 16 concerned contracts: favouritism in making, or negligence in fulfilling them. Particular interest was again shown in Warren's business of Göteborg masts, the expense of convoying contractors' ships, and in high prices paid for hemp and other commodities. Failures were alleged in the Board's book-keeping, and specifically about surveys, musters, and prize ships (3–10, 18). More controversial were charges that tickets had been issued and paid without proper checks (11–14, 17). Pepys was at his most assured in dealing with accounting processes, and silenced criticism with a battery of unanswerable detail. He was now particularly well practised in explaining the complexities of the ticket system. Where he had to admit failure (as over the regular surveying of stores), he had the reasonable excuse of wartime emergency. From time to time he asked for and received support from the King and the Duke. The King helpfully remembered that the convoys under discussion had been provided at the merchants' request, a point Pepys admitted he had not considered. More surprisingly Charles backed Pepys up over his paying insurance on a lost shipment of pipestaves for which Warren had no specific contract. He flatly refused to accept that Pepys would cash a ticket to himself in a matter of a few pounds. This issue was raised by Brereton on the final day of the hearing, and Pepys represents it as a derisory last thrust by the Commission which he and the King triumphantly parried.[26]

Brooke House came to nothing, though not because Pepys had routed Brereton's men. The debate itself had become buried in trivial details which, even if resolved, were never going to locate blame for the misfortunes of the war. It was, none the less, a significant development in Parliament's attempts to monitor naval spending. For Pepys it was a further advance on the public stage.

SIX

Rather like an Admiral

'We have not, at times, as large forces as we would like to carry the war to the enemy's front door.'

Admiral Sir Andrew Cunningham, 1 April 1942
[Simpson, *Cunningham Papers*, I, p. 594]

The parliamentary investigations into the war had further persuaded Pepys that it would be useful for him to enter the Commons. To the promptings already noted, his friend Thomas Povey added his voice when a general election seemed in prospect at the end of 1668, and Pepys set his mind to it: 'my great design, if I continue in the Navy, is to get myself to be a Parliament-man'. The qualification is important: it implies that Pepys had no political ambitions of a general sort, but saw membership of the Commons as a way getting a better deal for the Navy, and of enhancing his own status within its management. At its most simple, Pepys wanted to be part of the Westminster club, to which Batten and Penn belonged. For all the triumph of his March 1668 speech, this had been delivered from the bar of the House, reminding Pepys that he was an outsider. Seeing Penn sitting among the members reinforced Pepys's wish to belong there. More purposefully, Pepys genuinely felt that MPs' criticisms of the Navy Office were chiefly the result of ignorance, which his presence in their midst would dispel. With no territorial base of his own, he looked to represent one of the boroughs where the naval interest predominated. In the spring of 1669 he made enquiries at Harwich, to no effect. A vacancy then occurred at Aldeburgh through the death of Sir Robert Brookes, and Pepys's candidacy was immediately promoted by Sandwich. The local magnate was the Duke of Norfolk's heir, Lord Howard of

Castle Rising, to whom the Duke of York recommended Pepys as a man 'in an especial manner qualified' for the nomination. Pepys himself admitted to Captain Thomas Elliott, one of the town bailiffs, that he was 'wholly a stranger' and could claim no favours on his own account. Instead, he put himself forward entirely on the basis of the Duke's endorsement, with a promise to reimburse Elliott for buying the necessary votes. He then wrote to Lord Howard, mainly by way of dissuading him from favouring one of the other potential candidates. The Duke and Howard sent messages directly to the electors urging Pepys's cause. Other correspondence flowed from Whitehall to Suffolk; Matthew Wren argued that a seaport would be better served by the Lord High Admiral's man than by a local, however worthy. None of this satisfied the voters, who were reluctant to have a Court nominee foisted upon them, and on 9 November they elected Alderman John Bence. Pepys had been unable to attend the poll because of his wife's illness and death. That tragedy, and the business of the Brooke House report, allowed Pepys little time to dwell on his by-election defeat. The episode's significance is in signalling Pepys's growing attachment to the Duke of York and (quite incidentally) to the Catholic interest.[1]

Although Pepys's career did not advance at this point, he found much still to be done within his existing remit. The war and the subsequent enquiries had shown up deficiencies in the dockyard store accounts, which had to be addressed on two levels. The accounts themselves failed to itemise commodities with precision, and allowed a good measure of the King's goods to fall unobtrusively into private pockets. Reforms had been proposed in November 1668 by Francis Hosier, at that time Clerk of the Cheque at Gravesend. His orderly scheme of double-entry book-keeping naturally commended itself to Pepys, who retained an elegantly penned copy in his Library. At first even Pepys seems to have been taken aback by its complexity. Hosier assured him that his work was 'not so frightfull as you seeme to apprehend'; it was no more than the yard officers presently claimed to perform, and which the Principal Officers 'seeme to confesse their beliefe of being done'. In response, five Clerks of the Control were added to the establishment in February 1669, one at each of the chief yards and the other in the Navy Office. Hosier himself was promoted to this post at Deptford, and continued to give Pepys instances of inadequate record-keeping. In part this reflects Hosier's quarrel with John Uthwayt, Clerk of the Survey at Deptford; Pepys already suspected Uthwayt of malpractice, and was the readier to take Hosier's side. The matters at issue ranged from the general ('many issues of stores . . . where the storekeeper is not charged with any quantity at all') to the most particular ('not distinguishing between double and single portnails').[2]

While Pepys was agreeing with Hosier on the need for better organisation on the ground, he remained convinced that inefficiency would seep down from above so long as Mennes remained Comptroller. In June 1669 the Duke of York had explained that the post had been offered to Sir Thomas Allin, but he could not take it up until he had relinquished command in the Mediterranean. Allin had returned in April after his previous voyage, during which he had concluded a further treaty with Algiers. Even though he had been censured by the merchant interest for having, as Pepys put it, 'patched up a disadvantageous peace', he had been given a further tour of duty which kept him away from July 1669 to November 1670. In the event Mennes retained the Comptrollership to his death on 18 February 1671. As the old man lay dying, Pepys thought fit to remind the Duke of York that Mennes's successor would need 'a greater measure of integrity, experience, vigour of body and vivacity of mind' than any other public servant. This was so obvious a self-portrait that even James must have seen through Pepys's conventional disclaimer ('I have none . . . to name to you; much less the least ambition of having myself thought on'). It mattered nothing, since the promise to Allin was honoured, and he was appointed on 15 April. Allin had a distinguished career afloat, beginning as a royalist privateer captain operating out of his native Lowestoft at the start of the Civil War. After 1648 he had served in the official royalist fleet until he was sunk by Blake off Cartagena in 1650. He was court-martialled by his own side for cowardice, but escaped before sentence was passed. His loyalty was unshaken, and he was regarded as one of the most reliable officers by Charles II, from whom he received a succession of commands after the Restoration. He had enthusiastically carried out the secret orders to attack the Dutch Smyrna fleet in 1664, and had a fine record in the war which this action successfully provoked. Pepys had encountered him in November 1665, and found him 'very friendly . . . a good man I think, but one that professes he loves to get and to save'. Interestingly Allin records the same meeting in his official journal, but more prosaically ('dined with Squire Pepys and did some business with him'). Allin's acquisitiveness was touched on again in the aftermath of his 1668–9 voyage; he and his fellow officers were said to have followed 'more the trade of merchantmen' by carrying goods from port to port. This was a practice against which Pepys would legislate firmly when he was in a position to do so. But he recognised that Allin was 'in serious matters . . . a serious man', who discharged the Comptroller's duties energetically, if not always to Pepys's satisfaction.[3]

Allin's appointment to the Board was followed by that of Sir John Ernle, with the new portfolio of Comptroller of Storekeepers' Account (23 June 1671), to superintend the five new audit clerks. Ernle, though the father of a serving officer, had no naval experience of his own. When he was advanced to the Chancellorship of the Exchequer in 1676, his place on the Navy Board was not immediately filled. His arrival there may be said to have completed the main restructuring of the Office which Pepys had advocated. One further change among the Principal Officers occurred while Pepys remained at the Board; in June 1672 Middleton returned to a dockyard Commissionership (Chatham), and his place as Surveyor was taken by the shipwright John Tippets. Pepys never found such fault with Middleton as he had done with Batten; nevertheless he discovered him to be ignorant of the Lord High Admiral's most recent Instructions to Commanders, and negligent in overseeing the yard accounts. Most damning was the revelation that Middleton's office could not produce a complete list of the King's ships. Pepys had first met Tippets when he was Master Shipwright at Portsmouth in 1662. In February 1668 he had become resident Commissioner there. Pepys had suggested that neither Tippets nor John Cox (Master Attendant at Chatham, who was also being promoted to a yard Commissionership) should be put in charge where they had previously served. The Duke of York agreed that this was a sensible policy, and then chose not to implement it. Pepys was more successful in recommending that Tippets become assistant to the Surveyor, and later that he should succeed to the post. Tippets, as shipwright, had not entirely escaped Pepys's censures in the past, and would incur them again. However, Pepys was sure that Tippets's practical knowledge, and the 'vigour and method' with which he had run his yard, made him unquestionably the best qualified man for the Surveyorship. To this he was appointed on 5 September 1672.[4]

Penn had told Pepys in October 1668 that, for health reasons, he wanted to give up responsibility for the victualling accounts. Pepys accepted this confidence without comment, but was delighted to hear in the following month that Penn was indeed to leave the Board. He would instead join Sir Denis Gauden and his son Benjamin in a new consortium to run the victualling business itself. Penn could not be given a new post while he stood accused in Parliament of wartime misconduct, and the Duke of York allowed him to remain on the Board until the new victualling contract was completed. Pepys therefore had to wait till April 1669 for the satisfaction of attending Penn's farewell dinner. Penn died in September 1670. His place as Navy Commissioner and Comptroller of Victualling Accounts had been taken by Admiral Sir Jeremy Smyth on 17 June 1669. Smyth was a commander of considerable experience on land and sea, an old comrade of Albemarle. He was among those knighted after Lowestoft, and his courage was questioned only by Holmes (with whom, like Pepys, he came close to fighting a duel). Pepys found him 'an impertinent fellow' (that favourite term again) and a 'silly, prating, talking man', but a useful informant. He welcomed the appointment, though mainly because, as the Duke of York explained to him, it demonstrated that the Opposition was not as strong as had been thought, and James had been able to advance his preferred candidate. Pepys approved of

Smyth for being 'a seaman, no merchant'; but since he feared he was 'but very moderately qualified for this particular work', he had Smyth's warrant recalled, and redrafted it with more precise terms of employment. His doing so shows yet again how far, while still the lowest Principal Officer by rank, Pepys had in practice outgrown his office. By 1672 he had indeed achieved seniority by tenure, and was the only survivor of the Board as reconstituted in 1660.[5]

Anglesey's brief tenure of the Navy Treasurership was abruptly and contentiously ended in November 1668. Pepys correctly understood this as part of political manoeuvres to reduce the Duke of York's control of the Navy, perhaps even to replace him with an Admiralty Commission. Anglesey had recently hinted disapproval of a holiday which Pepys had taken. Pepys was unrepentant ('I care not a turd'), and indifferent to Anglesey's dismissal. From 1668–71 the Treasurership was held jointly by Sir Thomas Osborne and Sir Thomas Littleton, whom Pepys knew mainly as 'creatures' of the Duke of Buckingham and Lord Arlington. Osborne and Littleton had both been members of the Commons Committee for Miscarriages; Littleton in particular was a vocal critic of the Navy Board. Their appointment was therefore in line with the admirable principle of putting opponents of bureaucracy in charge of the largest spending department. They began by rather grandly announcing that they would pay out nothing whatever except by way of reducing the Navy's accumulated debt. Then, having been supplied with £20,000 by the Treasury, they proposed paying off tickets for 1666. This upset the Duke of York, who had to explain that many of those who served under him in 1664 and 1665 were still to be paid. Pepys, who had already been censured by these same men for favouritism in the honouring of tickets, fulminated that no 'plainer, or more scandalous and injurious instance' could be supposed than the Treasurers' scheme. Littleton and Osborne continued to provoke the corporate anguish of the Board, not least when they claimed precedence at the Office table. After a while, a working relationship developed (Pepys finding them 'mighty supple' and in some prospect of being brought to reason). Littleton left the Treasury in 1671, and took up responsibility for Navy victualling in succession to Penn. Osborne carried on as sole Treasurer until 1673. Pepys had found him more congenial, not least back in 1669 when he told Pepys that he represented 'the whole virtue of the office of the Navy', and that no man would be fitter to succeed Mennes as Comptroller. Greater distinction awaited Osborne, who, as Earl of Danby, headed the government from 1673 to 1678, and remained a significant fixture in the political firmament until the reign of Anne.[6]

Pepys was now recognised as the man who got things done, and all manner of people appealed to him for assistance. He had told Parliament in 1668 that one of the advantages of tickets was that payment could be made to the dependants of seamen unable to collect it themselves. Such a one was William Coe, boatswain of the fireship *Charles*, who found himself in Maidstone gaol for debt, while his wife was dying in child-bed. It was left to a friend, Anne Woodcock, to petition Pepys for Coe's ticket to be honoured. Then there was John Vyall, who had served on the *Cambridge* before being captured by Barbary pirates; he had an authorised attorney to collect his money, and the case was brought to Pepys's notice by one of the MPs who had condemned the ticket system, Sir William Doyley. Pepys's help was frequently sought by those anxious to avoid impressment. The press was only supposed to take merchant seamen, and there were always complaints from landsmen taken by accident or excessive zeal. Those legitimately pressed were often released through the connivance of local officers disapproving of the system. Conversely some magistrates used the press to offload their neighbourhood derelicts, who were no use whatever to the Navy. The best course was to apply to the Navy Board for formal protection, which could be claimed by those in what would now be called reserved occupations, and for other reasons. Pepys's surgeon Thomas Hollier certified that he had removed a kidney stone from a waterman called Robert Fenwick, and warned that his being pressed might reactivate the complaint; no appeal could have been better targeted, since Pepys himself had successfully undergone the same operation. Pepys was also well disposed to Sarah Young's request for her son John to follow his father as flagmaker to the Navy. This was very much a family concern (with granny in Norwich making up the cloth), and one for which old Young had long ago claimed a protection. Naturally those whom Pepys had helped in the past came back for more. Thomas Pointer, whom Pepys had made his clerk when he took over the victualling business in 1665, had gone on to work competently for Mennes. By 1671 he had got himself into debt, compounding his problems by staying away from the Office to avoid his creditors. He asked Pepys, as the one who had 'raised [him] from the dunghill', to smuggle out a number of official papers so that he could work from home. Among other awkward problems Pepys had to deal with was a complaint that the yard at Deptford stank of dead dogs and cats, and even nastier matter brought in on the tide.[7]

Such concerns punctuated the larger business of preparing the Navy for another war. The enemy was expected to be the French, not the Dutch (with whom England and Sweden had formed the Triple Alliance in 1668). This was a prospect which Parliament and the City welcomed and were prepared to underwrite. Charles II preferred an *entente cordiale*, and, like Edward VII, proceeded to negotiate it without troubling his ministers. The secret treaty of Dover in May 1670 provided Charles with a war-chest of French gold, and envisaged Anglo-French forces defeating the Dutch at sea, before invading their mainland. The latter was more on Louis XIV's agenda than it was on Charles II's. Charles had concerns of his own; the continuing detention, and indeed flaunting of the *Royal Charles* was a particular irritation. Charles looked to the possibility of an Orangist coup in the Netherlands, which would restore his nephew William to the quasi-monarchical status customarily held by his forbears. Charles optimistically supposed that William would show appropriate gratitude for his uncle's assistance. It was an uncharacteristic miscalculation: William preferred the role of Dutch patriot to that of Stuart client. For his part Charles was prepared to risk a good deal for the sake of alliance with his French cousin, but he could not yield on the issue of the Navy: 'The only thing', he told his sister, by way of addressing Louis, 'which can give impediment to what we both desire is the matter of the Sea, which is so essenciall a point to us here.'[8]

A statement of the Navy finances was presented to the King in Council on 11 May 1670, in the presence of the Duke of York and the Treasury Commissioners; the debt stood at £458,991, and current charges (including the finishing of five new ships) brought the total requirement to £906,172 13s 1¾d. The matter was referred to the Treasury Commissioners, who in August were able to promise a 'considerable sum' from the bankers to meet Pepys's estimates. In September the Duke of York was calling for a fleet of 50 sail to be made ready for the spring, as the secret Anglo-French treaty required. Pepys thoughtfully compared lists of English and French ships. What he still did not realise was that they would be fighting on the same side in the coming war.[9]

The assault on the Dutch was postponed until 1672. This allowed the evolution of a bolder French military plan, and although the combined naval operation was therefore of less strategic significance, the English had more time to prepare for it. Much effort had been made after the Second Dutch War to replace lost ships, and to match French and Dutch building. Priority was given to the great three-decker 1st- and 2nd-rates, which were felt to have proved their worth in the contests with the Dutch. Between 1668 and 1671 five new 1st-rates joined the fleet, as many as the total number hitherto serving the Stuart kings. The first to be launched was named in replacement for the chief casualty of the Medway raid; Pepys, who was present, wished her 'better luck then the former'. She was originally *Charles the Second*, which was soon recognised as a rather bad joke, and plain *Charles* was preferred. Of the three 2nd-rates fired by the Dutch and remaining as wrecks (*Royal Oak, Royal James, Loyal London*), only the last could be salvaged, re-emerging as the 1st-rate *London* in 1670. Also in 1670 came two newly built 1st-rates, *St Andrew* and *Prince*. Pepys had inspected the latter in October, a few days before her launch, finding cracks already opening up on her decks because green timber had been used. He also disliked her being upgraded from her original design as a 2nd-rate, which was the sort of thing which upset his estimates. She turned out to be unstable, which the Duke of York briskly resolved by lopping her masts and yards, whereafter she served notably as his flagship. Pepys acquired a journal of her service in 1672 from her lieutenant, John (later Sir John) Narbrough. The last of the 1st-rates launched before the war was a new *Royal James*, the first three-decker built by Deane, and in which Sandwich would fight his last battle.[10]

The shipbulding programme placed further strain on supplies of all sorts. A plan to exploit the timber resources of Scotland for the Navy came to nothing. The shipbuilder Phineas Pett had made extensive reconnaissance in 1666 and 1667, at, he claimed, considerable hazard and the neglect of his primary business. When some Scotch timber did arrive, it was dismissed in the dockyard as 'sorry firewood' (but the boatswain of the yard had already done a private deal to acquire the better stuff). Pepys reckoned that one shipment which cost £764 had brought in goods worth less than £390. However, he argued that the Board should not blamed, because they had been put up to it by the Court and Council (which he assumed meant the Scottish Secretary, Lord Lauderdale: an early example of misguided regional policy). Pepys gave much attention to the availability of timber rather closer to home, and conducted a survey of the royal forests.[11]

There was no significant commercial agitation, real or prompted, for another Dutch war. Merchants were still suffering from the slump in maritime trade which the last one had produced. The King demonstrated his disdain for the mercantile interest at the beginning of 1672 by suspending all service payments on government borrowing (the Stop of the Exchequer; which Pepys laconically dubbed 'the Post-pone'). This was intended to preserve funds for naval preparations, but Pepys, to whom the measure was a complete surprise, immediately saw that it compromised the Navy's day-to-day credit in the City. He urged the King and Council to distinguish between the banker, who lent 'with express condition of extraordinary profits', and the merchant, who supplied the Navy with goods at market price, and was obliged to accept securities for want of cash. Unsurprisingly, Pepys failed to change the King's mind. The Third war was, as contemporaries and later historians have generally agreed, an unambiguously political enterprise. It could not even have been justified on grounds of greed, and Charles II had to work hard to find a technical excuse for declaring it. He fell back on the ludicrous English claim to the sovereignty of the seas. When the yacht *Merlin* was bringing the wife of Lady Temple, wife of the English ambassador at The Hague, back to England in August 1671, a live round was fired to instruct the Dutch to strike their flags. This attempted provocation was thwarted by the courtesy of the Dutch, and their disbelief that a little pleasure boat was proposing to take on an entire squadron. So Charles turned to the stalwart Holmes, who duly though imperfectly attacked a Dutch Smyrna convoy off the Isle of Wight on 13 March 1672.[12]

The Duke of York was back in command of the fleet. Risking the heir-presumptive's life was even more questionable now that it seemed certain the King would have no legitimate children, but the Duke's rank made him the only acceptable SAC. Albemarle had died in 1670, and Rupert disliked, and was disliked by, the French. They would form the White Squadron, and their wishes had to be consulted. Sandwich, back from Spain, was given the Blue. Since there was no place for Rupert afloat, he was on 2 May given a novel appointment as the Lord High Admiral's deputy in London. James had taken Wren with him, and Rupert's existing secretary, Sir James Hayes, became effectively head of the Admiralty secretariat, and therefore the main link with Pepys at the Navy Board. Pepys had to supply Hayes with such elementary information as the names of those who captained the King's ships.[13]

On 28 May 1672 the main action of the war was fought in Sole Bay, off Southwold. A jingoistic spectator on the Dunwich dunes saw it as the greatest victory since the Armada:

> They batter'd without let or stay,
> Until the evening of that day,
> 'Twas then the Dutchmen ran away
> The Duke had beat them tightly.

In fact the English losses were greater, and though the Dutch did indeed withdraw, they had succeeded in their purpose of impeding an Anglo-French invasion of their mainland. A more realistic eye-witness was Pepys's friend the surgeon John Knight, who describes the rush to man the ships when the Dutch suddenly appeared over the horizon. In the course of the day the Duke had to shift his flag from the *Prince* to the *St Michael* and then to the *London*, as the first two were disabled. But it was Sandwich's *Royal James* on which Dutch attacks were concentrated. She was eventually destroyed by a fireship, and Sandwich was drowned in making his escape. From some reports it appears he may have been toppled from a longboat, which reached the shore with a suspiciously small number of men aboard. News of the loss of the *Royal James* was posted to London by 8 p.m., but it was the following day before Sandwich's death was reported. It is likely that Pepys was informed immediately, though at noon on the day after that, 30 May, he could not 'budge a step' from the Office, and anxiously asked for the latest news from the fleet. It was not until the evening of 10 June that Sandwich's body was washed up at Harwich, recognisable only from his Garter-star. Pepys went to pay respects to his cousin's body. This was embalmed by Serjeant Knight before the final journey to London and a state funeral in Westminster Abbey, at which Pepys bore a bannerol of arms. The days of their close association were long past, and the relationship never really recovered from a pompous lecture which Pepys had read to his senior cousin about an unsuitable mistress. One hopes that Pepys, who was so forgetful of his own marriage vows, would have forgiven Sandwich for (as local tradition has it) spending his last night on earth in the arms of a Southwold serving-girl.[14]

Among the other casualties of Sole Bay was Matthew Wren. Combat wounds aggravated an existing illness, and a few days after the battle he resigned as the Duke's secretary; he died on 14 June. Pepys did not want this plum to pass him by a second time, and while Wren was still alive he secured (so he thought) Coventry's support for his candidature. Coventry then had to explain that his own nephew, Henry Savile, who was the incumbent deputy, had in effect taken over. Coventry could realistically do nothing more, except pass on to Savile a generous message of support from the luckless Pepys, from whom, Coventry added, he could 'receive more help and learn more of the Navy . . . than from any man living'. Others still thought Pepys would get the job, or had even landed it. Pepys himself, writing to his brother-in-law Balthasar St Michel on 22 June, alluded obliquely to his continuing hopes. Three days later Anglesey provisionally congratulated Pepys on his new employment. Savile, however, was temporarily dug in, and Pepys soon had evidence of his slipshod paperwork. By 2 July the Duke had in any case replaced him with John Werden.[15]

Pepys's failure did not reflect any disfavour, though the Duke may well have been unaware of the strength of Pepys's wish to serve him more closely. At the beginning of August the Duke was promising Pepys his support in some unstated private business, and had another try at finding him a Commons seat. A by-election seemed likely at Castle Rising, Norfolk, by the promotion of Sir Robert Paston to the Lords. This was the Howard heartland, and Lord Howard was confident of delivering the nomination; but he had already promised seats to the King and the Duchess of Cleveland for their clients. With the county already grumbling about Court intruders, Howard did not want to risk a contested election against a local candidate, and while anxious to oblige the Duke, he found Pepys a stray piece in his electoral jigsaw. Pepys himself went into the high-fawning mode in which he was now so fluent (abasing himself to Howard as 'an humble creature of His Royal Highness'), but to no immediate purpose, since Paston's ennoblement was deferred for a year. Once again, therefore, Pepys's career seemed to have stalled. The only addition to his *curriculum vitae* for 1672 was promotion in Trinity House to the status of Elder Brother. Then on 29 January 1673 the Navy Office, which had escaped the general disaster of 1666, was burned down. Pepys's own lodgings were destroyed, and he lost many of the acquisitions of his early life. Some of his books were saved, as were the two of his specially designed book presses which had so far been made. As he moved into new and less attractive premises in Winchester Lane, he must have regretted the lodgings in Whitehall which might now have been his. It was, however, as well that he had not become so closely associated with the Duke of York, whose own career was about to founder.[16]

James's loss of the Admiralty in 1673 followed directly from the King's inability to control the House of Commons. When Charles confronted Parliament in February 1673, the task strained the sharp mind of Lord Chancellor Shaftesbury, who had to explain why supply voted in 1668 to meet a French naval threat had been spent on fighting the Dutch with French assistance. Shaftesbury (a republican, whom the King had appointed in an attempt to defuse the Opposition) revived the bogey of Dutch aspirations to 'an Universal Empire as great as Rome', at the same time warning that they were the 'common Enemies to all Monarchies'. The Commons could not be persuaded that their articulation of such sentiments back in 1664 constituted a standing order for the King to fight the Dutch whenever he felt like it. What did spur them was an ill-judged diplomatic attempt by William of Orange to enlist English supporters. In the face of this the Commons closed ranks, and agreed to vote supply. They kept the bill back from the Lords (which would have led automatically to its passage) until they had forced the King to withdraw his 1672 declaration of religious toleration, and to assent to a bill which required all public officials to pass the 'test' of Anglican correctness. Louis XIV was not prepared to bail out the English Catholics, and so increased the pressure on Charles, who was meanwhile having to equip the fleet at his own expense, to agree to the Test Bill. This was conceded on 29 March, and the Duke of York, as incorrigibly honest as he was Catholic, was chief among those who failed the test. We can be sure that Pepys was among those who crowded into the Chapel Royal on Easter Sunday to see if James would put public duty before his conscience, and take the worthless Anglican wafer. He did not, and on 15 June he laid down his baton. His hope of immediate reappointment as 'Generalissimo' was dropped on legal advice.[17]

Rupert would have been the most obvious candidate to succeed as Lord High Admiral. He was already in active command of the fleet, unsuccessfully attempting to co-ordinate a landing on the Dutch coast. Pepys, in what were his last days as Clerk of the Acts, received the customary amount of blame for inadequately supplying him. Rupert's displeasure with the Navy officers was so well publicised that a story circulated of his giving one or two of them an actual thrashing. Two days before James resigned, he presented the King and Council with a new set of instructions for the office of Lord High Admiral. Pepys retained three copies of this document; if he saw it in advance or indeed drafted it, he may have feared that Rupert was about to become his new superior. On 16 June Rupert was confirmed as commander of the current expeditionary force as Admiral of the Fleet. This was a post, not a rank, and not necessarily held by the Lord High Admiral. For this office there would be no personal appointee, but a Commission of thirteen. Rupert was the first named, though the style 'First Lord' was not yet adopted. The other original members were politicians, but included three former Navy Treasurers: Osborne, Anglesey and Carteret. Together they already constituted the Navy Committee of the Privy Council, and so it was all largely cosmetic. After some haggling over details, the formal process of appointment was begun on 22 June and completed by patent on 9 July. They met for the first time on 19 July.[18]

Meanwhile, Pepys had been chosen as Secretary to the new regime. This office was not conferred by patent, and the earliest mention of it occurs on 19 June, when Pepys announced that the King had 'been pleased upon his Royal Highness's resignation to call mee from the Navy Board to the place of Secretary to the office of Lord High Admirall'. This was in an otherwise routine letter which happens to be the first entry in the Letter Books of Pepys's secretariat. It was certainly a new beginning and a promotion for him, yet it grew imperceptibly out of his former work. He had so very largely extended the duties of Clerk of the Acts that many functions moved with him to his new appointment. Conversely the Clerkship resumed a lower profile. On the same day that Pepys penned his first Admiralty letter, Thomas Hayter and his own brother John, who had also been Pepys's Navy clerk, were appointed jointly to the Clerkship of the Acts. Both might have won the place on merit, but it was nevertheless a shameless exercise of jobbery by the promotee. Scarcely less blatant was Coventry's letter congratulating Pepys on his appointment; this consisted chiefly of a suit on behalf of the brother of one of Coventry's servants.[19]

The new Admiralty was therefore not quite as new as it seemed, and not without precedent. Charles I had kept the office of Lord High Admiral vacant from 1628 to 1638, and instead appointed an Admiralty Commission which was in effect a committee of the Privy Council. More recently there had been the Admiralty Commissions of the Commonwealth, to which full and lasting authority was delegated by the government. Charles II's Commissions of 1673–84 were different because the King only appointed them under political pressure; he distrusted many of the individuals he was obliged to nominate, and he reserved to himself a good part of the Lord High Admiral's traditional functions and perquisites. In particular he retained the nomination of sea officers (hitherto shared between the monarch and the Lord High Admiral), and would correspond directly with them and the Navy Board. He frequently chaired meetings of the Commission, and controlled the whole judicial side of the Admiralty. What part Pepys may have had in designing all this at the start is impossible to say, but in retrospect he stressed that the King ran the show, and that he himself was the King's servant first. Charles had, he recalled, 'put several parts of the . . . office into commission; retaining the rest in his own hands, and calling Mr. Pepys . . . from his charge of Clerk of the Acts, to that of Secretary to *himself* and the said commission'. Indeed in the immediate aftermath of the Duke of York's resignation, and before the Commission passed the great seal, Pepys worked directly to the King. It then soon became evident that the Duke would continue to take a proprietorial interest in naval matters. He remained Lord Admiral of Scotland (where the Test Act did not apply) and a Privy Councillor, and often Charles simply brought him along to Commission meetings. In the fleet this added to Rupert's frustrations, as he sensed that James was aiming to create a faction (or an extended 'following') among the officers. John Werden (now a baronet and a Navy Commissioner) was cast in the role of recruiting sergeant. More generally, it has been argued that interference from the King and the Duke contributed to Rupert's continuing operational failures during 1673. James's lurking presence is also found in trivial matters. Within a few weeks of his supposed resignation he was offering advice to a pilot, and ordering an enquiry into the fishery protection work of the Cinque Ports. James, in fact, never mastered the concept of retirement.[20]

All of this serves as a reminder that the Admiralty at this point was a personal office, not an institution. It had developed into the latter under the Commonwealth, when the Secretary and his two clerks were established public officials, with premises at Derby House in Westminster. This infrastructure disappeared at the Restoration, when James took his place as Lord High Admiral, and absorbed the administration into his own household. While the old system was wound up, its nomenclature lingered; several times during the latter part of 1660 Pepys speaks of the 'Admiralty' or 'Admiralty chamber' at the Duke's lodgings in Whitehall (and on one occasion wrote up his Diary there). Thereafter until 1673 the Admiralty scarcely existed as a separate department. The Duke's successive secretaries, Coventry, Wren and Werden, served him in a general capacity, though from September 1664 their special responsibilities were recognised by a salary of £500 out of the Navy vote, in lieu of fees previously exacted on commissions and warrants. The secretaries employed clerks on such terms as they chose, who might not necessarily be exclusively engaged on Admiralty business. Of these, only Coventry's clerk, James Sotherne (himself a future Admiralty Secretary) is known by name, and that from a chance remark by Pepys. The only dedicated Admiralty employee between 1660 and 1673 appears to be the Messenger, Alexander Harris. In the same time the Navy Office staff expanded until it numbered over thirty.[21]

Superficially, therefore, Pepys appeared to be moving from a well-structured concern to an amorphous one. Naturally he took with him the administrative method he had built up at the Board, and no doubt a good many actual books and papers. Principally, he took Hewer; probably from the very start, though his presence does not register in Pepys's correspondence until 22 December, and not until the following year is he specifically called Chief Clerk. Pepys also looked for independent premises, interestingly wanting to distance himself from the Duke's lodgings. In the first days of January 1674 he moved the Admiralty back to Derby House, which he also designated his official residence. It was an historic moment: in the precise sense in which administrative historians use the phrase, Pepys had taken the Admiralty out of Court. Only from this point can its existence as a separate department of state be surely charted. Pepys inherited the £500 salary which the Duke's secretaries had been awarded, a modest advance on the £350 he received at the Navy Board (and equal to the top salary he might have achieved there as Comptroller). This was nothing compared to the casual income from fees which still attached to his office, such as £5 on the renewal of every commission to administrative Vice-Admirals, and the like for the officers of the Admiralty Court. He acknowledged an additional £1,000 *p.a.* from these sources, and the reality was probably much higher.[22]

In 1673 Pepys at last achieved his seat in Parliament. In August the Duke of York had told him that Sir Robert Paston's promotion to the Lords was now going ahead, and so there would after all be a by-election at Castle Rising. Since Lord Howard had now become Earl of Norwich and Earl Marshal, Pepys's approaches to him were yet more oleaginous. He also cultivated his prospective constituency with presents, including £50 to the parish church. Having thus paid his dues, he was returned on 4 November, albeit having to fight off a local candidate. The loser, Robert Offley, then appealed against the result, and the ensuing dispute spoiled Pepys's arrival at Westminster. He was accused of being a closet Catholic (not true, though his aesthetic interest in Catholic ritual and artefacts played into his opponents' hands). Pepys's connexions with the Duke of York and the pro-French interest were real enough, and the Commons came close to annulling his election. Only prorogation saved his seat, which he retained until the dissolution in 1679. In that time he made over 70 speeches, almost all on naval matters; he sat on 24 committees, but that is dismissed as a modest tally by general parliamentary standards. He remained true to his longstanding objective, reiterated to Henry Savile in August 1672, that he sought election 'not so much out of any ambition as the just consideration of those opportunities it might give me of doing . . . better service in the station I am now in.' He was already aware of much prejudice the Navy had suffered for want of 'a few hands in Parliament thoroughly conversant in those affairs'. In this there was no false modesty, since he realised that he could come in only as a placeman. As such he remained, never entirely at home at Westminster, not really belonging to either of the emerging parties. He scorned the dull Tory squires who should have been his friends, while those whose cleverness and competence he respected tended to belong to the Opposition. MPs of all flavours were irked by his lecture-room manner ('Pepys has been heard three times over' complained one weary committee member). As he had done at the Brooke House hearings, Pepys deployed the Thatcherite tactic of burying debate under a mound of statistics. His hearers resented the style as much as the content of his performance, and rightly judged that he had little time for their ways and means.[23]

The most telling judgement came from Sir Robert Howard: 'Pepys here speaks rather like an Admiral than a Secretary'. It was not meant kindly, but it would not have displeased its subject, and it points to the innovative way in which he would serve the naval interest in Parliament. He came to combine many of the functions later shared between the First Lord of the Admiralty (that is, the Minister for the Navy) and the Permanent Secretary. He would look approvingly at the systems in France (where his opposite number ranked as a Secretary of State) and the Netherlands. He was convinced that the Navy was denied adequate funding because of 'the ignorance of our parliaments in matters marine': backbenchers had no understanding of the technicalities, and the King's ordinary ministers were not competent to enlighten them. The solution, Pepys saw, was a permanent, professional Admiralty administration with an authoritative voice in Parliament. He had had a taste of this in 1668 when he explained the ticket system from the bar of the House; now he stood at the despatch box, ready to defend every aspect of the King's naval affairs.[24]

SEVEN

Creating a Standard

'Unless we are authorised to commence building ships . . . we
should never be able to regain our present position without
incurring great cost and causing the very greatest suspicion
amongst the powers of the world.'
          Admiral of the Fleet the Earl Beatty, 15 December 1920
                    [*The Beatty Papers*, ii, ed. B. McL. Ranft
                           (NRS, CXXXII, 1993), p. 128]

Pepys came to the Admiralty in the dying months of a
disappointing war, one which he personally had special reasons
to deplore. Had he still been writing his Diary, he would surely have
confided to it the same sentiments as Evelyn did in his, condemning
'the folly of hazarding so brave a fleete, & loosing so many good
men, for no provocation in the World but because the Hollander
exceeded us in Industrie, & all things else but envy'. The Third
Dutch War produced a considerable body of polemical literature,
some of which Pepys bought and retained. He bound together *A
Justification of the Present War against the United Netherlands* and
its sequel *A Further Justification*, written at Arlington's request by a
former republican propagandist, Henry Stubbe. The main purpose
of these works was to refute the idea that the war was a Court
intrigue, and so to assure English dissenters that the quarrel with the
Dutch was the same as it had been under the Commonwealth. They
were therefore of a piece with the 1672 Declaration of Indulgence,
which was meant to defuse nonconformist opposition to the war by
offering freedom of worship. Indeed, Stubbe originally intended to
call his second work *An Apology for the King's Majesty's
Declaration* 'by an Old Commonwealth Man', identifying the

Declaration and the Stop of the Exchequer as pillars of the King's prudent government. It is unlikely that Pepys warmed to Stubbe's uncritical rhetoric. A much more thoughtful work which came his way was *The Interest of these United Provinces* (1673), by Joseph Hill, minister to the expatriate Scottish church in Middelburg. His book, published simultaneously in English and Dutch, urged England to disengage from the French alliance and make peace with the Dutch. The Dutch themselves were warned that Charles II was likely to get Parliament's backing for continued war, and so they should accept English terms rather than risk annihilation by Louis XIV. Hill accepted the Declaration of Indulgence as a genuine concession to dissenters, and dismissed fears that Charles intended to adopt Catholicism personally or politically. Pepys knew the author well. He had been a Fellow of Magdalene, and it had been in Hill's chamber that Pepys was once disciplined (the only known incident of his undergraduate career, and so recounted in every book about him except the present one). At the Restoration, Hill was ejected from his Fellowship and then chose voluntary exile. Pepys had enjoyed his conversation on church affairs ('though he is full of words'), and later found him helpful in identifying and searching for Dutch books on maritime subjects. He long remembered Hill's argument that the Dutch had as much cause to fear French naval expansion as did the English.[1]

Although controversy over the Dutch wars continued, the conclusion of the third was a major turning point. The alliance with the French had proved unsatisfactory even to its advocates, and collapsed in an argument about money. Danby and Pepys demonstrated that it would need almost £1½ million to fight on in 1674, and all that year's revenue was already spent. When the French ambassador, Colbert de Croissy, refused to accept the figures and accused the King of listening to demeaning counsel, Charles indignantly defended the competence and loyalty of his servants. Parliament was equally resolute in declining further supply, and the King was obliged to conclude the ignominious peace of Westminster in February 1674. Quite soon it was the French, not the Dutch, who were recognised as England's main rivals at sea. In political terms it is fashionable to speak of the 'long eighteenth century', stretching from the revolution of 1688 to the Reform Bill of 1832. The 'naval eighteenth century' might be said to last from Westminster to Trafalgar. The years immediately following the end of the Third War saw a series of reforming measures which contributed significantly to the professionalism of the Royal Navy, and so to the long and ultimately successful contest at sea with France. These initiatives, in the reform of the officer corps and in a co-ordinated shipbuilding strategy, were all promoted by Pepys in his first term as Admiralty Secretary, and to varying degrees were of his devising.[2]

A key element in the professionalisation of the officer corps was the regulation of volunteers, commonly known as 'reformadoes'. As far as Pepys was concerned they were gentlemen officers of the worst sort, 'persons of too great quality', who expected and sometimes received more deference than the regular officers. They fell into two categories, though the distinction was not always apparent. There were those for whom no established post could be found, but who were prepared to serve without pay until a vacancy occurred, or simply for the prospect of booty. A specific status of volunteer '*per* order' was introduced in 1661 by way of providing direct entry for young men of good family. These were nominated by the King (and so also called 'King's letter boys'), and were supposed to receive some technical training before being commissioned. They were paid as midshipmen, then ranking as petty officers. So although the '*per* order' system was designed to pack the Navy with men socially and politically acceptable to the Crown, it went some way to bridging the gap between the amateurs and the professionals. Predictably it brought in a good few aristocratic wasters; on the other hand some officers managed to get their personal servants taken aboard under the guise of volunteers. Similar abuse was made of the actual rank of midshipman, into which captains' trumpeters, fiddlers and barbers were on occasion intruded. In a similar vein, Captain Charles O'Brien (himself a former '*per* order' volunteer) took his mistress for a Mediterranean cruise by putting her in man's clothes and on the books of his ship, the *Leopard*. Pepys's sense of humour quite failed him at this point, and while still at the Navy

Board he had tried to codify and therefore control the carriage of all 'supernumeraries'.[3]

In wartime all help was more or less welcome, and this was recognised in October 1673 by allowing volunteers the same scale of compensation for wounds which had been set for regular officers in the previous year. Between wars the Navy found itself with a large surplus of officers. Until quite recently such men would simply have returned to civilian life. The schemes now devised to retain and pay them mark a decisive shift towards the creation of a truly professional naval service. After the Second Dutch War, former captains and lieutenants were sometimes appointed as 'midshipmen extraordinary,' to assist the commissioned officers under whom they served, and standing ready to take over from them if necessary. In November 1674 the Board took note of Pepys's report that these places were swamped by servants and other supernumeraries; it was ordered that the practice of restricting them to former regular officers should be enforced. Yet the problem persisted, and Pepys wanted a limit on the numbers according the rate of each ship. Even where the system operated as intended, there was resentment that appointees were too grand to do any useful work aboard ship. In April 1676 Pepys again raised the issue with the King and the Board. He was more concerned about volunteers 'too old and too long practised in the liberties and pleasures of the shore', but he also spoke disparagingly of the midshipmen extraordinary. There and then he produced a set of rules he had devised for both categories, which was immediately approved. As issued on 8 May, this regulated pay, and established maximum numbers of volunteers and midshipmen extraordinary for ships of 3rd- to 6th-rates; the larger ships were presumed capable of absorbing unspecified quantities. It was once supposed that by this means Pepys actually invented the cateogory of midshipman extraordinary. This is no longer tenable, and neither were the final regulations entirely of his own making. A clause obliging the midshipmen extraordinary to keep personal journals had been added on the suggestion of the Navy Board. Pepys's influence is surely evident in the precise stipulation that the midshipmen extraordinary were to deliver these journals to the Secretary of the Admiralty before they could claim their pay, and that they were to set out 'in distinct columes' the ship's position every day at noon, and to record all 'extraordinary accidents hapning in the voyage'. In the following December the Admiralty issued a general order for reformadoes to be examined in navigation, and Pepys instructed the Navy Board to test several individuals.[4]

Of all the achievements of Pepys's first Admiralty secretariat, the establishment of examinations for officers is by far the most important. Had Pepys done nothing else, this would justify the esteem in which the naval service has ever since held him. His admirers have always pointed to it with special enthusiasm, and its significance appears undiminished by more critical scrutiny.[5]

The first move had been the requirement that captains of 6th-rates, who acted as their own masters, should pass the existing master's examination run by Trinity House. The proposal, originating with the Navy Board, was put by Pepys to the Admiralty on 14 November 1674, and was immediately approved. An exception was at first made for those who had previously commanded higher rates, but the examination was extended to them on 1 September 1677. At the latter meeting the Duke of York, in commending this firmer qualification for the captains of 6th-rates, and recalling the establishment already in place for volunteers, urged the necessity of examination of prospective lieutenants (and thereby of future captains). He suggested that Trinity House or the Navy Board might certify candidates. Pepys pointed out that lieutenants' duties had never actually been codified, and that this should now be done, and proper instructions issued to them. When all this was approved, Pepys drafted the instructions and devised a form of examination.[6]

Possibly the idea really came from Pepys, and the Duke agreed to front the proposal to the Board. In the course of the next few months Pepys consulted a number of prominent serving commanders. Sir John Narbrough, C-in-C Mediterranean, provided a timely instance of a foul-up aboard the 3rd-rate *Sapphire* in the absence of a qualified lieutenant. In reply, Pepys acknowledged the general problem ('Lieutenants having hitherto been brought into the Navy without any certain assignment of what is their duty, or any inquiry before hand into their qualification to perform it'), and assured Narbrough that the King and Board had resolved to tackle it. Pepys duly presented his proposals to the Board on 1 December, when they were accepted in all but two details. Following the Duke's suggestion, Pepys had wanted Trinity House to participate in the examination. He had a special concern, having in 1676–7 served a first term as its Master. The Corporation was the acknowledged authority on navigation (in which the examination would chiefly consist), and already examined masters and pilots in the River, including those of the King's own ships. But the Lords of the Admiralty thought prospective lieutenants should not be interrogated by mere technicians, and instead recommended flag officers or captains of 1st- or 2nd-rates as examiners. The Admiralty also disapproved of Pepys's recommendation that the would-be lieutenant should serve a year as an ordinary midshipman (something Their Lordships considered 'beneath the quality of a gentleman to go through'). This was left to consideration by the Navy Board and such senior captains as were in London.

Meanwhile, Pepys continued to take soundings of his own. He invited Sir John Kempthorne, the Commissioner at Portsmouth, to consider what would happen 'when the few commanders . . . now surviving from the true breed shall be worn out'; what sort of captains could be made from unqualified lieutenants, most of them ex-volunteers with limited service at sea? At the same time Pepys was reluctant to abandon the idea of involving Trinity House, whom he saw as providing just that technical expertise which the Admiralty still thought demeaning. Eradicating the distinction between 'gentlemen and others' was a principal part of the exercise. On 8 December Pepys reported to the Admiralty on discussions between the Navy Board and the senior sea officers, who had liked the idea that lieutenants should have served a year as midshipmen, and were finally persuaded to it by the future Lord Dartmouth. When asked if *he* had served such an apprenticeship, he said he had not, and it had 'cost him many an aching head and heart since to make up the want of it'. The Lords accepted this, though exempting volunteers who had served at sea three years, and removing certain discrepancies between the proposed establishment and the existing instructions to commanders. Nothing more was heard of Trinity House being party to the examination. The new regulations were formally published on 18 December. Candidates had to be aged twenty or above, and to have served three years at sea, one of those 'in the quality and . . . duty of' midshipmen (though this did not apply to those who had served two years as volunteers). All candidates were required to provide testimonials from the captains under whom they had served. A viva voce examination would then be held at the Navy Office before a Navy Commissioner who had held sea command, a flag officer, and the captain of a 1st- or 2nd-rate. No actual curriculum was stipulated, and the questioning would reflect the concerns of the examiners, ranging from mathematics to practical seamanship.[7]

On 24 January the results of the first examination under the new system were announced (four passes, one fail), encouraging the Lords of the Admiralty to welcome 'the good breed of lieutenants, and consequently of commanders, which may hereafter be expected in the navy'. Pepys took great satisfaction in the operation of his scheme. Within six months he was confident that 'we have not halfe the throng of those of the bastard breed pressing for employments which we heretofore used to be troubled with'. The dimmest applicants gave up altogether, while the more hopeful had some serious cramming to do. Among the latter was Pepys's nephew Samuel Jackson, who persuaded Matthew Jane, yeoman of the powder room aboard his ship the *Foresight*, to tutor him in navigation. Another kinsman afloat, John Pepys, was grateful for his captain's encouragement as the examination loomed. The unsuccessful were allowed to try again. One such was Edward Dering, who was failed for not being able to calculate high water at London Bridge from given astronomical data. His examiners, Sir John Chicheley and Sir Richard Haddock, told him to go back to sea, which he did, and he pretty soon obtained his commission. Pepys understood that Dering had only made one voyage before his original candidature, and he saw the case as a bending of the rules. Their strict observance was, he believed, not only the best way of promoting good men, but would also provide commanders with unexceptionable grounds for not advancing the unworthy.[8]

The status of a profession depends on the qualifications by which it is entered, and the rewards which it brings. On both counts the profession of sea officer was established in Pepys's time. Before then officers were always appointed for some specific service, and very few were more or less permanently employed. The system was much the same as that which until very recently obtained for professional cricketers; however regularly a man was selected as a member of the England team, he was only paid as such for the duration of a particular match or series. In the Navy the move to a permanently salaried officer corps began with an Order in Council on 17 July 1668 which assigned half-pay ('pensions') on a graduated scale to flag officers and captains of flagships who had served in the Second Dutch War, and for whom no employment could be found. Similar provision was made on 26 June 1674 relating to the Third War. Meanwhile, on 6 May, all captains of 1st- and 2nd-rates who had seen active service were given such retainers, based on their best previous employment. It was necessary to explain that this did not apply to those who merely sailed battle-damaged great ships back to port, and various other qualifications were introduced. On 6 March 1675 the Admiralty decided to extend half-pay to those commanding squadrons of twelve or more men-of-war, and this was authorised by the Council on 19 May.[9]

This was one issue on which Pepys's opinion decisively shifted. In his early days at the Navy Board he had been concerned to show that captains' and lieutenants' pay was traditionally calculated only when their ships were victualled for sea. He thought that paying them even for 'rigging time' was a bad innovation of the First Dutch War. When the Duke of York had promoted the first regulation for half-pay in July 1668, Pepys followed Coventry in disapproving of the whole idea. Earlier that year full pay had rather generously been allowed to captains fitting out during what proved to be a false alarm, and Pepys felt that the Duke was being too free with his brother's money.

By the time he came to the Admiralty, Pepys accepted that regular payment was not an abuse, but was as necessary for the professionalisation of the service as controlled entry. While all the regulations of 1674–5 were issued through his means, he was directly responsible for assigning half-pay to masters. His original proposal (20 January 1675) was limited to those of 1st-rates, to whom the Admiralty added those of 2nd-rates; the regulation was published simultaneously with that for squadron commanders on 19 May.[10]

At the same time as he was making regulations for the sea officers, Pepys was giving similar attention to the naval chaplaincy. Ships' chaplains were supposedly supported from the deduction of a groat (4*d*) per month from the pay of every man aboard. Since these sums were collected whether or not any chaplain actually existed, this money was frequently retained by captains and pursers. In his early days at the Navy Board Pepys had been shocked to learn that even such respectable figures as Carteret, Penn and Allin had effectively pocketed large sums from this source. Allin, for example, had offered to 'recover' unspent deductions for the Crown, and was duly given £1,000 from the surplus funds he identified. Pepys was even more scandalised that Lawson ('one of the greatest criers up of religion and zeal') should have sued for and been awarded £2,000 in a similar fashion. Pepys put the matter to the Bishop of London (whose jurisdiction covered clergy outside the normal diocesan structure), and by this and no doubt other means an Order in Council was procured on 10 January 1668 which diverted unallocated chaplains' groats to the Chatham Chest. Although a better idea than giving the spare cash to Admirals, it did not supply the spiritual guidance for which the seamen had paid. The problem had to be approached from its other end, the appointment of chaplains. This was originally at the discretion of captains, tempting them, like any ecclesiastical patron, to keep the livings vacant and enjoy the fruits. A central system of recruitment was first tried in 1665 under the Archbishop of Canterbury's authority, but it was not until Pepys gave his mind to it again in the 1670s that a lasting arrangement was made. In December 1676 he drew the Admiralty Commissioners' attention to the frequency with which captains failed to appoint chaplains, and the general ignorance and debauchery of those chaplains who did serve. He was asked to prepare a paper for one of the meetings at which the King would preside. This took place on 3 February 1677, when Pepys's draft proposals were agreed: (1) none of HM ships should go to sea without a chaplain; (2) no chaplain should be employed until he had been approved by the Archbishop of Canterbury or the Bishop of London; (3) no chaplain should serve aboard ship without a warrant from the King, grounded on the Archbishop's or Bishop's certificate; (4) if no already-approved chaplain offered to serve in a ship being sent to sea, the Admiralty Secretary was to apply to the Archbishop or Bishop to recommend a fit person; (5) subject to the above, captains' preferences would be considered.[11]

A revised version was presented to the Board on 8 December, and issued on the 15th. This established that: (1) no chaplain was to be admitted aboard ship or allowed the monthly groats unless appointed by the King's warrant, and the warrant to be exhibited to the captain of the ship and the Comptroller of the Navy; (2) no one was to be eligible for the King's warrant before delivering to the Admiralty Secretary the Archbishop's or Bishop's certificate of his learning, piety, conformity, and other qualifications; (3) the Secretary was to give the Archbishop or Bishop the names and rates of ships being set to sea, their complements and the names of their commanders; the bishops would then recommend and certify suitable persons; captains might select any chaplain approved within the preceding three years, without need for further episcopal certificate. A common form of the King's warrant was also devised. Pepys also appears to have issued a kind of prospectus for would-be chaplains outlining their idyllic prospects: expense-free living, leisure to study, his captain's conversation and ('upon his good behaviour') table, free travel, and the prospect of future royal patronage.[12]

Pepys's interest in the naval chaplaincy was not simply administrative, and he was genuinely interested in the spiritual well-being of the seamen. This he believed was best served by their adherence to the doctrines and practices of the established church, even though the many seamen from nonconformist communities were unsympathetic to the official chaplains. The regulations he devised in 1677 formed part of his general programme of codification, but it may well be that two particularly unsatisfactory naval chaplains had sharpened his concern. One was Titus Oates, who was chaplain of Captain Robert Rooth's *Swiftsure* in 1673–4. In 1675 Oates sailed, again with Rooth, aboard the *Adventure* to Tangier, and it was seemingly from this ship that he was put ashore after conviction of sodomy. He was no more than a civilian passenger on this voyage, but his former status as a naval chaplain has coloured accounts of the incident, if indeed he was not dimissed from his actual chaplaincy for the same reason. Although there is no evidence of it, Oates's case must certainly have come to Pepys's attention at the time. He was certainly aware of the even more outrageous behaviour of George Bradford, chaplain of the *Sweepstakes*, who when he was not drinking, gaming and streaking with his cronies, spent all morning 'catterwoolding' with his wife. Yet here was a chaplain whom Bishop Compton of London had duly examined and approved. Admittedly this was but one aspect of a total breakdown of discipline aboard this particular ship. Pepys's 1677 regulations did not in any case address the problem of misbehaviour by chaplains duly appointed, or impose any element of superintendence. This was first introduced at Tangier in 1683, when Lord Dartmouth wanted a chaplain in his flagship *Grafton* who would exercise moral leadership over the other chaplains on the station. Pepys, who was present as Dartmouth's adviser, secured the post for the distinguished divine Thomas Ken. Five years later, when Pepys had returned to the Admiralty, and Dartmouth was C-in-C, they proposed the more formal appointment of a senior chaplain, and Pepys offered the place to the Master of Magdalene, John Peachell. Since Peachell was under a cloud for disobeying James II, and was generally quite unsuitable, the nomination reflects poorly on Pepys, and he was lucky that Peachell turned it down.[13]

The achievement of which Pepys himself was most proud was his persuading Parliament to finance a building programme of thirty new ships. This was an unprecented investment in defence hardware, all the more notable because the need was not obvious.

Although it was not immediately evident to contemporaries that the Third Dutch War was the last of the series, nobody wanted to provoke a Fourth. And while the last war had been wholly wasteful, it had left England with a fleet of unprecedented size. Most impressively there were six 1st-rates afloat, and a replacement for the one wartime loss (the *Royal James*) was nearing completion. But there were only 18 ships of 70 guns or more, of which the French had 22 and the Dutch 34. Moreover, the French and Dutch had mostly new ships, whereas at least half the English fleet was over twenty years old. In the immediate aftermath of the war it seemed to many (Pepys included) that the Dutch were still the main threat, and since the French alliance had proved militarily and (even more so) politically unworkable, independent superiority to the Dutch was essential. Ideally the Royal Navy had to be prepared for a renewal of the Franco–Dutch alliance it had faced in the war of 1664–7. Charles was chastened by the events of 1672–4, and was unreceptive to Pepys's first briefings on the Navy's postwar requirements ('he is more thoughtfull of getting out of debt for what is past . . . then willing to entertaine any proposition that may tend to the encreasing of it'). The King had entrusted the administration to the staunchly Anglican and anti-French Osborne, created Earl of Danby in June 1674. Danby's abilities had been demonstrated by his time as Navy Treasurer, and he remained committed to the support of the Navy. This found direct expression in the one day a week he regularly spent with Pepys at the Admiralty. In general his astute fiscal policy would generate conditions favourable to Pepys's ambitious agenda. By identifying French naval expansion as the main peril to England's commerce, Danby's administration could make an authentic appeal for public funds.[14]

When Parliament met in April 1675, Charles asked in general terms for appropriate supply, leaving Pepys to fill in the details. He pitched in on 24 April with a bid for forty new ships (two 1st-rates, seven 2nd-, the remainder 3rd- and 4th-rates). He had circulated enquiries to a number of those whose expertise and judgement he valued: Deane, Tippets, Hayter, Gibson and Hewer. The most radical response came from Sir Richard Haddock, who argued the

1 Pepys, as one of the Barons of the Cinque Ports, supporting the canopy beneath which James II processed to his coronation in Westminster Abbey on 23 April 1685. The sharply drawn figure ahead and to the left of the King is an unmistakable portrait of Pepys at the summit of his own career. Detail from an engraving in Francis Sandford's *History of the Coronation*. [*Pepys Library, Magdalene College, Cambridge*]

2 The Earl of Sandwich: politician and naval commander, Pepys's cousin and first patron: 'And I in good esteem, I think, as any man can be with him' (Pepys, *Diary*, 31 December 1662). An anonymous pen and ink drawing in Pepys's collection. [*Pepys Library, Magdalene College, Cambridge*]

3 Sir William Penn: 'a man of very mean parts, but only a bred seaman'; Pepys nevertheless thought him 'the ablest man in England' for promotion to the Comptrollership of the Navy (*Diary*, 10 October 1664, 22 August 1666). Pepys saw this portrait in Sir Peter Lely's studio on 18 April 1666 (*Diary*, that day). [© *National Maritime Museum, London*].

4 Sir John Mennes: 'a fine gentlemen and a very good scholler' (Pepys, *Diary*, 8 November 1661). Much as Pepys admired him personally, he repeatedly urged his removal from active duty at the Navy Board. Pepys knew him as a much older man than the dashing Cavalier here painted by Sir Anthony van Dyck. [*By courtesy of the National Portrait Gallery, London*]

Ireton

5 Charles II: 'the King doth not look after his business himself, and thereby will be undone, both himself and his nations' (Pepys, *Diary*, 31 October 1666). Pepys continued to regret that the King's application did not match his ability. A mezzotint by Jan van der Vaardt after William Wissing, in Pepys's collection. [*Pepys Library, Magdalene College, Cambridge*]

6 The Battle of Lowestoft, 3 June 1665: 'a great victory, never known in the world' (Pepys, *Diary*, 8 June). The noise of the engagement may have been heard by Pepys in London, over a hundred miles away. A pen and ink drawing by Willem van de Velde the Elder, *c.* 1674. [© *National Maritime Museum, London*]

7 James II: 'We owe a great deal of the strength of our Navy to [the] D[uke of] Y[ork]'s getting ships to be begun' (Pepys, *Naval Minutes*, p. 159). Pepys served James loyally for a quarter of a century, and shared his fall from power. A mezzotint by John Smith after Sir Godfrey Kneller, in Pepys's collection. [*Pepys Library, Magdalene College, Cambridge*]

8 Prince Rupert: 'the boldest attaquer in the world for personal courage; and yet . . . wanting the patience and seasoned head to consult and advise for defence' (Pepys, *Diary*, 4 June 1664, endorsing the opinion of Sir William Coventry). An engraving by Robert White after Sir Godfrey Kneller, in Pepys's collection. [*Pepys Library, Magdalene College, Cambridge*]

9 Sir Thomas Allin: 'would poison the fleet or let them starve rather than lose . . . his own profit' (Pepys, *Navy White Book*, pp. 242–3). Pepys gleefully recorded this malicious gossip, but nevertheless respected Allin's abilities as a commander. His forceful personality is evident from this engraving by Pieter van der Banck after Sir Godfrey Kneller, in Pepys's collection. [*Pepys Library, Magdalene College, Cambridge*]

10 William III: 'a Prince whose genius seems bent to land-action only' (Pepys, *Naval Minutes*, p. 394). Pepys accepted orders from him as head of government after the Revolution, but would never swear allegiance to him as King. A mezzotint by John Smith after Sir Godfrey Kneller, in Pepys's collection. [*Pepys Library, Magdalene College, Cambridge*]

11 One of the 3rd-rates of the 1677 building programme, probably the *Hampton Court*: 'I may truly challenge [*claim*] to myself to have been the chief, if not the only occasion of this last parcel of the best ships that ever were built in England' (Pepys, *Naval Minutes*, p. 13). Painting by Willem van de Velde the Younger, *c.* 1680. [*Birmingham Museums and Art Gallery*]

12 The Pepys Library, Magdalene College, Cambridge: 'a pleasant sight to me, to see my whole study almost of one binding' (Pepys, *Diary*, 5 February 1665). The first two book presses were made in the following year. The collection was completed in twelve presses, and first occupied this room in 1724; the central desk had also belonged to Pepys. [*Photograph: Pepys Library, Magdalene College, Cambridge*]

need for forty new ships, drawing particular attention to the limited usefulness of the existing 5th- and 6th-rates ('not able to stand the shocke of a battaile'). This seems to have provided Pepys with his manifesto, which he backed up with a mass of other documentation. On this occasion his statistical barrage did not achieve its effect, and Opposition MPs were unimpressed by his claims to privileged information. They merely suggested that he tap the existing customs revenues, which were indeed buoyant after a year of peace. In reply Pepys asserted that the Navy already absorbed all that was available. These exchanges reflect the enhanced political profile of naval issues in the 1670s. This owed something to Pepys's presence in the Commons, and his professed mission of instructing the MPs in the Navy's mysteries. More generally, there were genuine fears that the King and his brother (whose lingering presence Pepys so obviously represented) were filling the Navy with Catholic officers. The Opposition were as concerned to restrict the King's control of this force as their predecessors had been to wrest the militia from his father. The session ended on 9 June without any better resolution. When the MPs returned to Westminster in October, they debated Pepys's proposal for three weeks, and agreed in principle to half what had been asked: one 1st-rate, two 2nd- and fourteen 3rd-rates, for which £300,000 was voted. However they again insisted that this be a charge on the customs, of which they agreed to appropriate £400,000 to the use of the Navy. The King was irritated by this and other (as he saw it) obstructive debate in the Commons, and seized on an intercameral squabble as the excuse for a further prorogation. The supply was consequently lost.[15]

Parliament did not reassemble until February 1677. By chance the delay helped Pepys's cause, because when the Opposition peers Buckingham, Shaftesbury, Salisbury and Wharton claimed that a dissolution was automatically triggered by a statute of Edward III requiring annual meetings, they were imprisoned for contempt. Their followers in the Commons, unsympathetic to the argument for their own redundancy, were temporarily embarrassed, and Danby seized the moment to push through the shipbuilding programme. MPs generally were now ready to accept that French expansion had to be met with the thirty new ships for which the King now asked. Pepys carried the House with an impressive speech on 23 February, the most important of his political career. He had prepared a highly technical analysis of the functions and costings of the various rates. 1st-rates were necessary to fight the French (and, he might have added, for prestige). The 4th- and 5th-rates were dismissed as useful only for convoys and anti-piracy, and no more of these smaller vessels were needed. It was the three-decker 2nd-rates, combining advantages of height and manoeuvrability, which Pepys identified as the most effective strike weapons. By the same token, he argued for broader, stronger ships, which would sail better and have more protection against enemy shot, while carrying their own ordnance higher. The speech as delivered seems to have diverged from Pepys's draft framework; clearly he was so much the master of his material that he could adapt it to the temper of the House. As a result, he was prepared to accept some reduction in his proposals, and the day ended with a resolution to vote up to £600,000. Despite his concessions, this allowed rather more than the rates and tonnages strictly required. The funding was then discussed in committee, where Pepys was required to give further reassurances on supply of materials and the construction process. On 5 March the supply was voted on a 17 months' assessment, incorporated in an enabling Act on 16 April. The actual sum of £584,976 2s 2½d was assigned for building, over a period of two years, of a 1st-rate (1,400 tons), nine 2nd-rates (1,100 tons apiece), and twenty 3rd-rates (900 tons apiece). Pepys knew at once that this was a major achievement, 'the raiesing of a new stock of ships of more value then was ever at once undertaken by this nation'.[16]

The parliamentary campaign was but the overture to the great work which now began, and of which Pepys and the King may be said to have been co-directors. While Pepys was, of course, the manager, Charles played an active part in the design process and, as Pepys recalled, himself paid for improvements to the statutory specifications. What the King and Pepys most keenly urged was the advantage of mass production. Years before Pepys had enunciated the simple maxim of 'Husbandry in building a smaller vessel at the time of building a greater', because so many leftovers ('leavings') from the one could serve for the other. Building to a standard took this principle further. Ships were to be launched as soon as possible, and (following Continental practice) to lie afloat together while they were finished. Meanwhile the next ship could be laid down. Existing repair commitments made some compromises necessary from the start, and only half the new ships could be begun immediately. It was originally hoped that all thirty would be built in the King's own yards, as the 1st-rate and the 2nd-rates indeed were. One of the first 3rd-rates was, however, put to a contractor in Bristol, underwritten by Hewer, and four from the second batch were built in private yards on the Thames. These arrangements were conceded reluctantly because of the pervading belief that private contractors cut corners to support their profits. Much though Pepys and his contemporaries were concerned to regulate work done in private yards, their oversight has been judged inadequate by the standards of modern defence procurement.[17]

Needless to say the capabilities of the King's own dockyards were severely tested by the building programme initiated in 1677. It was immediately recognised that impressment would be necessary to supplement the workforce, and hopes that full employment would induce an atmosphere of cheerful industry proved over-optimistic. The Admiralty did make one concession. In 1674 dockyard workers had been forbidden to take away waste wood ('chips'). This was a longstanding perquisite, which Pepys viewed with particular disfavour, and its abolition was a further instance of his reforming hand. Naturally it was very unpopular, and an attempt by the Admiralty to *sell* the men what they had previously carried home free was a predictable flop. By way of encouraging work on the new ships, the 'ancient practice of carrying out lawful chips' was restored in May 1677, though by 'silent connivance' and 'as little publication . . . as the nature of the affair will admit', Pepys hoped, unrealistically, that the concession would not be interpreted as an entitlement.[18]

The issue of 'chips' was in any case trivial in view of the great quantities of timber now required in the yards. Only a fraction could be supplied from the royal forests, and for the rest the King's officers were authorised to search private estates, and to requisition appropriate transport. By May tenders were being invited through the *London Gazette* and by public notices for timber and other supplies, and imports were being negotiated. These were matters for the Navy Board, and so no longer Pepys's direct responsibility. He was more closely concerned to ensure that the Ordnance Office supplied his uniform ships with corresponding standard weaponry, for which an estimate was ready by 10 May.[19]

Despite co-ordination between the naval and ordnance authorities, the one 1st-rate of the 1677 programme was not a success. The *Britannia*, launched in 1682, was built by Sir Phineas Pett with a generous beam (16 inches beyond specification) to allow for higher batteries – just as Pepys had envisaged in his 1677 speech. Nevertheless the upper tier of her armament had to be reduced from demi-culverins to sakers, giving her overall a ratio of weight of ordnance to weight of shot poorer than that of Pett's previous 1st-rate, the *Prince* of 1670. *Britannia* was notoriously unstable, and she was only risked in action after girdling in 1690. At Barfleur in 1692 she at last did what she was built to do, and fought a French opponent of equivalent size, the *Soleil-Royal*. A distant spectator of this mutually crippling engagement was the exiled James II, who remained perplexed by the fact that he and the Royal Navy were no longer on the same side. Pepys's *Britannia* (if she may be so termed) survived, still crank, into the reign of George I. Five of the 2nd-rates were delayed until the 1680s, and the programme was completed by the launch of the *Coronation* in 1685. All those which remained until the early eighteenth century were broken up and rebuilt. The longest survivor was the *Neptune* of 1683, renamed *Torbay* in 1750, which after a fashion links the Navy of Pepys's day with that of Nelson.[20]

All but one of the twenty 3rd-rates were finished within the two years laid down by Parliament; the final one was ready in 1680. Pepys kept specially bound sets of accounts for the two first to be completed, both built by John Shish at Deptford. The *Lennox* was begun on 25 June 1677 and was launched on 12 April 1678;

Hampton Court followed on 10 July. It was aboard one of their sisters, *Grafton* (named after the first Duke, the King's son by Nell Gwynn), that Pepys sailed to Tangier in August 1683. The rather dour journal he kept of the voyage gives no hint of the pride this circumstance surely brought him. A little earlier he had been interested in the destination of models of *Grafton* and another of the 3rd-rates, *Captain*. On the return from Tangier in March 1684 the *Grafton* mischievously sprang a leak in her larboard bow, and her begetter must have spent an anxious hour while the hole was stopped. The 3rd-rates of 1677 have been described as the best-looking warships ever built, an aesthetic appeal which the brushwork of the Van de Veldes does much to promote. The paintings show that some individuality of design was allowed to the builders, while the family likeness is never in doubt. The Younger's *Hampton Court in a gale* (*c.* 1680) (plate 11) is both a technical *tour de force* and a virtual certificate of seaworthiness for the whole class. The Elder's contrasting image of *English warships becalmed* (National Maritime Museum) might rather be titled *The English maritime deterrent at work*. It is perhaps as the King hoped his Navy might be: magnificent, usefully occupied, and at peace. For a moment in 1678 he seemed to be prepared to use it against the French, and allowed a full mobilisation. It was a mere parade, and chiefly for domestic consumption. Pepys knew this well enough, though he sympathised with the officers who were denied the opportunity of service.[21]

EIGHT

The Uses of Adversity

'So little care there hath been to this day to know or keep any
history of the Navy.'

Pepys, 16 January 1668 [*Diary*, IX, p. 26]

Twice in Pepys's career, high achievement was swiftly followed by
reverse. In 1689 the reverse would be terminal. A decade earlier
the prospects had seemed just as bleak when, with the great
shipbuilding programme still continuing, he was driven from office.
For five years he was not so much in opposition as in limbo. Not that
he was idle; he employed much of his time in scholarly pursuits which
may properly be seen as the continuation of his naval life.

It is better to view Pepys at this stage not as a civil servant whose
career was untowardly disrupted, but rather as a politician who
suffered the cyclical vengeance of the electorate. The origins of his
downfall lay in his entry into Parliament in 1673 as a client of the
Duke of York and the Howards. The attempt to annul his election
on grounds of popery had failed, with his accuser Shaftesbury
staging a tactical retreat. Pepys had survived his personal exclusion
crisis, and in any case the matters objected against him had no
substance. That counted for little to Shaftesbury, who knew that the
same slander would eventually find its target. Meanwhile he
docketed Pepys as 'vile', and then 'thrice vile'. As the Duke of York's
obvious nark, Pepys was a prime target for those who imagined that
the King and his brother were intent on establishing a French-
backed Catholic dictatorship. It infuriated him that the genuine
efforts he promoted to match French naval expansion were
misinterpreted, and he had no truck with those who (remembering
how the Third Dutch War had begun) would vote no supply unless

the King declared what alliances he had made. In Pepys's own view this did not amount to 'arbitrary government'; on the contrary, that was risked by those who opposed more spending on the Navy, and so left the country open to French invasion. A decade later, when the the Duke of York had succeeded to the throne, Pepys thought it 'very fitt . . . that the King should be at liberty to dispense with, as well as make his own Rules'. This high view of the royal prerogative was already formed in February 1678, when he told the Commons: 'The best expression of the divinity of a Prince is to take good Counsel; the King has taken it, and executed it, and it stays with you to enable the King to go through with it.'[1]

Pepys's constitutional theory, and the hectoring manner in which he expressed it, continued to irritate his fellow MPs. When in June 1678 Sir John Knight indignantly questioned the level of naval expenditure, Pepys replied so sharply that he had to apologise to the House. High-handedness of that kind played into the hands of the Opposition, who were resolved that the haughty Secretary of the Admiralty should be removed from the political arena along with the Duke his master. As a result Pepys and the naval administration were caught up in the carefully orchestrated anti-Catholic mania known as the Popish Plot. This developed from allegations made by the former naval chaplain Titus Oates of a conspiracy to murder the King, and so hasten the accession of his Catholic brother. The incident which triggered a state of red alert was the discovery on 17 October of the presumed murder of Sir Edmund Berry Godfrey. Godfrey was the London magistrate to whom Oates had made his depositions, and the circumstances of his death made him a Protestant hero. On the day of Godfrey's funeral, which was turned into a political rally, Pepys alluded to 'attendance elsewhere' (meaning Westminster) keeping him from his regular business. The Admiralty Commissioners themselves were so fully occupied in Parliament that they did not meet again as a body until 4 January 1679. All the more burden consequently fell on Pepys, who as well as having to mind his own political back, had to implement the increased security measures which the crisis generated. His first instruction (25 October) was for the commanders at Portsmouth and the Downs to search urgently for a fellow in a brown wig, maybe squinting with both eyes, who was suspected of being a Jesuit. This man, later identified as Father Simons ('a considerable Instrument in the said Plott'), more usually called himself Colonel John Scott. He was no more a colonel than he was a priest, but an agent of Shaftesbury and Buckingham, and his involvement in the plot was real enough. He escaped Pepys's dragnet, and as a result the ports and ships were watched with greater strictness. In November Oates invented a sub-plot which envisaged a Catholic seizure of the Navy, and MPs took up the hue and cry. Pepys immediately instituted a survey of the Anglican rectitude of the sea officers, and was satisfied by the assurances he received. The exercise, although addressing no real issue, did something to restore public confidence. Sir Richard Beach, Commissioner at Chatham, was impressed by Pepys's 'industry both to prevent Papists getting into the Navy and to secure the Navy against any attempts from them'.[2]

What most concerned Pepys personally was the attempt by his political opponents to implicate his clerk, Samuel Atkins, in Godfrey's murder. Atkins was arrested on 1 November 1678 and immediately interrogated by the parliamentary Committee looking into the plot. It was, as Pepys well knew, a 'manifold contrivance', in which he himself was the real target. Indeed the Opposition may have been intending to incriminate Pepys directly, substituting Atkins because Pepys had an inconveniently watertight alibi. Pepys was meanwhile doing all he could to prepare a defence for Atkins. One of his most admirable qualities was the support he gave his staff, and none had more cause to be grateful for this than Atkins. The most circumstantial allegation was that Atkins had been seen with Godfrey's body; Pepys was able to produce reliable testimony that at the time in question Atkins had been spending a boozy evening aboard the yacht *Catherine*. Atkins's unedifying but inconsequential activities during the whole period under investigation were established by Pepys with his usual thoroughness.[3]

Meanwhile one of Shaftesbury's agents in the Commons, Thomas Bennett, threw in a further charge that Atkins had given a passport to a Jesuit. Since the Admiralty did not issue passports, Pepys fielded that easily enough. In what were to be the last weeks of the Cavalier Parliament, he appeared to be hunting with the pack, serving on a Commons Committee to prevent the growth of popery, and another which examined the incriminating papers of the Duke and Duchess of York's secretary, Edward Coleman. In fact Pepys's political position was now very fragile, all the more so when, at the end of December, Danby's authority was undermined through an unholy alliance of French diplomatic pressure and Opposition tactics.[4]

In January, with the public mood still volatile, the King decided to try his luck with a general election. Parliament was dissolved on 24 January, and writs sent out for a new assembly on 6 March. Pepys hoped to be returned again for Castle Rising, but his application to the town was not answered. Instead he looked to represent either Portsmouth or Harwich on the Admiralty ticket. Sir Robert Holmes, now governor of the Isle of Wight, also offered him one of the constituencies at his disposal there. Pepys was touched by this kindness from the old rogue, not least because in the prevailing political climate 'Court-dependence' was an electoral liability. Even so, he preferred to keep his other options open. In fact the King asked him to let the Chancellor of Exchequer, Sir John Ernle, take the safe seat at Portsmouth, and it was at Harwich that Pepys (along with Sir Anthony Deane) was elected without contest on 5 February. By the time Pepys was back from the poll, Atkins had already made his first appearance in King's Bench. Pepys was there the next day to stand by his man, and to drill the defence witnesses whom he had, quite improperly, summoned in the King's name. The court dismissed the evidence of a renegade naval officer, Captain Charles Atkins (no relation of the accused) in which an attempt was made to link the murder to Pepys himself. Matters were effectively settled by the evidence of the captain of the yacht, and Atkins was acquitted on 11 February. The case against him was so flimsy that in normal circumstances it would never have been heard; in the current paranoia the outcome was remarkable, and, had Atkins been left to his own devices, would probably have been different. Though Pepys

131

derived much satisfaction from his clerk's acquittal, he knew that his own battle would now have to be fought.[5]

In the new House of Commons Pepys was one of just thirty or forty members on whose support the King could rely. The much larger body of Opposition MPs, unsatisfied by Pepys's investigation into the religious complexion of the Navy, took up again the allegation that the service was infiltrated with Catholic (especially Irish) appointees. Throughout the brief life of this Parliament, the naval administration was under attack, with Pepys manning the barricades. He assured the House in February that the fleet was in excellent condition, and could be at sea within three months. As ever he defended his department resolutely at the despatch box, though in his correspondence he recognised that 'the generall Scandall of Popery' stuck to all those, himself included, who owed their places in the Navy to the Duke of York.[6]

In a constitutional development of far-reaching consequence, the King was obliged to reconstruct his ministry to reflect the results of the general election. The principal casualties were Danby, who resigned on 16 March, when his office was put in commission, and the Duke of York, who was sent out of the country. Opposition leaders were admitted to a remodelled Privy Council, including Shaftesbury as Lord President. When the new Councillors were sworn in on 20 April, Charles announced his further intention of revoking the Admiralty Commission. He nominated a new seven-man Board, headed by Sir Henry Capel, who was himself admitted to the Privy Council. The new Commission, as originally drafted by Pepys and Lord Chancellor Finch, was phrased in the same terms as that of 1673, in which much had been reserved to the King. Capel and his colleagues insisted upon being granted powers as full as had ever been exercised by a Lord High Admiral, and these were written into their patent of 14 May. This carried what Pepys termed 'clauses reflective' implicitly criticising the King and the previous Commission by alluding to a prevailing state of abuse, disorder and disobedience. Shortly before the arrangements were completed, Pepys reported to the Duke of York in Brussels. He was, as the Duke had predicted, now in trouble on his master's account: 'For, whether

I will or noe, a Papist I must be, because favoured by your Royall Highness.' Some of the new Admiralty Commissioners wanted him to stay on as Secretary, though he suspected this was only until they made themselves familiar with the work. The majority had seemingly been hand-picked from the Navy's critics. These were men with whom he had 'for many years lived in a constant state of war', and for whom his Secretaryship was a continuation of the Duke's Admiralty by other means. Rather optimistically, Pepys suggested that he might exchange his office for a place on the Commission. James had given some encouragement to this idea, and now put it to the King. His endorsement sounds mercenary ('the easiest and less chargeable way of doing something for him that can be thought on'), but this was simply James's rather wooden candour. At the same time, he (and indeed Pepys) showed little appreciation of the delicate political machinations in which the King was involved. In theory Pepys would have made a most suitable Admiralty Commissioner, and he would surely have viewed the Commission's record rather differently had he been a member of it. As things were, there was not the smallest chance that Charles would risk further parliamentary rumpus by appointing him.[7]

In any case, Pepys's immediate future was not to be of his own choosing. The Commons continued to complain of all and every imagined disorder in the Navy, and on 28 April they had appointed another Committee to investigate miscarriages. Its chairman, William Harbord, had his eye on Pepys's job as well. The Committee was packed with Pepys's other political opponents, and receptive to the allegations which were now being articulated. It was immediately apparent to one MP that 'Mr Pepys, however prepared, must certainly be destroyed'. The overt accusers were John Scott, returned from France, and Pepys's former butler, John James. Both men had personal grudges against Pepys, though these were incidental to the political motivation of Buckingham and Shaftesbury, working through the likes of Harbord, Sir John Hotham, Thomas Papillon and Roderick Mansell in the Commons. The principal issue was a visit made to France by Deane and Hewer in 1675 to take over two pleasure boats for the lake at Versailles. Scott claimed that at the same time naval secrets had been passed to the French, and that Pepys had been a party to the whole business. Specifically, Pepys was said to have sent over draughts and models of the best English ships, extensive lists of the fleet, and a 14-page document identifying weaknesses in England's naval defences. It was well known that Pepys manufactured such things by the yard, so the inventory had a certain plausibility. Scott swore he had seen the incriminating material in the office of the Treasurer-General of the French Navy, Georges Pélissary; this was true enough, since Scott had concocted and delivered much of it himself. Although all this had been while the English and French were allies, it could readily be represented as treasonable. John James's role was to sketch in suitably damning details about Catholic practices and objects in Pepys's household. A further charge concerned the *Hunter*, a privateer operated by Deane and Pepys's brother-in-law St Michel during the Third Dutch War, and which had attacked English shipping. Pepys was said to have supplied the *Hunter* from the King's stores at Portsmouth, and to have procured the letters of reprisal. It did not matter that Pepys's involvement in the alleged piracy was tangential; it would help in prosecuting the more serious charges. Even his friend Sir Robert Southwell had to concede that 'how slender soever the proofs be', he and Deane would 'taste of the bitter cup'.[8]

Pepys's tenure of the Secretaryship had not been created by the 1673 patent, and so was unaffected by its revocation. For a while, therefore, he continued to act for the new Commissioners. Save for recording their appointment on 21 April, he made no further entries in the Board's minute book (the 'Admiralty Journal'). In other respects the administrative machine ground on, as Pepys waited to see if he would be kicked upstairs, or simply out of office. It was known that the new First Commissioner wanted Harbord as Secretary, and so it was particularly galling for Pepys that he had to answer to Harbord in his capacity as chairman of the Miscarriages Committee. Even after Pepys had told the Committee he would resign, the regular stream of orders to ships and commanders continued to flow from Derby House. On 16 May, the day that the new Commission formally passed the great seal, Pepys was looking forward to the imminent launch of the latest of the new 3rd-rates. Next day he was concerning himself with the precedency of captains in an outbound fishery protection convoy. Yet the day after that, 17 May, he circulated the news that the King had accepted his resignation, and advised the Navy Board and commanders to address further correspondence to the Admiralty Lords. It was a pre-emptive move. On 20 May Harbord's Committee reported to the House, weaving together the fabrications of Scott and James into a threefold charge of treason, espionage and piracy. Pepys could do no more from the floor of the House than plead not guilty, and cast some preliminary aspersions on his accusers. Such friends as he still had were mindful of their own necks, and said little. Pepys and Deane were immediately arrested. Pepys was first required to return to Derby House with the Serjeant at Arms, presumably to empty his desk under supervision. His immediate worry was over the relatively minor business of provisioning the sloop *Hunter*. He remembered that a Navy 5th-rate with the same name had been refitting at Portsmouth at the time in question, and asked for urgent clarification from the Navy Board. His recollection was correct: it was the King's *Hunter* for which he had ordered supplies at Portsmouth in July 1673, though it is not clear if some genuine or deliberate confusion had resulted. In any case Pepys was not going to escape by quoting a file at his accusers. On 22 May he and Deane were committed to the Tower by the Speaker's order. Pepys had at least the satisfaction that his place at the Admiralty was taken not by the venomous Harbord, but his long-serving clerk Tom Hayter.[9]

After twenty-nine years of continual service, Pepys had suddenly ceased to work for the Navy. All the managerial and diplomatic skills which he had developed in that time were now to be applied to a different purpose. The operation he had conducted in Atkins's defence had to be repeated on a much larger scale on his own account. Even while he remained a state prisoner in the Tower, he set his own agents to work gathering information, and in due course he compiled a massive dossier establishing his innocence. In two folio volumes which he called his 'Book of Mornamont' (named after a country seat which was another of John Scott's fantasies)

Pepys documented the whole conspiracy against himself, and dismantled it step by step. Much of the evidence he assembled served simply to discredit Scott, James and their associates, and had no bearing on naval affairs. One detail of maritime interest may serve to illustrate Pepys's thoroughness. Among the documents which Pepys supposedly leaked to the French naval authorities was the journal of Sir Richard Munden's ship *Assistance*, describing the capture of St Helena in 1673. This certainly added a circumstantial touch to Scott's charge, though it is not clear why it was considered a specially sensitive document. In any case, Pepys obtained Munden's sworn statement that the only copy of the *master*'s journal remained in his hands; he said nothing of his *own* journal, perhaps because he knew that Pepys did indeed have a copy of that. The process of gathering such depositions became easier when, after a spell of less daunting custody in the Marshalsea, Pepys was released on bail on 9 July. He had lost his official residence at Derby House, so Will Hewer invited him to share the elegant lodgings he had just taken at York Buildings off the Strand. There followed an anxious year during which Pepys and Deane pressed for their case to come to trial. No prosecution was ever brought, and on 28 June 1680 Pepys and Deane were formally discharged. It was something of an anti-climax: Pepys, who keenly collected printed and manuscript accounts of all the Popish Plot trials at Old Bailey and elsewhere, was denied the opportunity of starring in his own show.[10]

The lifting of the charges against him restored Pepys's good name; it did not recover his lost offices. For five years Pepys had no formal employment, and received nothing beyond the modest income of his Brampton estate. There was no obvious prospect of resuming his professional career, and although his savings protected him from immediate financial concern, he needed something to occupy his mind. From time to time he was tempted by the academic life, and he had some reminders of his Cambridge connexion. Magdalene was putting up a new building (the one which in time would bear his name), and Pepys did his duty as *alumnus* with a subscription and a loan besides. In return he prevailed on the Master of Magdalene to help advance a kinsman at one of the other colleges.

In August 1681 there was a tempting prospect of his becoming Provost of King's. This was in effect a Crown appointment, and with the King's assistance Pepys could have overcome his formal disabilities (being neither in deacon's orders, nor an Etonian). This particular aspiration anticipated by about three hundred years the fashion of appointing retired public figures as heads of houses at Oxford and Cambridge. Pepys would have fitted the requirements admirably in the 1980s; as things were, he accepted that his intellectual credentials were inadequate, and did not allow his name to go forward. Despite this shrewd self-appraisal, he had already decided to apply his mind to a great scholarly project, a history of the Navy. Although no part of this was ever written, the research material which Pepys collected and preserved is in itself a massive contribution to the subject, and has placed all its subsequent historians in his debt.[11]

The genesis of Pepys's scheme is well established. It was on 13 June 1664, as Pepys and Coventry were glumly discussing the imminence of a Dutch war, that their talk turned to the idea of a naval history of England. Their more immediate idea was for a book about the previous Dutch war, which Coventry thought Pepys should write. Coventry offered to procure permission for 'searches to all records &c.'; no doubt envisaging a partnership of Pepys's spadework overlaid with his own opinions. Some passages in the Navy White Book reflect just that relationship. Pepys was delighted by the proposal; it was 'a thing I much desire and sorts mightily with my genius' (by which he meant no more than 'natural ability'), and something which, done well, would advance his career. This was in truth what users of Cambridge University Library would call a 'tea-room project'. In the 1660s Pepys's time was already very adequately filled, not least in the writing of one of the world's greatest books. Nothing came of this history of the First War, which in any case was not a subject for which Pepys had yet much interest. In the ten printed volumes which now contain the Diary and the Navy White Book, there is reference to just one action of the war (the battle of Kentish Knock), and only by way of retailing a story abusive of Sir William Penn. Blake, the First War's most illustrious

General-at-Sea, is recalled chiefly as land commander. When, with the coming of the Second War, Pepys began to compare its costs and administrative arrangements with those of the first, he was prompted by the immediate concerns of his office rather than by the prospect of historiography.[12]

The Second Dutch War itself was a different matter. Even before its formal declaration, Pepys was urging Coventry to have an eye to 'the recording of what shall pass worthiest remark in the great affair'. Rather unnecessarily he also recommended that Coventry's clerks should preserve the relevant papers as materials for a future history, 'if God send leisure and a good issue'. Although the outcome was far from satisfactory, Pepys resolved to write it up. To this end he began to make his own copies of office papers, and when early in 1669 his place seemed threatened by the post-war enquiries, his worries were compounded by fear of losing access to the records. So for a time he put all his leisure and all the secretarial help he could commandeer to stocking his own files. Many of his manuscript compilations served for current reference and as a basis for future history. The Navy White Book was clearly written with both functions in mind; its random entries about the frauds of employees and the vagaries of his colleagues give way to longer, more reflective passages in which Pepys sets down views he developed in conversation with Coventry, Wren and Gibson about the origins and conduct of the Second War. His personal Diary also has a place in this category; it enabled him to assure the Brooke House Commission in 1670 that he could account for every single day he had spent in the Navy's employment up to the end of the war. He knew he had created a major historical record.[13]

By then he had come to accept that, much as a complete naval history of England was wanted, he might not be able to do it. He was still toying with the more limited idea of a book on the First Dutch War, and he meant to draw attention to 'many things worthy imitation' in the way it was conducted. This much he told the King, no less. It is doubtful if Charles warmed to that idea, but he did ask Pepys to publish a defence of the financing of the Second War, by way of rebutting the accusation that Charles had embezzled the parliamentary supply. No more was heard of this particular idea. The general project, however, gained momentum as Pepys's career advanced. Greater prosperity meant that he could expand his library, and he also acquired material and information from his increased circle of contacts. He asked the historian of the peerage, Sir William Dugdale, about the social background of naval commanders (Drake in particular), and about the origins and precedence of Admirals. Sir John Cotton, an MP supportive of Pepys's shipbuilding programme, gave Pepys ready access to the great library established by his grandfather Sir Robert. Towards the end of his first Admiralty secretaryship Pepys was thanking one of his older friends, the Huguenot merchant James Houblon, for 'those folios of assistance you daily give me', which would make a substantial contribution to the naval history of England, should he ever have time to write it.[14]

Time enough came after Pepys left office, once he was finished with the immediate business of documenting his own recent past. Then, and the more so as the prospects of return to public life receded, he gave his attention to the projected naval history. This was now envisaged as nothing less than a maritime history of the world. Every day, he told Sir William Petty in 1683, he did something on ship design or sailing. For guidance he turned principally to Evelyn, whom he knew to have a great store of relevant knowledge, ancient and modern. For his part, Evelyn urged Pepys to occupy his 'Recesse . . . and calme from publique businesse' with a mammoth work, bringing together the military and administrative history of navies, the science of navigation, and the theory and practice of naval architecture. This encouragement was genuine enough, though no doubt Evelyn was the freer with his material because a project of his own had been stillborn. In 1670 he had been commissioned by the King to write an official history of the Second Dutch War, and was given access to State Papers. In the last months of the Third War, the King asked for the preface to be published right away as part of the propaganda offensive. Unfortunately, by the time this little book, *Navigation and Commerce*, was printed later in 1674, England and the Netherlands had made peace. Evelyn's reiteration of the contentious issues of salutes and fishing limits outraged the Dutch ambassador, and to mollify him, Charles ordered copies of the book to be seized. Evelyn was much put out by this, and abandoned the rest of his war history. So now in the 1680s Pepys, like a dockyard worker carrying home wood chips, was looking for leftovers. Evelyn obliged, though with some cautionary words on the tedium of historical research, ploughing through an ocean of papers: 'so much trash there was to seift and lay by'. Pepys did not retain Evelyn's MS, and what use he made of it is uncertain. He did at least save a copy of *Navigation and Commerce* from the shredder. For his part, Evelyn recycled a good deal of the book's contents in his letters to Pepys.[15]

The range of topics floating in Pepys's mind is evident from the queries he put to Evelyn. Some were particular details, of the sort with which scholars forever pester one another. Could Evelyn describe the maritime sculptures on Trajan's column? Indeed he could, with reference to the work of Alfonso Ciaccono. Where could Pepys find more about the battle of Lepanto, or the voyages of Sebastian Cabot? Back came the relevant information. Just occasionally Evelyn was stumped; he could not give Pepys the name of Henry VIII's chief military engineer, and could not find the MS journal of Drake's which Pepys asked to see. Instead he sent two other Elizabethan journals: of Frobisher's voyage to the North-West and Edward Fenton's to the South Atlantic. The latter was never returned. Some of Pepys's other enquiries were vast in scope. What had been written on naval strategy? Were naval defeats to be explained by inadequate intelligence? And was the Spanish Armada a case in point? By what inventions has English commerce prospered? Why have some nations, more renowned than the English in other arts and sciences, been inferior in developing maritime skills? It almost seems that Pepys meant to anticipate the nineteenth-century American historian A.T. Mahan's *Influence of Sea Power upon History*. Needless to say Pepys did not have the modern historian's professed impartiality; his book would have celebrated England's maritime achievements and justified her current pretensions. To this end (and in the process revealing the weakness of his general historical knowledge), Pepys asked Evelyn for all instances of English naval defeats and foreign invasions since the Roman Conquest, 'more especially from the French'. Evelyn replied to all this in a scholarly, meandering way. Thus when his account of naval attempts on England arrived at 1545, he remembered that the French had at that time deployed rowbarges. That led him back to a consideration of the tonnage and manpower of the Greek bireme, on which he advised Pepys to check his Herodotus, Thucydides, and Pliny.[16]

At the outset Evelyn had given him a stiff general reading list, to which Pepys's attention can in some measure be gauged. Pepys had a solid grounding in the classics, and would have had no difficulty in following up references to the principal sources. He must have been thrown by Evelyn's more arcane allusions, some of which have defeated modern scholars. The faint thought that Evelyn was sometimes winding Pepys up should be dismissed as unworthy. Pepys's library was already well stocked on maritime subjects, and he was always extending it, but his knowledge did not come entirely from his own shelves. He was, as Evelyn knew, thoroughly familiar with the argument over the freedom of the seas propounded by the Dutch jurist Hugo Grotius in his *Mare Liberum* and answered by John Selden's *Mare Clausum*. Pepys had read up this debate in 1661, and frequently returned to it, though he retained only Selden's work, and was scornful of the author's 'straining of arguments'. Evelyn was also confident that Pepys knew the works of Lazare de Baïf, master of requests to Francis I of France, but that does not mean Pepys had yet bought his copies of the *De Re Navali* of 1537 and the *Annotationes* of 1549. Pepys would have recognised Evelyn's 'Marisotus' as Claude Barthélemy Morisot, whose *Orbis Maritimi* of 1643 he acquired and studied. Another standard author Pepys already knew was Georges Fournier; he had been unable to afford his *Hydrographie* when he first saw it in John Martin's bookshop, but later added it to his collection. What Evelyn recommended as 'Furniere' in 1681 may, however, have been *Fortifications*, which Pepys did not buy. The 'late *Architecture Navale* publish'd in French' was undoubtedly the work of Dassie. Pepys bound his copy with a broadside version of a splendid engraving, also in Fournier's *Hydrographie*, of a French royal ship. Evelyn thought the 'most perfect extant' work on the mechanics of shipbuilding was by the Dutchman Nicolaas Witsen, a view shared by Pepys's colleague Lord Brouncker. Another work recommended by Evelyn was the *Arcana del Mare* by Robert Dudley, illegitimate son of the Elizabethan Earl of Leicester, and himself Duke of Northumberland by the Emperor's creation. Pepys would have had some account of Dudley from his friend Bullen Reymes, who met the author at Florence in 1634. Although Pepys later used and admired Dudley's work, he never had his own copy.[17]

Among the acquisitions during this first period of dedication to the naval history project, the greatest prize was Anthony Anthony's illuminated MS of Henry VIII's Navy. Anthony was a clerk in (and later Surveyor of) the Ordnance Office, and had presented his work to Henry in 1546. It comprised three vellum rolls, containing paintings of each of the King's 58 warships, together with their ordnance inventories. Two of the rolls were given to Pepys by Charles II in 1680; the other was lost until 1690, by which time Pepys was not in a position to angle for it. Pepys does not explain precisely how the rolls came to him, which has led to some speculation that he pilfered them. It is more likely that the gift followed from an audience Pepys had with the King at Newmarket in September 1680. Pepys was hoping for financial compensation for his loss of office, and perhaps for some future employment. It was during this encounter that Charles dictated his wartime escape story. They would certainly have discussed Pepys's work on naval history, so perhaps the King saw a way of responding handsomely to Pepys's suit at no cost to himself. Pepys already knew of the Anthony Roll's existence, and may well have asked for it there and then.[18]

The visit to Newmarket did not usher in the rehabilitation and reward which Pepys had hoped for, but it usefully sustained his contacts with the Court. While still in the Tower he had written to the Duke of York, ingeniously abhorring the faith to which the Duke openly adhered, while suggesting that they were fellow-victims of the same persecution. Shortly afterwards, Pepys had been brought from the Marshalsea to speak to the King; what was said we do not know. Some further correspondence with the Duke of York, on Trinity House business, took place in 1681. Pepys could still exercise some influence in naval appointments, but he was itching to get back to the Admiralty, which Hewer told him was 'in such a Pickle' compared with the Duke's time. Pepys was again at Newmarket in March 1682, and had some dealings with the Duke himself. From this encounter came an invitation to accompany James to Scotland, where the King was now sending him as viceroy. Pepys was meant to sail with the Duke in the *Gloucester*, but he preferred the better accommodation aboard the yacht *Catherine*. His choice may have saved his life, since the *Gloucester* ran aground, and many of the Duke's attendants were lost. The accident was blamed on the obstinacy of the pilot, who refused to listen to those (James included) who warned that they were holding too close to the shore. Pepys saw it as, by extension, the fault of the Navy Board in not appointing a better pilot, adding to his growing conviction that the service was falling apart in his absence.[19]

Pepys had no official status on this trip, though (to his satisfaction) he was in attendance at two meetings of the Privy Council, and approved of the Duke's statesmanship ('absoluteness, and yet gentleness': the Stuart dream). His return to public life effectively began when, in August 1683, he was appointed to accompany the expedition which was to evacuate the garrison at Tangier. The King had eventually accepted that this was economically and militarily untenable. Pepys had no part in this decision, having given up his Treasurership of the Tangier Committee along with his Admiralty post in 1679. Indeed it was not until they were three days out of Portsmouth in the *Grafton* that the commander, Lord Dartmouth, informed him of the real purpose of the mission. Pepys had simply obeyed a summons at short notice, and was glad just to be back aboard a good ship and in congenial company. He marked the occasion by beginning a new journal. Like the others he kept after 1669, it is a poor cousin of the great personal Diary, though it is the chief record of the expedition. In this Pepys's principal duty was the repatriation and compensation of the residents. He discharged this task with his customary competence, setting a benchmark for those who in more recent times have administered the end of empire. His Tangier business had always been closely related to Pepys's naval career without strictly forming part of it, and this was equally true of the last episode. Rather more significantly, the expedition was Pepys's comprehensive re-introduction to the concerns of the Navy, and to many of its serving officers. He regretted the need to evacuate the garrison, but his part in the process set him and Dartmouth at odds with the blue water strategists, and those who had simply found Tangier a congenial posting.[20]

Behind this lay a political contest for the Duke of York's favour between Dartmouth and the Mediterranean C-in-C, Arthur Herbert, which Dartmouth was winning. Pepys had a grudge against Herbert for denying a lieutenant's place to his protégé Samuel Atkins. Dartmouth, as an advocate of gentlemen captains, had originally been no more to Pepys's taste; but, as we have seen, he had come to recognise the usefulness of the examination system Pepys promoted. He had also formed a low opinion of the existing Admiralty Board, on which Herbert sat as a supernumerary. Pepys was therefore already inclined to Dartmouth's camp, and during the expedition of 1683–4 they became firm allies. It was an alliance which, Pepys hoped, might bring about his own return to power. To that end he did all he could to denigrate Herbert, filling his 'Journal' and related papers with every kind of malicious tittle-tattle that he could find. Some of his accusations (that Herbert never kept a proper journal, or appointed captains who had not served as lieutenants) were simply false. Allegations which may have had some basis in fact were elaborated to serve the interests of Pepys and Dartmouth, coloured by some of Pepys's particular prejudices. Other evidence was, according to Pepys's most stringent modern critics, simply manufactured. Pepys was in fact prepared to use any convenient weapon to beat his path back to the Admiralty, and it was on the Tangier station that the naval politics of his second Secretaryship took shape.[21]

NINE

Top Gun

'The Admiralty must be in a position to say what they want, order it and pay for it.'

Admiral of the Fleet the Earl Beatty, 19 March 1922
[Ranft, *Beatty Papers*, II, p. 212]

As they sailed back from Tangier in March 1684, Pepys and Dartmouth talked long about the current disorders they detected in the Navy, which they blamed squarely on the incumbent Admiralty administration. They were critical, too, of the King and the Duke of York, for indulging commanders in the 'good voyages', the carrying of commercial cargoes aboard the King's ships, for which the Mediterranean provided rich opportunities. But primarily it was the Admiralty's retrenchments in a 'pretence to reformation' which Dartmouth and Pepys deplored. Dartmouth himself doubted if on their return he would have any influence in naval politics, where the King's son the Duke of Grafton appeared to be the rising figure. Grafton had succeeded Rupert as Vice-Admiral of England, and although not a member of the Admiralty Board, he had formed close links with the First Commissioner, Finch (who had himself become Earl of Nottingham). Dartmouth thought that Grafton might prevent any attempt by or on behalf of the Duke of York to recover the Admiralty. So he encouraged Pepys to think that between them, and with York's connivance, they could form a counterweight to the Grafton and Nottingham faction.

Unknown to his would-be campaign managers returning from the Mediterranean, York had already aligned himself to this purpose with the Earl of Sunderland and the King's French mistress, the Duchess of Portsmouth. The political tide was running in favour of this grouping when Dartmouth and Pepys returned to England on 30 March. They were met by curt orders from the Admiralty, prompting Hewer to lament that nothing would be well with the Navy 'untill his Royall Highness shall thinke fitt to take it into his care'. Pepys had an interview with Sunderland on 6 April, and was pleased to find, against expectation, that he was supportive. After Dartmouth was cordially received at Court on 11 April, he and Pepys, assisted once again by Samuel Atkins, began canvassing support for changes in the Admiralty regime. At first there seemed to be the possibility of an assault from within. The death of Lord Brouncker on 5 April created a vacancy which Dartmouth hoped Pepys might fill. The promotion instead of Herbert (already elevated as Rear Admiral of England) to full membership of the Commission was a setback, but incidental. More significant was the departure of Grafton on a visit to France. By the beginning of May the King was ready to dissolve the existing Admiralty Commission, although, as he liked to surprise people, he allowed its members to carry on their routine business until the last moment. On 11 May the patent of 1679 was revoked, and was not replaced. Charles II became his own Lord High Admiral, as James II, and indeed Elizabeth II, would be. While Charles lived, his brother gave advice and assistance on Admiralty affairs without a specific office.[1]

This arrangement affected the status to which Pepys now advanced. Had the King chosen to issue a new Commission, Pepys might indeed have been appointed to it as Dartmouth had envisaged. Dartmouth had also proposed that the Secretary of the old Commission, John Brisbane, who was additionally damned by his friendship with Herbert, should be replaced by one of his own people, the military engineer Henry Shere. Brisbane's secretaryship would end with the dissolution of the Commission he had served, but that did not automatically allow for Pepys to be returned to his old post. Previous secretaries had been appointed by the Admirals or Commissioners of the day; this holds good even for 1673, when the King was acting informally as Admiral, and brought in Pepys as his personal assistant. There was no clear precedent for the post under a monarch who was his own permanent Admiral. The logical course was to give the Admiralty Secretary parity with the King's existing Secretaries of State, and to this end a warrant was issued on 1 June 'for erecting an office of Secretary for the affairs of the Admiralty', and granting it to Pepys at £500 a year during pleasure. A patent to this effect was issued on 10 June. Much has been made of the singularity of the office thus achieved by Pepys, which was never again bestowed in such form. Actually it is no more than a reflection of the personal Admiralty of Charles II and James II. Since no other Secretary held office by patent, there is no model by which to assess the terms of Pepys's appointment. It should be noted that his salary (always a good indication of status) remained as it had been before. This is not to deny the distinctive character of Pepys's second secretaryship, to which he brought the full weight of his personality and experience, and when he enjoyed the wholehearted support of the successive Kings. In this culminating period of his career, Pepys is rightly said to have held an authority equivalent to that of Colbert as Louis XIV's *homme de confiance* and Minister of Marine.[2]

This did not take instant effect. Pepys was back in business at Derby House from 23 May, some days before the formal process of his appointment was initiated. He resumed the 'Admiralty Letters' register on 29 May, pointedly opening a new volume (X), leaving volume IX blank after the place where he had been interrupted five years before. By chance he was soon dealing with one of the same matters (Newfoundland fishery convoys) that had been on his desk in the last days of his previous tenure. From September he worked mostly at home, so York Buildings became effectively Admiralty HQ. His first half-year back was spent taking stock, and more particularly, in preparing a comprehensive denunciation of the out-going Whig administration: 'making myself on the King's behalfe maister of the then state of the Navy, and the disorders and distress it had been suffer'd to fall into under that commission'. This involved a series of visits to the dockyards, where what most distressed him was the evident decay and disrepair of the new ships of 1677. His initial melancholy turned to indignation when it was suggested that weak Baltic or unseasoned English timber had been used in their construction. Pepys satisfied himself that the defects arose entirely from incompetent maintenance during the regime of 1679–84, which meant of course that no blame attached to him. This argument was developed by Pepys and reiterated at every opportunity during his second term. In its final form it dominated the *Memoires* he published in 1690 when, driven again from office, he was still defending his record against that of the Whig Lords. Since then it has passed into legend, assisted by Pepys's emotive description of the mouldering battlefleet:

> . . . some of theyr buttock-plankes being started from theyr transums, theyr treenailes burnt and rotted, and plankes thereby ready to drop into the water . . . under the danger of sinkeing at theyr very moorings . . . I have seene toad-stooles growing in them as bigg as my Fists; some never once heel'd or bream'd since theyr building, but exposed in hott weather to the sunn, broileing in theyr buttocks and elsewhere for want of liquoring and cooleing them with water . . .

Generations of Dartmouth cadets have been required to commit a version of this to memory, its suggestive juxtaposition of fist and buttock briefly enlivening the dull years between Drake and Nelson. Only recently have Pepys's opinions been seriously examined, and their factual bases tested against data other than his own. What emerges is that the 1679–84 administration was by no means as incompetent as Pepys maintained, that certain residual defects could be traced back to his own previous management, and overall, that Pepys was condemning his predecessors for failing to sustain a defence strategy which his day had required, but theirs did not.[3]

The first version of Pepys's stocktaking report was presented to the King on 1 January 1685. Charles had no opportunity to discuss it with his senior ministers before he died on 6 February. The Duke of York's accession as James II, the first professional Navy officer to wear the crown, ensured that naval affairs would have the highest priority in the new reign. James's elevation incidentally exalted Pepys, since no one now stood between the King and his Admiralty Secretary as James himself had done in his brother's last year. Within a few days Pepys was invited to read his paper; first in instalments to the King alone, and then in full with Lord Treasurer Rochester present. At the King's request, Pepys spent the rest of 1685 trying to see if the problems he had identified might be resolved through current funding, and by the officers (meaning the Navy Board personnel) whom James had inherited. He concluded that the service could not be rescued from its 'continu'd declensions and hopelesnesse' without radical overhaul of the fiscal and administrative structure. He reported verbally to the King at the end of the year, outlining a programme of refurbishment which he believed could be achieved within an annual budget of £400,000. The King asked him to put this in writing, and on 29 January Pepys presented a 'Memorial and Proposition' which, after rehearsing much of the matter about the decay of the fleet, went on to specify targets for a quarterly supply of £100,000 for three years: (1) the whole ordinary charge of the Navy ashore; (2) the extraordinary repairs then necessary, and the completion of three 4th-rates then building; (3) sea stores for six months; (4) a fleet with 3,000 men at sea; and (5) the building of two new frigates each year. To oversee this programme the existing Navy Board would for the same period be replaced by a body of newly selected Commissioners. Pepys had been examining the terms of the 1618 Commission, which served as the model for the scheme he submitted on 5 February.[4]

The King immediately gave his approval, instructing Pepys and the Attorney-General to define the Commissioners' duties. Pepys himself effectively nominated his own team, which included his companion Will Hewer and his brother-in-law Balthasar St Michel. Hewer was now a substantial figure in the City as well as a naval official of great experience, so his inclusion was unexceptionable. St Michel features prominently in Pepys's Diary as a callow and luckless parasite. He had matured since those days, and had done solid work as a muster-master. Even so, his appointment (as Resident Commissioner at Deptford and Woolwich) was more a reward for serving as Pepys's private detective in 1679–80. Pepys also brought in two experienced seamen, Sir John Berry and Sir John Narbrough; Narbrough was already a close friend, though Pepys's original selection had been Captain Henry Shales, who declined.

Three members of the existing Navy Board were retained: Sir Phineas Pett (who had been Comptroller of Storekeepers' Accounts), Sir John Godwin (whom Pett replaced as Resident Commissioner at Chatham), and Sir Richard Beach (who remained Resident at Portsmouth). Pepys said he would not presume to meddle with the Navy Treasurership. The ineffective Lord Falkland continued in office, though Pepys commandeered his house at Deptford for St Michel's use. The other principal members of the old Navy Board, Sir Richard Haddock (Comptroller), Sir John Tippets (Surveyor) and James Sotherne (Clerk of the Acts) were not appointed to the new Commission. Instead, Pepys proposed that they should be re-employed to audit outstanding Treasurer's, victualling, and shipbuilding accounts. The key figure in Pepys's scheme was to be Sir Anthony Deane, who had sourly resigned his Navy Board post in 1680. He now had a lucrative private practice, and needed considerable persuasion (including the promise of £500 a year above the Commissioners' standard salary of £500) before returning to the public sector. In order to convince the King of the need for such a costly headhunt, Pepys submitted an outrageous set of character sketches in which the alternative candidates were aspersed as incompetent or inexperienced ('never built a ship in his life' was said of several). It appeared that all the shipbuilders in England were too old or too young, and most of them were illiterate drunks. Even Tippets and Pett, whom Pepys was recommending for further administrative work, were supposedly disabled by gout from doing anything out of doors. Astonishingly the King accepted all this; Deane was hired, and along with the other new Commissioners, received his patent in March. At the end of the month they corporately assured the King and the Lord Treasurer that the assignment could be completed within Pepys's estimate. It was well known that Pepys had orchestrated the whole affair.[5]

Pepys was not himself appointed to the Commission; he directed its work by virtue of his existing patent. It was, however, all the more important that as the King's Secretary he should represent his department in the new Parliament. James had wanted him to sit for one of the Cinque Ports. Pepys was duly returned at Sandwich, only to have his election contested by burghers disenfranchised by the Crown's streamlining of local government. The King then instructed Sunderland and the Duke of Albemarle, as Lord-Lieutenant of Essex, to ensure Pepys's election at Harwich. It is likely that the very large portrait now at Magdalene was commissioned to mark Pepys's return to his old constituency. He was further honoured by appointment as a Deputy Lieutenant for Huntingdonshire on 1 April; this was, however, as far as Pepys would rise in county society. It was as a Baron of the Cinque Ports that he attended James at his coronation on 23 April; he is clearly if unflatteringly portrayed in one of Sandford's engravings of the ceremony (Plate 1).[6]

The Special Commission was able to report that in its first full year, to Lady Day 1687, routine maintenance had been carried out for 70 ships (30 more than planned), and attention was being given to those ships which were in need of 'extraordinary repairs', some of them scarcely able to stay afloat. Once restored, ships were protected by cutting apertures on the gundecks, keeping the ports open and otherwise encouraging the flow of fresh air, and by watering the sides day and night. The omission of these elementary precautions was, as Pepys had already asserted, the chief cause of the decay he found in his ships of '77. The repair programme had been sustained despite a shortage of timber, and although the cost of residual repairs was increasing apace, the Commissioners were confident of finishing on schedule at the end of 1688. It was already possible to put to sea a Channel Guard of ten ships, manned by 1,310 men, in place of the three small ships with a combined complement of 270 which had lately done the job. This, it was claimed, was better than in any year of peace for the previous twenty years. Without having to seek additional funds, the Admiralty would set out a fleet under Grafton which escorted Pedro II's new bride to Portugal, and went on to treat with the Barbary States. Substantial building work had been done on shore installations; in particular storage facilities had been improved as a means of combating embezzlement. All this had only been possible, as the Commission readily conceded, because of the King's support, and the regularity of the payments begun by Lord Treasurer Rochester. They might have added that the confidence which, against all the odds, James commanded in the 1685 Parliament ensured that adequate supply was voted in the first place. In the Commons Pepys briefly enjoyed the part of a spending minister in a government with a solid majority.[7]

The Special Commissioners made their second report on 31 August 1688, covering the year which had ended at the previous Lady Day. They warned that the state of the ships had been worse, and the repair proportionately larger, than their original estimate. They also complained that they had been hampered by 'many obstructions and hardshipps put upon us (both from sea and shore)' from those to whom their good husbandry was an unattractive replacement for the laxness of the recent past. Nevertheless they certified that all carpentry work on ships ready for sea had been completed, to the satisfaction of the carpenters themselves, the yard Commissioners, and several of the King's shipwrights. (Evidently the latter had recovered from the debilities of drink, illiteracy, age or youth with which Pepys had severally indicted them two years before). In addition to £15,000 earmarked for emergency stores, £4,000 had been saved from the overall budget, and had been spent on canvas, hemp, masts, deals, anchors and principal requirements. At Lady Day 1687, after the Commission's first year, the fleet numbered 168 ships (130 in harbour, 38 at sea), of which 65 were in repair. A year later the total had reduced to 162. Of these, all 40 of those at sea and 98 of those in harbour were in repair. Of the remaining 24, work was in progress on 11, leaving just 13 for attention. The Commissioners expected that by Michaelmas 1688 all the work would be completed, they would be able to close their account six months ahead of schedule. This neat conclusion was not quite achieved; four ships remained under repair and four more were awaiting repair when, on 12 October the Commission was formally dissolved. At the same time the customary Navy Board offices of Comptroller, Surveyor and Clerk of the Acts were revived, with Haddock, Tippets and Sotherne resuming their duties.[8]

152

The King was so pleased with the work of the Commission that he tried to give it a vestigial life. He suggested the creation of 'inspectors marine' on the French model, and wanted to keep Hewer and Deane in that capacity. James's parliamentary agents have been likened to *intendants*, and a further borrowing from Louis XIV's system appealed to him. Hewer would have none of it, arguing that the work would be unnecessary if the under-officers did their jobs, and frustrating if they did not. Pepys was asked to put the idea out of the King's mind. It will be remembered that when he was at the Navy Board, Pepys was a firm advocate of the traditional government through the Principal Officers. His suspension of that structure after he had moved to the Admiralty should not be condemned as inconsistency. He extended the remit of both departments in turn, absorbing Admiralty responsibilities while at the Navy Board, and keeping an eye on Board matters from the Admiralty. His work moved with him.[9]

That Pepys's Commissioners of 1686–8 did indeed perform virtually all they set out to do, within estimate, and somewhat ahead of time, is not now disputed. Immediately after the Revolution, when Pepys's battlefleet was at last facing the French, and none too convincingly, the effectiveness of the Commission's refits and new building was called into question. It was to meet these criticisms that Pepys published his *Memoires* in 1690. During 1691–2 a parliamentary Accounts Commission examined the whole work of the 1686–8 Navy Commission, and although there was some dissent on political grounds, William III's men concluded that Pepys and his team had answered contract. Their verdict is endorsed by Professor Ehrman in his lucid analysis of the figures (from which the details following are derived). The reserve of stores lasted rather less than Pepys had claimed it would, though a good stock of timber was in hand at the end of 1688. Pepys was 'not very far beyond the truth' in claiming that the 54 dockyard storehouses (and minor works ashore) which the Commission had built in two and a half years were more than had been done by all previous Kings of England together. (Henry VIII, after all, is noted for building *two*.) Necessarily it is for the shipbuilding and repair programme that

James II's Commission is chiefly judged. The intention to build two new frigates a year could not be fulfilled, but the three new 4th-rates were finished, and three fleet auxiliaries were built. During William III's enquiry there were some suggestions that the repairs had been inadequate, but this looks chiefly to have been an attempt by Haddock and Tippets to discredit the body from which they had been excluded. Since only a further £624 was spent on the hulls of the thirty Pepysian ships between 1688 and 1691, the soundness of the 1686–8 work seems to be confirmed. The Commission's opponents were unable to substantiate claims that the certificates of repair has been improperly obtained. Pepys had assumed an income of £1,200,000 over three years, and estimated a further £90,787 would be needed. Since the Commission was wound down six months early, its projected income was reduced by one sixth. The actual sum made available was £932,563, of which £929,871 was eventually spent. By deducting certain 'extraordinary' charges, Pepys was able to represent a 'saving' of £307,570 on his original estimate. The true surplus of £19,892 would in fact seem the better demonstration of his careful cost analysis.[10]

Pepys's copies of the Commission's reports are particularly fine specimens of penmanship, and the accountancy has been found, by contemporary and modern scrutiny, to be as good. However, while it is allowed that the Commission was a remarkable success on its own terms, it is no longer possible to swallow the whole rhetoric with which Pepys championed it against the regime of 1679–84. Until recently Pepys's views have been taken at face value, channelled (as he fully intended them to be) through statistics in his own assembled papers and published *Memoires*. The first exponents of Pepys's naval career, J.R. Tanner and Edwin Chappell, relied unashamedly on their man's own testimony. W.A. Aiken expressed the received view that few of the Whig Lords 'had the slightest knowledge of the matters . . . entrusted to their care', and 'their inefficiency exceeded all expectations'. Only recently has a balanced view emerged from a pioneering study by J.D. Davies, employing the earlier Commission's own archives and the private papers of the successive First Commissioners, Sir Henry Capel and Lord Nottingham. There is no denying that the Commissioners of 1679–84 were generally as ignorant of naval affairs on appointment as Pepys himself had been when he joined the service. Pepys's complaints about the toleration of 'good voyages' and the promotion of gentlemen officers were drawn from his standing armoury, and were in effect a veiled criticism of Charles II for indulging his favourites. Pepys also unfairly blamed the Admiralty Commissioners for economies which were required of them by the Treasury. There is also some new evidence that not quite all of the original timber for the 1677 ships was as sound as Pepys and Deane maintained.[11]

What most plainly appears is that Pepys's discussion of the fleet strength is a shameless juggling of numbers to suit his own purpose. He claimed he left the Admiralty in April 1679 with 12,040 men aboard 76 ships; on his return in May 1684 he found 24 ships, with a combined complement of 3,070. In fact there were 39 ships in service at the latter date, and they represented a normal and appropriate Summer Guard for time of peace. By contrast the fleet of 1679 had been mobilised for an anticipated war with France, the hypothetical challenge which had brought forth Pepys's thirty new ships. Admiralty lists actually show 86 ships in pay at one point just before Pepys's departure. By then the immediate emergency had already passed, though as usual the ships could not be stood down until there was money to pay them. Once Charles II recovered the political initiative after 1681, there was even less likelihood of an Anglo-French naval war. That did not mean the Navy had nothing to do. Operations against Algiers, which had resumed in 1677, continued until 1683. S.R. Hornstein has shown that during 1679–84, despite financial shortages, the Admiralty maintained between 40 and 44 ships at sea, whereas between 1675–9 and 1684–8, under Pepys's direction, the number never rose above 37 except in 1679. The 1679–84 Commissioners are now also credited with developing a system of convoy protection through regional squadrons. Useful work of this kind needed fewer and smaller ships than those of a battlefleet designed to fight a general action against the French or Dutch. In hindsight it has to be observed that Pepys's 1677 shipbuilding programme was an over-reaction, and his outrage at the ships' redundancy was misplaced.[12]

The crusade against 'good voyages' also now looks slightly off-target. In July 1686 James II issued a regulation which prohibited the carrying of plate (along with coin, bullion, jewels and any kind of commercial goods) aboard his ships. By way of compensation the captains' wages were to be increased by about 9 per cent *pro rata*. Carriage of coin had previously been allowed, and indeed gave security to international finance. Pepys thought the practice merely encouraged captains to trade in a general way. He had long been gathering instances of captains lingering in port, sometimes undertaking bogus repairs, while awaiting a payload. He had therefore determined to remove what he considered a practical and moral blemish on the service. In the event the captains did not receive their increment, and Professor Rodger suggests they had some reason to resent the withdrawal of their trading perquisites. The handsome fees which Pepys received for issuing passes to ships trading in the Mediterranean seemed much easier money to those who actually had to sail in its waters. In truth the 'good voyages' were not invariably bad, and might be considered a marine extension of process by which the Royal Mail carried private correspondence.[13]

By the time the Special Commission of 1688 closed its books, the consuming crisis of James II's reign was already well developed. The King's religious mania and the political miscalculations which this induced have always seemed adequately to explain his dethronement. Now even his limitations as an Admiral are considered a factor, adding to the irony that England's most nautically experienced monarch was the one who lost his kingdom to a seaborne invasion. Pepys's role in the events of 1688–9 also has its curiosities. Interpretation is difficult because of a significant dearth in his private correspondence at the time, and the circumspection which he afterwards observed as a grudging but obedient subject of William III. Pepys's admirers, who praise his unswerving loyalty to Charles II and James II, find it strange that he was prepared to serve William. It can seem puzzling that the King's own Secretary for

Admiralty affairs should not have had a larger influence on events. His public position should not be exaggerated: he was not a Privy Councillor nor a member of James's inner circle of Catholic cronies. In the broad history of the Revolution he is not a significant figure. Only in its naval aspects does he have a high profile, since it fell to him to keep the King in touch with the fleet, and he drafted many of the most vital despatches.[14]

The sequence of events which ended Pepys's career began in January 1688 with the news that James II's Queen was pregnant. The birth of a son, sure to be raised as a Catholic, would displace the King's Protestant daughter Mary, the current heiress-presumptive. Mary had been married to William III of Orange as part of the reconciliation after the Third Dutch War, and James's opponents had been consoled by the fairly imminent expectation of Mary's succession. William suddenly saw his own prospects disintegrating. He had no ambition to rule in England, or to preserve its people from popery, but he keenly wanted his wife's inheritance to support his own country's struggle against Louis XIV. Such modest military aid as England was giving him was withdrawn by James, also in January 1688, giving the Dutch reasonable grounds for suspecting an Anglo-French alliance against them. William was now persuaded to contemplate direct intervention in English affairs. As the year progressed the level of Dutch naval preparations was monitored in England, and Pepys co-ordinated the response. In early May he inspected the fortifications between Chatham and Gillingham, shortly after the King had done the same. Dartmouth had wanted all the great ships behind the protection of the chain, but had been overruled by James and his flag officers, who were confident in the efficiency of the shore batteries. Pepys's survey suggests that this optimism was misplaced ('No men bredd to the guns, but depend on the Navy'). The birth of the King's son on 10 June increased the probability that those guns would shortly be needed. For the moment it was necessary only for Pepys to order a celebratory salute throughout the fleet. Some defections occurred, the most significant being that of Arthur Herbert. He had fallen out with James the year before, and now carried to Holland the appeal from seven opposition leaders which William took as his invitation to England.[15]

At the start of August Pepys was actually expecting that the number of ships at sea could be run down over the next three months, but very shortly the King was ordering a concentration of forces in the Downs. Before the month was past, Pepys was urgently preparing the King's ships for action, 'it being the time in our whole lives wherein the same can be of most use and importance to him'. Even so neither he nor the King was yet convinced that the Dutch preparations were directed against England. As late as 3 September he wrote: 'I find both his Majesty and his ministers under a good degree of conviction that we shall not need to apprehend any great attempts, or indeed any at all from them [*the Dutch*] at this time.' It was only on 24 September that the King received convincing intelligence to the contrary. He immediately cancelled the writs for a new Parliament, and in a belated move to restore confidence in the naval command, he demoted his Catholic C-in-C, Sir Roger Strickland, and replaced him with Dartmouth. Pepys for one was delighted, because, quite apart from the religious issue, Strickland had pestered him interminably about his right to wear the union flag. Dartmouth joined the fleet at the Buoy of the Nore on 2 October, and at once reported to Pepys, initiating a series of exchanges which are a fundamental source for the ensuing events. Pepys generally had the better intelligence, though Dartmouth was occasionally sceptical of it. It was expected that William would land in the east or north-east; and with a high seas engagement in mind, the fleet was moved to the Gunfleet anchorage off Harwich on 15 October. Since it is now clear that William had not yet rejected this option in favour of the south-west, the English move was tactically reasonable. What James and his advisers (presumably including Pepys) failed to appreciate was that William's strategic premise was the avoidance of a battle, not the winning of one.[16]

It was late on 26 October that the King heard that William was at sea, but also likely to be kept on his own coast by a rising storm. At 2 a.m. Pepys was on hand to send the King's recommendation to Dartmouth to 'try whether any advantage may be taken' by attacking the Dutch where they lay. Dartmouth had formerly proposed just that, but now he feared being driven on to the enemy coast by the same winds which had kept the Dutch there. Late on 29 October Pepys passed to Dartmouth a plausible eavesdropping from William himself, identifying the Humber as the Dutch target. Overnight the wind veered ENE, and on the following day, in the expectation that the Dutch would be on the seas again, Dartmouth weighed anchor to intercept them. He did not so much as clear the Galloper. By 31 October the 'Protestant' wind had arrived from the East, allowing William to sail unmolested on the following day, and immuring Dartmouth in his anchorage for the rest of the piece. Even before he heard that the Prince was at sea again, Pepys knew 'the very being, as well as honour' of the Crown and government was in the balance. By 11 p.m. on 3 November the Admiralty had sightings of the Dutch fleet passing westwards of Dover and the Downs. After midnight Pepys left the King and his generals, who had rolled up their maps of Yorkshire and were urgently (but still needlessly) preparing to defend Portsmouth. It was with 'not a little Surpriseing' and no doubt some embarrassment that Pepys told Dartmouth that all the recent intelligence had been wrong. He can be wholly exonerated. William had not opted for a landing in the west until he was actually at sea. His fleet initially sailed north-west and came within 100 miles of the Yorkshire coast. Only on the night of 2/3 November did they turn for the Channel.[17]

The movement of the Dutch towards their eventual landfall at Brixham was monitored by Pepys and duly passed on Dartmouth. He conveyed the King's specific assurance to the C-in-C that no blame attached to him for the failure to intercept. Dartmouth was merely ordered to proceed to the Downs to await developments. This was not quite the end, because by 11 November Pepys understood from captured papers that the Dutch had fewer ships than had been previously reported, and when this intelligence had been evaluated, Dartmouth was authorised to proceed against them. Once again the weather prevented the fleets from meeting. In any case, with William safely disembarked and apparently marching on London, the immediate problem was military not naval. On

17 November the King left London for Salisbury. Pepys came tagging along as far as Windsor, where he saw fit to present James with an extraordinary document requiring the Treasury to pay him an unspecified sum for services rendered over an equally unspecified period (on the strength of which Pepys subsequently claimed a cool £28,007 2s 1¼d). James signed it, as he would have signed the Thirty-Nine Articles at that moment had they been put in front of him. Doubtless Pepys was owed something, but it was an act of staggering insolence to intrude his private concerns upon the King at such a time. He clearly saw the regime disintegrating, and optimistically hoped that its successor would honour this blank cheque payable to himself. It looks like a rare instance of a rat presenting a bill to the captain of a sinking ship.[18]

Rat week it was, though Pepys did not desert. With no expectation of 'any more action . . . this season', there was little to do openly at the Admiralty except cancel impressment and the fitting out of additional ships. Other business had to be done covertly. Once the King had returned forlornly to London, Pepys was involved in plans to evacuate the Queen and the infant Prince of Wales. On 4 December he drafted a warrant for the King's signature, authorising the captain of the yacht *Isabella* to take the Comte de Lauzun to Flanders or France; it was to de Lauzun that the King entrusted his son. Dartmouth thought this such political folly that he prevented the use of a royal yacht, and the Prince's escape had to be even more furtive.[19]

The King left Whitehall in the early hours of 11 December, intending to follow his son to France, though he got only as far as Rochester. When the provisional government met at Guildhall later that day, Pepys was ordered to transmit their message to Dartmouth for preventing hostilities between the Prince's ships and his own, and for the removal of all Catholic officers. Next day Pepys was required to see to the examining of all ships passing below Gravesend. While he was so engaged, a letter which the Prince of Orange had written on 29 November reached Dartmouth at Spithead, proposing a union of their fleets. To this he immediately agreed, and a council of war on the following day (13 December) endorsed the decision. The

Fourth Dutch War was over, and the Dutch had won. It was apparently only at this point that Dartmouth received Pepys's message from the Guildhall assembly, and a day later still (the 14th) that a last and now redundant letter from the King arrived. This had been written at Whitehall on the 10th, just as James was about to take to his horse. Pepys was blamed by Dartmouth for sending this by the common post; but even the express delivery which Pepys employed could not keep pace with events. On 15 December Pepys attended the Lords to explain the procedure for stopping the ports. Next day James surprised everyone by returning to London, and countermanding the Lords' orders. His readeption lasted just forty-eight hours. William allowed him to escape properly, and then began to assume a kind of regency. He was, however, scrupulously careful to retain as many as possible of his uncle's officials. Pepys was summoned to attend him on 19 December, and undertook to accept the Prince's orders. At this time James was deemed merely to have 'withdrawn', and Pepys could accept political reality without compromising his allegiance.[20]

So he remained at the Admiralty a little longer. He hoped to represent Harwich again in the Convention which was summoned to settle the constitutional crisis, but was roundly defeated at the election on 16 January. He was therefore prevented from giving his voice in the deliberations which resulted in the accession of William and Mary on 13 February. Most of James II's adherents were now dismissed, and even if Pepys had been able to mould his conscience as some others did, it is unlikely that he would have been wanted. He resigned on 20 February, though he was tidying his files until 1 March.[21]

TEN

The Oracle of the Navy

'So hard is the business of the sea, to be at once thoroughly and
rightly comprehended.'

Pepys, July 1693 [*Naval Minutes*, pp. 312–13]

Pepys lived on till 1703. He had taken over Hewer's property at
York Buildings, and there he remained until in his last months
he again joined Hewer at Clapham. Towards the end of his second
secretaryship he had ostentatiously displayed the Admiralty shield
outside his door, which encouraged the successor regime to claim the
property from him. Pepys very properly stayed put. William III's
government twice interned him as a suspected Jacobite: from 4 May
to 15 June 1689, and then again from 25 June to 14 July 1690. The
second imprisonment was occasioned by a menacing French naval
presence in the Channel, and attempts were made to link Pepys with
Jacobite hopefuls in Portsmouth. Pepys later bought a pamphlet
which explained the alleged plot, listing him among the political
prisoners in the Westminster Gatehouse. He was technically a 'non-
juror': one who would not swear allegiance to William and Mary,
but did not actively oppose them.[1]

Although Pepys had co-operated with his designated successor,
Phineas Bowles, in the transfer of business, he retained a good many
official books and papers, and the new Admiralty Board (which
Herbert headed) was soon asking for them. The matter was delayed
by Pepys's first imprisonment, but by 12 July 1689 a substantial
transfer had been made. Even so, not everything clearly identifiable
as a public record left York Buildings. Most notably Pepys retained
the fourteen large folios which register his out-letters as Secretary
between 1673–9 and 1684–9. The later Admiralty Secretary, Josiah

Burchett, was trying to recover them in 1699 and again in 1700, reminding Pepys of an Order in Council of 1673 requiring retention of the department's records. Pepys clearly had no intention of parting with these volumes, which remain in his Library at Magdalene. The Public Record Office has only an incomplete set of copies. Pepys himself had copies made of some of the volumes he did surrender in 1689, and the more significant of these were added to his Library. Some official documents which were evidently not wanted by the Admiralty, together with those which Pepys did not think worth incorporating in his Library, passed with a large quantity of Pepys's other papers to the Bodleian Library. Pepys's refusal to hand over the 'Admiralty Letters' was perhaps a matter of personal pride. It is unlikely that he was merely trying to withhold material from his opponents' eyes. He would certainly have wanted to keep them as reference in any future debate, and eventually for writing the history of his own time. Pepys also retained for the Library several volumes which had been part of his office equipment, but which he reasonably regarded as his personal property.[2]

The immediate purpose for which Pepys wanted these materials was the composition of his *Memoires*, justifying the appointment and operation of the Special Commission of 1686–8. Evelyn greeted the publication with enthusiasm, and a spoof review in his heaviest manner. Every copy of this little book has its typographical errors corrected by hand: not actually by Pepys, but probably at his direction. He was nevertheless pleased enough with his publication to consider having it translated into French. After 1690 he was left alone by the government. This was a measure of the stability of Revolution; by the same token, it was becoming ever less likely that Pepys would regain office. A last thought of returning to Parliament was abandoned. He nevertheless remained fascinated by politics, and followed the naval events of King William's war with a discerning eye. He still had, of course, many friends in the Navy, but increasingly it was with learned folk that he associated and corresponded. The two worlds met in his continuing role as a governor of Christ's Hospital, which is documented in a 700-page dossier which Pepys assembled. He had assisted the foundation there in 1673 of the Royal Mathematical School, which provided technical training for future seamen. On his visit to Spain in 1684 he had been impressed by the equivalent seminary created by Carlos II, and was the more determined to encourage nautical education at home. He used his contacts in the Royal Society (of which he had been President in 1684–6) to add very high-powered support to his patronage of the Mathematical School. His work was honoured by the award of the Freedom of the City in 1699. Principally, in a retirement sustained by ample means and tolerably good health, he turned back to the related projects of completing his Library and his naval history.[3]

The history was never written. Its intended compass is indicated in the 'Naval Minutes', a commonplace book which Pepys kept between 1680 and 1696. The extant MS is written out neatly by Pepys's clerks, though it retains the jumbled and repetitive sequence of original notes. Many of these are simply memoranda to consult a particular book or person ('Buy Matthew Parris'; 'Consult Mr. Shere for his notes upon Noah's Ark'; 'Read Geraldus his chapter *De Navigiis*'). Others allude to topics he meant to pursue ('Few English engineers'; 'the presumptuous claims of King Edgar and King John to Sea-Dominion'; 'felony for a soldier or seamen to beg'). There are also many observations on his own time, including a much-quoted description of Charles II, the Duke of York (and Sandwich) as 'the most mathematick Admirals England ever had'. Predictably there is a good deal of self-justification. Pepys also notes what he has been told, as, for example, by Gibson and Deane about the relative merits of English and foreign shipbuilding. Here he marshals the evidence and develops a line of argument; one can see parts of a book taking shape. Nothing more extensive ever seems to have been drafted, and no overall scheme for the book was devised. The 'Minutes' serve best as a guide to Pepys's reading during his two chief periods of scholarly activity.[4]

As his reading list grew, the writing was deferred; a common authorial dilemma. By way of organising his sources (seen and as yet unseen) he compiled in 1695 his 'Bibliotheca Nautica', an analytical bibliography of English works on navigation. To the same MS he appended lists of the Spanish and Portuguese literature, supplied to him by Dr Hans Sloane from Nicolás Antonio's *Bibliotheca Hispaña* (Rome, 1672). For the French authors, extracted from *La Bibliothèque du Sieur de la Croix-du-Maine* (Paris, 1584), he was indebted to Dr Francis Bernard. Pepys already knew the principal Dutch works in English translation. Since 1663 he had owned the 1588 edition of Anthony Ashley's *Mariners Mirror*, translated from the work of Lucas Janssen Waghenaer which gave to all such navigational guides the name of 'waggoner'. Now the bookseller Richard Mount guided Pepys through the home waters of Dutch maritime publishing. Further assistance came from Pepys's Magdalene mentor Joseph Hill, who promised to search out particular titles.[5]

Yet perhaps this exercise was counter-productive, persuading Pepys that he would never master so much technical material. From this time allusions to the great work become more guarded. He continued to add naval material to the Library, chastising himself for a small lapse in keeping up to date. More ominously, at the end of 1696 Evelyn was cautiously asking what progress had been made, urging Pepys to send a few drafts, however imperfect. Evening, he reminded his old friend, was now upon them. Three years later, with still nothing written up, Pepys lost the regular services of his long-standing library clerk and copyist Paul Lorrain. He wanted a new assistant to revise the catalogue and for the larger task of 'garbling up' the notes for the naval history. His nephew John Jackson came to help with the catalogue, but of the history there is no further mention.[6]

The Library had proved to be occupation enough, and much of the time which Pepys might have spent in writing his history was devoted to its extension and ordering. For that we should be grateful, since the collection he has passed to us is an incomparably greater thing than any book he might have written. It is a library which more than any other bears its creator's mark. Pepys not merely designed it on a scale which he considered appropriate for a scholar and a gentleman; he also took great care that it should remain intact. Having no children of his own, he left his books in the first instance to his favourite nephew, John Jackson, and then to his old college at Cambridge. Magdalene's tenure was strictly circumscribed in a codicil to Pepys's will: nothing might be added to the collection, nor disposed of; the books were to be kept separately from the College's existing library, and not to be borrowed (save that the Master might take volumes to his Lodge). Trinity College was enjoined to monitor the observance of these rules, and stood to inherit the whole collection should Magdalene default. It has to be said that a few books went astray in the early eighteenth century (including one naval MS), and in 1806 the College improperly sent several volumes to London for scrutiny by a naval enquiry. Trinity has never exercised its right of inspection, and might now have some difficulty in contesting Magdalene's long use.[7]

The Library therefore came to Magdalene in 1724, the year after Jackson's death, and has stayed there. At Pepys's request it was first housed in the new building to which he had subscribed; it has not always been there, but since 1959 it has resumed its original home, the elegant room which occupies the larger part of the first floor. Here the 3,000 volumes are preserved in the twelve glass-fronted bookcases (called 'presses') which Pepys had designed for them. The first two were made by Thomas Simpson, master-joiner at Woolwich and Deptford, and their arrival in July and August 1666 was a great moment. As the books multiplied, so more presses were constructed, though the presses themselves exerted a control on accessions. Having eliminated the displeasing clutter which his books had previously created, Pepys was severe in discarding items for which no shelf space was available. He disposed of most duplicates (often replacing what would now be regarded as a more valuable edition by a later one), and ejected some books which he considered unworthy of preservation. Some items were left out of the Library simply because they did not fit the shelving scheme, including several important but awkwardly sized volumes of naval accounts from Elizabeth's reign. These are among the MSS now in the Bodleian.[8]

Pepys's library system has a sublime simplicity. The books are numbered in a single sequence, from 1 to 3000, and are arranged in ascending order of height. They spiral upwards through the twelve presses, and then descend at the rear of the same shelves. Larger volumes are kept in separate cupboards below, and the largest of all have places in a central desk. By chance the first (and therefore smallest) book is one of the most treasured nautical items: a set of printed tide tables with a MS map, all on vellum leaves, published in France in 1546. Because of the inscription 'F. Drak' it is known as Drake's pocket book. As with most of Pepys's other books there is no sure provenance, because he did not keep an accessions register. The growth of his Library is well documented in the Diary, but after 1669 we have only occasional references in his correspondence, and a few inscribed dedications. Pepys himself very rarely wrote in his books. This was in keeping with his general tidiness, and it should not be inferred that he did not study what he acquired. There is ample testimony to the contrary. The very orderliness of the Library, and the immaculate and tranquil conditions in which it is now preserved, can be deceptive. The gilt-blocked books lie massed behind the glass like three thousand dead goldfish in twelve tanks. Visitors occasionally suspect that some sections are pure sham, behind which would be found bottles or more recondite pleasures. This is not the case, though the aesthetic arrangement of the Library can make its contents seem bewilderingly diverse to the casual observer.[9]

Subjects are dispersed through the shelves as the rule of size requires, though, wherever possible, kindred matter of the same size stands together. Pepys also mixed printed matter and manuscript; some volumes contain elements of both. Naval and maritime subjects, which are but one of the Library's themes, necessarily cut across these divides. Best known are the manuscript records of Pepys's own professional life, essential to the historiography of the Restoration Navy. The Library also contains a valued collection of maps and charts, which have now been fully catalogued. Less familiar, because hitherto not considered as a group, are the printed books on navigation and naval history. Pepys's Library was already well known to the scholarly public in his own lifetime, and the manuscripts were listed in the catalogue of British and Irish MS collections published by Oxford University in 1697. Pepys had been diffident about the inclusion of his material ('how farr a Masse of Papers, for the most part unconnected, and . . . out of any of the trodden Roads of common Reading, can bee thought convertible to publick use . . . I cannot see'). His cringing disavowal of academic distinction was the politeness of the day, and in reality Pepys certainly intended his Library to be a public resource. A few literary and illustrative pieces from it were published in the course of the eighteenth century. An engraving by James Basire of the *Henry Grace à Dieu* from the Anthony Roll was the first nautical item to appear. The Admiralty had not forgotten that the Library contained a significant chunk of its own archives, hence the application for papers to be sent up in 1806. The publication of selections from the Diary in 1825 brought Pepys a new and lasting celebrity, but the other riches of the Library were only slowly revealed. Publication of the whole Diary was long impeded by the erotic passages, and the Master and Fellows were from time to time obliged to deliberate solemnly over which obscenities might be revealed. Only with the edition of 1970–83 by Robert Latham and William Matthews was a complete and reliable text established.[10]

Latham's predecessor as Pepys Librarian, R.W. Ladborough, surprisingly suggested that scholars had paid less attention to the naval books than to the music. It was unfortunately the case that one distinguished naval historian had previously been denied access. Michael Oppenheim, while writing his definitive *History of the Administration of the Royal Navy*, was refused permission to use the MSS on the grounds that 'a member of the university was working at them'. This was a reference to J.R. Tanner of St John's. Oppenheim may also have been socially and politically unwelcome; but for whatever reason, he was never allowed near Pepys's papers, and so was unable to take his own work beyond 1660. Yet more surprising was the College's refusal in 1895 to allow the Navy Records Society to reproduce the illustrations from the Anthony Roll; as a result an edition of the MS intended by Francis Elgar had to be abandoned, and it was a century before the project was carried through by other hands. The Navy Records Society has played a major part in making Pepys's papers accessible. Nine of the Society's volumes derive wholly or largely from material in the Pepys Library, and another (*Tangier Papers*) is from the Rawlinson MSS.[11]

The Pepys Library's naval MSS may be loosely classified as (1) 'official', those generated by Pepys's work at the Navy Board and Admiralty (whether 'originals' or copies made for Pepys's own use), and (2) 'historical', matter collected specifically for his naval history. There are also some curiosities belonging to neither category. Of the few in the first group which are true 'originals', pride of place goes to the 'Admiralty Letters' which Pepys so resolutely declined to surrender after his resignation. These volumes (amounting to over 6,000 pages, say 3¼ million words) are still only partially published. Tanner begin to summarise them as part of his *Descriptive Catalogue of the Naval Manuscripts in the Pepsyian Library* for the NRS, but in two of his own volumes he dealt with only the first four (numbered II–V) of the MSS, covering the years 1673–8. Proposals for a resumption of the work have been laid before the Council of the Navy Records Society; in the mean time the remaining ten volumes, including the whole period of Pepys's second secretaryship, have to be consulted in manuscript. Serious scholars will in any case always need to go behind Tanner's calendar to read the full letters.[12]

Tanner had begun his *Catalogue* with an introductory volume in which he presented a digest of his great knowledge of the Pepys MSS. This remains the fullest analysis, re-worked by Tanner in four lectures he published in 1920. To his introduction to the *Catalogue* he appended two of Pepys's most basic working texts, his Registers of the Royal Navy (ships) and of Sea Officers, 1660–88. In the fourth part of the *Catalogue*, Tanner diverted from the 'Letters' to present in a yet more massive volume the minutes ('Journal') of the Admiralty Commission from 1673–9. Tanner also edited the 'Naval Minutes' for the NRS; this was not part of the *Catalogue*, and may have attracted his attention simply because the MS volume stands next in place after the 'Journal'. That Tanner had by no means exhausted the 'official' group of naval manuscripts is shown in his necessarily briefer *'Sea' Manuscripts*, which outlines the contents of some 115 manuscripts wholly or partially of maritime interest. This was Tanner's contribution to *Bibliotheca Pepysiana. A Descriptive*

Catalogue of the Library of Samuel Pepys, an unfinished project for which various parts were issued by the College between 1914 and 1940. Tanner's *Sea MSS* descriptions were absorbed and in some cases extended in the *Catalogue of Modern MSS* (i.e post-medieval MSS on all subjects), which forms part of the new *Catalogue of the Pepys Library* completed under the general editorship of Robert Latham between 1978 and 1994.[13]

The deceptively titled *Report on the Pepys Manuscripts* edited by E.K. Purnell for the Historical Manuscripts Commission deals only with the three volumes of 'State Papers', which Pepys acquired from Evelyn. There is matter of interest here for the naval history of the Civil War, including Charles II's time on Jersey under the protection of Sir George Carteret. However, a fair amount of this merely summarises papers now lost, and there is frequently little more to be had from the extant MS than is provided in the *Report*. Apart from the 'State Papers', the largest of Pepys's collections of discrete original MSS are the 'Naval Papers collected for Parliament'. These comprise over 200 letters, lists and other items, mostly from 1660–79; only a few of them are in Pepys's hand. Little from this collection has been published (save that there are a few original printed items), and for this reason a full calendar was provided in *Modern MSS*.[14]

Pepys naturally preserved copies of the main reports and papers he drafted; those of which he was particularly proud were given a distinctive dark blue binding. A small pudgy volume with 'Diary Naval' on its spine attracts attention. This is devoted to the proceedings of the 1686–8 Commission, and does indeed contain a diary section. Like the other later Pepys diaries, it disappoints those hoping to find the old flame rekindled. Even so, and though Bryant made extensive use of it, a full edition might be welcomed. The Commission's two reports, 1687 and 1688, are, as already noted, fine and intricate documents, and would test the skills of any editor or printer. Among the more important volumes illustrating the earlier part of Pepys's career is his report to the Duke of York on the workings of the Navy Board, with the responses of its members and the Duke's further 'reflections' on them. Pepys made a similar collection of the defences he submitted for the parliamentary enquiry after the Second Dutch War. His 750-page 'Naval and Admiralty Precedents' brings together many of the reports and 'establishments' of his own time, with a few earlier items. The 'Day Collection', begun in 1684, is a more compact collection of key documents of his first and second secretaryships; in this case a protective binding indicates that it was kept at his desk for regular reference.[15]

Some manuscripts acquired in the course of Pepys's professional duty could be accounted his own property. Among those actually dedicated to Pepys were Francis Hosier's 1668 proposals for reform of storekeepers' accounts, and Edward Battine's treatise on shipbuilding written in 1684. Deane's larger work on shipbuilding, written at Pepys's request in 1670, belongs in this group. Another item of special interest was Captain Richard Bolland's illustrated account of Tangier and its fortifications (1676), describing a place with which Pepys already had a long connexion but had not yet seen. Pepys also acquired a good collection of ships' journals, many of them well-illustrated with charts and drawings of coastal features; those of Sir John Narbrough are the most visually pleasing, and those of Sir Robert Holmes probably the most lively reading.[16]

The naval manuscripts which are here loosely grouped as 'historical' include items which came to Pepys, and those which he compiled with his own writing project in mind. Of the former, the oldest, and the only item of naval interest from among his thirty-six medieval MSS, is the late-fifteenth century 'Libel [*little book*] of Englysch Policie' a poetic tract in support of England's maritime trade. The most celebrated of Pepys's naval manuscripts is the Anthony Roll of 1546; although we must now regret Pepys's ruthless scissoring of the original vellum rolls to create a codex which could be accommodated in his Library, in doing so he produced a bibliographic treasure in its own right, embellished with a luxuriant burgundy binding and exotic multi-coloured endpapers. The 'Fragments of Ancient English Shipwrightry', begun by Elizabethan royal shipwright Matthew Baker, has illuminations as famous as those of the Anthony Roll. Its text (fragmentary indeed, but comprising the earliest known technical manual on shipbuilding in English) is only now being studied in detail. Pepys, like most of his contemporaries, looked back wistfully to the maritime glories of Elizabeth's reign. Of these he had a tangible trophy, the *Libro de Cargos*, listing the provisions and munitions of 81 of the ships of the Spanish Armada, and itself presumably taken from one of them. He also had a MS translation of Petruccio Ubaldini's account of the Armada campaign (as well as a set of the engraved maps by Augustine Ryther which accompanied the printed version), and a treatise, dedicated to Lord Burghley, on the means of preventing any subsequent invasion.[17]

The greatest concentration of historical material is the eleven folio volumes of the 'Miscellany of matters historical, political and naval'. These are Pepys's research files, containing the material he had copied from other repositories in the 1690s when he was able to pay for transcriptions to be made. They are therefore fair copies made by clerks, though not always very systematically arranged. The first volume contains material relating to the foundation of Trinity House, and the journal of the shipbuilder Phineas Pett (printed by W.G. Perrin for the Navy Records Society). The second and third volumes contain copies from the papers of Sir Julius Caesar, Judge of the Admiralty (d. 1636). The fourth was taken wholly from the commonplace book of Thomas Bedford, who was the deputy and reversionary Registrar of the Admiralty Court from 1679 to his death in 1705. Almost all of volume VII was copied from the State Papers, from those of Henry VIII to the time of the Commonwealth.[18]

The whole of volume IX concerns colours and salutes, and the issue of the dominion of the seas which these symbols so potently reflected. This includes material from Pepys's own administration, and his historiographical memoranda and queries. A good many of his friends contributed to the volume: Haddock, Narbrough and Deane provided notes on salutes, Samuel Hunter collected memories of the colours worn in Charles I's time, and Sir William Dugdale supplied his designs for banners flown by the newly married Prince and Princess of Orange in 1677. Pepys's friend the Serjeant-Surgeon John Knight wrote a complete history of the cross of St George, with some illustrated designs for the better marshalling of squadronal colours.[19]

Most of all Pepys took copies from the Cottonian manuscripts, that 'inestimable library' which he called one of the jewels in the English crown. Principally, his Miscellany volume VIII is a complete transcription of Cotton Otho E 9, and volume IX contains most of Otho E 7. In 1731 there was a major fire in the Cottonian Library, then at Ashburnham House beside Westminster Abbey, and very many of the bound MSS were burned around the sides. As a result, virtually everything subsequently printed from these volumes is liberally and frustratingly peppered with [...]s. Pepys's copies can, however, help to fill the gaps, as has now been done for an important selection of letters relating to the Spanish Armada. Even where the Cotton MSS (now in the British Library) or other originals survive intact, the Pepysian transcripts can help to resolve uncertain readings. Wherever the originals can no longer be located, Pepys's copies assume the status of primary sources.[20]

Printed books on maritime matters are generally dispersed through the Library by the strict rules of size. Pepys did however form sub-collections on certain subjects, where he bound together smaller books and pamphlets of related concern. Among his four volumes of 'Sea Tracts' are works of the sixteenth-century writers on navigation William Borough, William Bourne, Martin Cortés, Thomas Hood, Robert Norman, and others. Some of these books would have delighted Pepys with their 'volvelles' (revolving charts), an early exercise in interactive publishing. Also here is the murkier side of science, Simon Forman and John Dee. Rather misplaced among these technical writings is Robert Kayll's economic treatise *The Trade's Increase*, to which Pepys also had the unhappy MS sequel, 'The Trade's Decrease'. A further group of 'Naval Pamphlets' mostly contains reports of actions, including those of the 1690s (demonstrating Pepys's continued interest in current naval affairs). Here also is *A Rough Draft of a New Model at Sea* (1694, but probably written in the 1660s). Pepys surprisingly failed to identify this as the work of Halifax, and supposed Robert Harley to be the author.[21]

Although Pepys only produced one publication, he assisted numerous others, and was the dedicatee of several, including two on naval matters. Nathaniel Butler's *Six Dialogues* was dedicated to Pepys by its publisher Moses Pitt. An edition of Narbrough's collected journals came with a map inscribed in Pepys's honour, and a graceful general encomium from the publishers Samuel Smith and Benjamin Walford; they were also generous with complimentary copies, and Pepys had his own sumptuously bound.[22]

The Library at Magdalene contains only the cream of the Pepysian literary inheritance. Much of his official correspondence is in the Public Record Office, and should be held to include letters he wrote as Clerk of the Acts on behalf of the Navy Board, as well as those over his individual signature. Items from the main series of State Papers can be read in summary in the *Calendar of State Papers, Domestic*; a great deal else lies in the uncatalogued departmental records of the Admiralty. Of the papers which remained with him at his death, a large selection of those most relevant to his professional and public life were acquired by the antiquary Richard Rawlinson, and by him left to the Bodleian in 1755. Selections from this collection were published with the early editions of the Diary (from 1825), and it forms the basis of R.G. Howarth's *Letters and the Second Diary of Samuel Pepys* (1933). Howarth's 'Second Diary' is Pepys's Tangier Journal, which should be consulted in the far superior NRS edition by Edwin Chappell (1935). Another great batch of Pepys's correspondence remained with his collateral descendants the Pepys Cockerells, selections being printed by Tanner as *Private Correspondence . . . 1679–1703* (1926) and (perversely) *Further Correspondence . . . 1662–79* (1929). In 1931 the Pepys Cockerell MSS were auctioned, and most were bought privately. The volume from which *Further Correspondence* derived, and which has substantial naval interest, was bought by the National Maritime Museum. Shorthand matter from it, not used by Tanner, was transcribed and edited by Chappell as *Shorthand Letters* (1933). H.T. Heath's selection of Pepys's family letters (from several collections) includes correspondence with St Michel of some naval interest. Pepys's correspondence with Evelyn, also from various sources, was edited by C. Marburg (1935); this is replaced by G. de la Bédoyère's *Particular Friends* (1997).[23]

The survival of so great a quantity of his own writing, and his preservation for us of so much else, surely absolves Pepys from the failure to compose a naval history. Such a work might well have been a disappointment. Had it been completed along the lines which the research indicates, it would have been of staggering proportions, and nowadays unreadable for that reason alone. He would have displayed the fruits of his wide reading in classical sources and modern history, and have added a great deal of first-hand *reportage*. While his writing would inevitably have been coloured by the prejudices of his day, he would have been refreshingly dismissive of the more fanciful English pretensions. He would have celebrated the Navy as 'safeguard of the seas', the guarantor of England's political independence and commercial livelihood. Yet he showed surprisingly little interest in English advances upon the broader oceans, and his work might not have inadequately reflected the colonial ventures in which so many of his associates were involved. His work would also have taken him into areas technical and historical where he had no expertise. Naval historians are severe on their own kind, and unforgiving of the landsmen who presume to interpret their mysteries. As one of the greatest of them wrote to another: 'the moment shore historians touch salt water a mist comes over them'. Pepys, for all his long service to the Navy, was still a civilian ('Squire Pepys') to a real man of the sea, and his naval history might have been judged too much a view from the shoreline. Those of us who can claim no maritime experience whatsoever must presume no further. It is enough to respect the unrelenting industry with which Pepys followed his professional calling, and to acknowledge the great fund of materials he left us. Pepys remains for us, as he was to his contemporaries, 'the *Oracle* of the Navy'.[24]

Abbreviations

Including short titles of certain principal sources more fully described in section (ii) of the Bibliography

Allin, *Journals*	*The Journals of Sir Thomas Allin*, ed. R.C. Anderson (NRS, 1939–40)
AntJ	*Antiquaries Journal*
APC	*Acts of the Privy Council of England*, ed. J.R. Dasent (1890–1907)
BIHR	*Bulletin of the Institute of Historical Research* [continued as HR]
BL	British Library
Bodl.	Bodleian Library, Oxford
Br. *Naval Documents*	*British Naval Documents*, ed. J.B. Hattendorf *et al.* (NRS, 1993)
Cat. PL	*Catalogue of the Pepys Library*, ed. R.C. Latham (Woodbridge and Cambridge, 1978–94)
CHJ	*Cambridge Historical Journal* [continued as HJ]
CJ	*Journals of the House of Commons*
CSPD	*Calendar of State Papers Domestic*
CSP Ven.	*Calendar of State Papers Venetian*
Diary	*The Diary of Samuel Pepys*, ed. R.C. Latham and W. Matthews (1970–83)
DNB	*Dictionary of National Biography*
EHR	*English Historical Review*
Evelyn, *Diary*	*The Diary of John Evelyn*, ed. E.S. de Beer (1955)
Further Corr.	*Further Correspondence of Samuel Pepys*, 1662–1679, ed. J.R. Tanner (1929)
Grey, *Debates*	*Debates of the House of Commons . . . by . . . Anchitell Grey* (1794)
Heath	*The Letters of Samuel Pepys and his Family Circle*, ed. H.T. Heath (Oxford, 1955)
HJ	*Historical Journal* [continuation of CHJ]
HMC	Historical Manuscripts Commission
HMC, *Buccleuch*	*Report on the Manuscripts of the Duke of Buccleuch and Queensberry* (HMC, 1899–1903)
HMC, *Dartmouth*	*The Manuscripts of the Earl of Dartmouth* (HMC, 1887–96)
HMC, *Downshire*	*Report on the Manuscripts of the Marquis of Downshire* (HMC, 1924–42)
HMC, *Finch*	*Report on the Manuscripts of Allan George Finch*, II (HMC, 1913–22)
HMC, *Hodgkin*	*The Manuscripts of J. Eliot Hodgkin* (HMC, 1897)
HMC, *Lindsey*	*Supplementary Report on the Manuscripts of the . . . Earl of Lindsey* (HMC, 1942)
HMC, *Ormonde*	*Calendar of the Manuscripts of the Marquess of Ormonde*, new series (HMC, 1902–20)

HMC, *Pepys*	*Report on the Pepys Manuscripts* (HMC, 1911)
Howarth	*Letters and the Second Diary of Samuel Pepys*, ed. R.G. Howarth (1933)
HR	*Historical Research* [continuation of BIHR]
HT	*History Today*
Letters to Williamson	*Letters . . . to Sir Joseph Williamson*, ed. W.D. Christie (Camden Soc., 1874)
LJ	*Journals of the House of Lords*
LP Henry VIII	*Letters and Papers . . . of the Reign of Henry VIII*, ed. J.S. Brewer, J. Gairdner and R.H. Brodie (1862–1932)
Maps	S. Tyacke (comp.), 'Maps', in *Cat. PL, IV, Music, Maps and Calligraphy* (Cambridge, 1989)
Marsden, *Law and Custom*	*Documents relating to Law and Custom of the Sea*, ed. R.G. Marsden, II (NRS, 1946)
Memoirs	*Memoirs of Samuel Pepys*, ed. Lord Braybrooke (1825)
Milward, *Diary*	*The Diary of John Milward*, ed. C. Robbins (Cambridge, 1938)
MM	*The Mariner's Mirror*
Modern MSS	*Cat. PL, V, Manuscripts, ii, Modern*, comp. C.S. Knighton (Woodbridge, 1981)
Monson, *Tracts*	*The Naval Tracts of Sir William Monson*, ed. M. Oppenheim (NRS, 1902–14)
N&Q	*Notes and Queries*
Naval Minutes	*Samuel Pepys's Naval Minutes*, ed. J.R. Tanner (NRS, 1926)
Navy White Book	*Samuel Pepys and the Second Dutch War*, ed. R.C. Latham (NRS, 1995)
NMM	National Maritime Museum, Greenwich
NRS	Navy Records Society
Part. Friends	*Particular Friends: The Correspondence of Samuel Pepys and John Evelyn*, ed. G. de la Bédoyère (Woodbridge, 1997)
Penn, *Memorials*	G. Penn, *Memorials of . . . Sir William Penn* (1833)
Pepys, *Memoires*	S. Pepys, *Memoires . . . of the Royal Navy of England* (1690)
PL	Pepys Library, Magdalene College, Cambridge [volumes printed and MS and numbered in a single shelf sequence 1–3000]
PLB	Pepys Library Buffet [supplementary material acquired by gift or purchase; not part of the Pepys bequest]
Priv. Corr.	*Private Correspondence . . . of Samuel Pepys*, 1679–1703, ed. J.R. Tanner (1926)
PRO	Public Record Office, London
Rupert and Monck Letter Book	*The Rupert and Monck Letter Book*, ed. J.R. Powell and E.K. Timings (NRS, 1969)
Sandwich, *Journal*	*The Journal of Edward Montagu*, ed. R.C. Anderson (NRS, 1929)
Shorthand Letters	*Shorthand Letters of Samuel Pepys*, ed. E. Chappell (1933)
Smith, *Correspondence*	*The Life, Journals, and Correspondence of Samuel Pepys*, ed. J. Smith (1841)
Tangier Papers	*The Tangier Papers of Samuel Pepys*, ed. E. Chappell (NRS, 1936)
Tanner, *Naval MSS*	*A Descriptive Catalogue of the Naval Manuscripts in the Pepysian Library*, ed. J.R. Tanner (NRS, 1903–23)
Tanner, *Sea MSS*	*A Descriptive Catalogue of the Library of Samuel Pepys*, I, 'Sea' *Manuscripts* ed. J.R. Tanner (1914)
TRHS	*Transactions of the Royal Historical Society*
Wing	*Short-Title Catalogue of Books printed in England, 1641–1700*, comp. D. Wing, 2nd edn (New York, 1972–98)

Notes

Chapter One

1. *The Journal of Edward Montagu, First Earl of Sandwich, Admiral and General at Sea, 1659–1665*, ed. R.C. Anderson (NRS, LXIV, 1929), pp. 33–4. B.S. Capp, *Cromwell's Navy: The Fleet and the English Revolution, 1648–1660* (Oxford, 1989), pp. 109, 336–9. R.L. Ollard, *Cromwell's Earl: A Life of Edward Montagu, 1st Earl of Sandwich* (1994), pp. 65–9.
2. Howarth, pp. 11–12, 15, 16, 17–18. *Memoirs of the Life of Colonel Hutchinson . . . by his widow Lucy*, ed. C.H. Firth (1885), II, p. 235. Capp, *Cromwell's Navy*, pp. 342–4.
3. *Diary*, I, p. 1.
4. *Ibid.*, pp. 65, 71, 75, 77, 81, 82–3, 85–6.
5. *Ibid.*, pp. 86, 90, 95–6, 98. *DNB* (Creed, John).
6. *Diary*, I, pp. 97, 99–100, 102–3, 104, 109. Capp, *Cromwell's Navy*, pp. 357–60. J.D. Davies, *Gentlemen and Tarpaulins: The Officers and Men of the Restoration Navy* (Oxford, 1991), pp. 121–6.
7. *Diary*, I, pp. 86, 105, 108, 112–13, 123–5, 126. G. Penn, *Memorials of the Professional Life and Times of Sir William Penn* (1833), II, p. 210. G. Trease, *Samuel Pepys and his World* (1972), p. 32.
8. *Ibid.*, pp. 131–2, 134, 135, 136–9. Capp, *Cromwell's Navy*, pp. 368–9. Penn, *Memorials*, II, pp. 220–1.
9. *Diary*, I, pp. 143–4, 152, 154–5, 157. PL 2141 (Charles II's escape); printed in *Charles II's Escape from Worcester*, ed. W. Matthews (1967), pp. 34–84.
10. *Diary*, I, pp. 104, 158–9, 160, 167, 169. *Navy White Book*, p. 258. Davies, *Gentlemen and Tarpaulins*, p. 128.
11. *Diary*, I, pp. 174, 177, 184, 185, 189, 191, 210, 216; VII, p. 31; VIII, pp. 63, 227–9; IX, pp. 145, 325, 329, 334–5. Cf. *Particular Friends: The Correspondence of Samuel Pepys and John Evelyn*, ed. G. de la Bédoyère (Woodbridge, 1997), p. 98. PL 2820 (see below, pp. 34–5).
12. *Diary*, pp. 188, 191, 192–3, 194. Orders in Council of 4 July: PRO, PC 2/54, ff. 54–5; copies PRO, SP 29/7, no. 43 (*CSPD 1660–1*, p. 110, where Batten mistakenly as 'Baker'); PL 2611, pp. 113–16; 2867, pp. 350–1 (first order only); Penn, *Memorials*, II, pp. 243–5 (the first order, mistakenly dated 2 July), 246; others listed in *Diary*, I, p. 191 n. 2. Tanner (*Naval MSS*, I, pp. 6, 7 n. 1) thought the Pepys MSS misdated the first order, but later (*Sea MSS*, p. 34), corrected himself. The second order says the committee reported to the Council on 2 July, from which the heading in the Penn copy may be derived. *Navy Board Officials, 1660–1832*, comp. J. M. Collinge (Office-Holders in Modern Britain, VII, 1978), p. 1 & n. 1. G.E. Aylmer, *The King's Servants: The Civil Service of Charles I, 1625–1642* (2nd edn, 1974), p. 208. R. Hutton, *The Restoration: A Political and Religious History of England and Wales, 1658–1667* (Oxford, 1985), pp. 137–8.

13. Collinge, *Navy Board Officials*, p. 129. PRO, SP 38/19, p. 14 (*CSPD 1660–1*, p. 139; warrant for appointment of Clerk of the King's Ships, during pleasure, with notional stipend of £3 6s 8d). F.W. Brooks, 'William de Wrotham and the office of Keeper of the King's Ports and Galleys', *EHR*, XL (1925), pp. 570–9. C.F. Richmond, 'English naval power in the fifteenth century', *History*, LII (1967), pp. 6, 9, 11–12. *The Navy of the Lancastrian Kings*, ed. S. Rose (NRS, CXXIII, 1982). *British Naval Documents, 1204–1960*, ed. J.B. Hattendorf *et al.* (NRS, CXXXI, 1993), pp. 33–4, 42–3. D. M. Loades, *The Tudor Navy: An Administrative, Political and Military History* (Aldershot, 1992), pp. 15–17, 36. N.A.M. Rodger, *The Safeguard of the Sea: A Naval History of Great Britain*, I, 660–1649 (1997), pp. 53, 128–30, 158–9. PL 2871, pp. 87–8.

14. *Naval Minutes*, pp. 60, 153, 234 382. Loades, *Tudor Navy*, pp. 50, 81–4. Rodger, *Safeguard of the Sea*, pp. 222–5. *LP Henry VIII*, XX, ii, Appendix, no. 27 (iii); XXI, i, no. 718 (1, 2, 5, 6, 8–10). *Br. Naval Documents*, pp. 90–1, 95–6. A.W. Johns, 'The principal officers of the Navy', *MM*, XIV (1928), pp. 32–54. C.S.L. Davies, 'The administration of the Royal Navy under Henry VIII: the origins of the Navy Board', *EHR*, LXXX (1965), pp. 268–88.

15. *Calendar of Patent Rolls 1549–51*, p. 309. Baeshe papers in PL 2875–6, *passim*. Order of 8 January 1557: PRO, PC 2/7, pp. 565–6 (*APC*, VI, pp. 39–41); SP 11/10, no. 1 (*CSPD Mary I*, p. 259); *Br. Naval Documents*, pp. 70–1 (from PC 2/6, pp. 487–8). T. Glasgow, Jnr, 'Maturing of naval administration, 1556–1564', *MM*, LVI (1970), pp. 3, 7–9.

16. *Naval Minutes*, p. 119. Pepys had a copy of the patent naming Hawkins and Benjamin Gonson joint-Treasurers (18 November 1577): PL 2876, pp. 181–5; other papers relating to Hawkins as Treasurer in PL 2875–6, 2878, *passim*. J.A. Williamson, *Hawkins of Plymouth* (2nd edn, 1969), p. 200. William Borough, *A Discourse of the Variation of the Compass* (1581); Pepys owned the 1585 and 1596 editions: PL 1077(6), 1078(4). Cf. *Naval Minutes*, pp. 229, 378. Borough as administrator: PL 2876, pp. 423–4; 2878, pp. 526–7; Drake's complaint (21 May 1587): PL 2876, p. 273. Cf. J. S. Corbett, *Drake and the Tudor Navy* (1898), II, pp. 79–80, 87–8, 89, 101, 105–7. G.M. Thompson, *Sir Francis Drake* (1972), p. 207.

17. *LP Henry VIII*, XX, ii, Appendix, no. 27 (iii). *Diary*, VI, pp. 307–8 & n. 1. Bodl. MS Rawlinson A. 200–7, incl. Gonson's accounts for 1562–3, 1570 and 1574 (A. 200–202); others listed in D.794, f. 1 (I am grateful to Prof. D.M. Loades for checking these details). Papers relating to Gonson: PL 2875, pp. 93–4; 2876, *passim*. *Navy White Book*, p. 379.

18. *Diary*, I, p. 318; III, p. 40; IV, p. 96 & n. 4; V, p. 177; IX, pp. 482, 486. Papers relating to Buck: PL 2876, p. 670; 2878, *passim*. R. Lockyer, *Buckingham: The Life and Political Career of George Villiers, First Duke of Buckingham, 1592–1628* (1981), p. 76. Cf. M.B. Young, *Service and Servility: The Life and Work of Sir John Coke* (Woodbridge, 1986); *The Jacobean Commissions of Enquiry, 1608 and 1618*, ed. A.P. McGowan (NRS, CXVI, 1971). Papers relating to Coke: PL 2873, 2875, *passim*. Report of 1618 Commission: PL 2735, pp. 44–109. *Naval Minutes*, pp. 95–6, 109 & n. 6, 271, 278.

19. PRO, SP 12/15, no. 4; SP 14/90, no. 98 (*CSPD 1547–80*, p. 165; *1611–18*, p. 438). PL 2611, pp. 1–63 (instructions said to be given by the *Marquess* of Buckingham as Lord High Admiral, which would date them to 1619–23). BL, Sloane MS 3232, ff. 87–138 (Northumberland's instructions, dated 14 November 1646, at which time his position was senior member of the parliamentary Admiralty Commission: in modern terms, both First Lord and First Sea Lord); ff. 139–191v (Buckingham's instructions, undated). *The Naval Tracts of Sir William Monson*, ed. M. Oppenheim (NRS, XXII x XLVII, 1902–14), III, pp. 389–418. Those of the Duke of York are in PL 2611, pp. 129–90; 2867, pp. 357–99; Bodl. MS Rawlinson A. 466, ff. 14–37v; printed as *The Œconomy of His Majesty's Navy Office* (1717). The Duke's covering letter: PL 2611, pp. 127–8 (also PL 2867, pp. 356–7), printed Penn, *Memorials*, II, pp. 265–8. *Navy White Book*, pp. 285, 289, 331.

20. Johns, 'Principal officers', pp. 49–50. A.C. Dewar, 'The naval administration of the interregnum 1641–59', *MM*, XII (1926), pp. 406–30. D.E. Kennedy, 'The establishment and settlement of Parliament's Admiralty, 1642–1648', *MM*, XLVIII (1962), pp. 276–91. M.L. Baumber, 'Parliamentary naval politics 1641–49', *MM*, LXXXII (1996), pp. 398–408. Rodger, *Safeguard of the Sea*, p. 422.
21. *Diary*, I, p. 193; IX, p. 524. *Further Corr.*, p. 232 & n. 2. *Navy White Book*, pp. 331, 371. *Naval Minutes*, p. 252.
22. Capp, *Cromwell's Navy*, pp. 9–10. Cf. *Diary*, V, p. 59 & n. 4, 328 n. 3; D.C. Coleman, 'Naval dockyards under the later Stuarts', *Economic History Review*, 2nd ser. VI (1953–4), p. 136. PL 2589, pp. 117–18, cited in *Diary*, VII, p. 307 n. 5. *Navy White Book*, pp. 276, 284–5, 289–90, 406, 409, 418. *Further Corr.*, pp. 3, 56.

Chapter Two

1. *The Memoirs of James II: His Campaigns as Duke of York, 1652–1660*, ed. A.L. Sells (1962), p. 57. J. Callow, *The Making of King James II* (Stroud, 2000), pp. 70–3, 84. *Naval Minutes*, p. 257. *Diary*, III, p. 122; VI, pp. 38, 45, 54, 118; VIII, p. 294 & n. 1. *Navy White Book*, p. 221. Collinge, *Navy Board Officials*, p. 86. PL 1455: John, 1st Baron Berkeley of Stratton, *Memoirs* (1699). *Clarendon's Four Portraits*, ed. R.L. Ollard (1989), pp. 22–42, 107–23. PL 2504 (HMC, *Pepys*), *passim*.
2. G.R. Balleine, *All for the King: The Life Story of Sir George Carteret (1609–1690)* (St Helier, 1976). *The House of Commons, 1660–1690*, ed. B.D. Henning (1983), I, pp. 28–31. *DNB*. PL 1399(1), 1431(25): J. Dunton, *A True Iournall of the Sally Fleet, with the Proceedings of the Voyage* (1637). *The Barbary Voyage of 1638 . . . from the original Manuscript of Sir George Carteret*, ed. B. Penrose (privately printed: Philadelphia, 1929). K.R. Andrews, 'William Rainborowe and the Sallee rovers', in his *Ships, Money and Politics: Seafaring and Naval Enterprise in the reign of Charles I* (Cambridge, 1991), pp. 160–83. S.E. Hoskins, *Charles the Second in the Channel Islands* (1854) I, p. 179. PL 2504 (HMC, *Pepys*), *passim*. *Diary*, I, pp. 295–6; VIII, p. 117. *Navy White Book*, pp. 114, 119–23.
3. Henning, *The Commons 1660–90*, I, p. 607. *DNB*. B.S. Capp, 'Naval operations', in *The Civil Wars: A Military History of England, Scotland, and Ireland 1638–1660*, ed. J.P. Kenyon and J. H. Ohlmeyer (Oxford, 1998), pp. 158–86, and his *Cromwell's Navy*, *passim*. D.E. Kennedy, 'Naval captains at the outbreak of the English Civil War', *MM*, XLVI (1960), pp. 195–6; *idem*, 'The English naval revolt of 1648', *EHR*, LXXVII (1962), pp. 247–56. R.C. Anderson, 'The royalists at sea in 1648', *MM*, IX (1923), pp. 34–46. Dewar, 'Naval administration of the interregnum', pp. 418, 423. Baumber, 'Parliamentary naval politics', pp. 399–400. A.W. Johns, 'The Constant Warwick', *MM*, XVIII (1932) pp. 254, 260–1. PL 2504 (HMC, *Pepys*), *passim*. *Diary*, V, p. 169 & n. 1. W.R. Chaplin, 'The history of Harwich lights and their owners, *The American Neptune*, XI (1951), pp. 5–12.
4. *Diary*, I, p. 280; III, pp. 101–2, 148, 172, 197; IV, pp. 182, 201; V, pp. 83, 105, 117, 122, 196, 301, 316–17; VII, pp. 214, 242, 252; IX, pp. 149–50. *Navy White Book*, pp. 9–10, 15–16, 54, 65–6, 67, 74, 88–9, 95–6, 102–3, 117–18. *CSPD 1667–8*, pp. 589, 592
5. *Navy White Book*, pp. 184, 197. *Diary*, III, p. 252; IV, pp. 194–5; VII, p. 301 & n. 1; VIII, p. 463.
6. Collinge, *Navy Board Officials*, p. 129. *DNB*. Henning, *The Commons 1660–90*, III, pp. 222–3. Penn, *Memorials*. Cf. M.R. Brailsford, *The Making of William Penn* (1930). I have been unable to consult L. Street, *An Uncommon Sailor: A Portrait of Admiral Sir William Penn* (Bourne End, 1986). *Diary*, I, p. 226; VIII, pp. 226–8.

7. PL 2611 (Penn's naval collections).

8. *Diary*, II, pp. 54. 103–4, 108; VII, p. 189; VIII, pp. 30, 36, 349. *Navy White Book*, pp. 143–8, 244–5.

9. Collinge, *Navy Board Officials*, p. 138. *DNB*. PL 2193, pp. 125–63 (Slingsby's Discourse), printed *Discourses of the Royal Navy*, ed. J.R. Tanner (NRS, VII, 1896), 325–59, along with Holland's Discourses of 1638 and 1659, the MSS of which are PL 2193, pp. 1–22 and PL 2835; other copies of Slingsby's work in PL 2871, pp. 683–97; BL, Harleian MS 6003, ff. 160–9; Add. MS 9335, ff. 51–60v; Slingsby's career described in Tanner, *Discourses*, pp. lxx–lxxxii. *CSPD 1660–1*, p. 16. *Diary*, II, p. 20 & n. 3, 42 & n. 2, 76 & n. 1; III, p. 286. *Naval Minutes*, pp. 53, 90, 117–18, 137,

10. *Documents relating to the Civil War, 1642–1648*, ed. J.R. Powell and E.K. Timings (NRS, CV, 1963), pp. 15–17. *Diary*, II, p. 70; IV, p. 124. Collinge, *Navy Board Officials*, p. 122. G.A.R. Callender, 'Sir John Mennes', *MM*, XXVI (1940), pp. 276–85.

11. *DNB*. Henning, *The Commons 1660–90*, III, pp. 229–30. *Diary*, IV, pp. 227–8; VII, p. 186. *CSPD 1665–6*, p. 455. *The Rupert and Monck Letter Book 1666*, ed. J.R. Powell and E.K. Timings (NRS, CXII, 1969), p. 74. F.L. Fox, *Great Ships: The Battlefleet of King Charles II* (Greenwich, 1980), p. 69 identifies 'Peter . . . praying' in the original figurehead of the *Royal Charles* (ex-*Naseby*) as Pett himself, but it more probably represented Hugh Peters, Cromwell's favourite preacher: *Diary*, IV, p. 418 & n. 2.

12. *Diary*, I, pp. 286–7; II, p. 12; IV, p. 227; V, p. 28. *Navy White Book*, pp. 27, 115–16. PL 2870, pp. 483–503; 2874, pp. 1–30; 2934, pp. 35–6.

13. G.E. Aylmer, *The Crown's Servants: Government and Civil Service under Charles II, 1660–1685* (Oxford, 2002), pp. 179–83. Monson, *Tracts*, III, pp. 407–8.

14. *Diary*, III, p. 159. *Navy White Book*, pp. 213–15. PL 2940 (register of ships), printed in Tanner, *Naval MSS*, I, pp. 153–306; Fox, *Great Ships*, pp. 173–83, is largely based on it. PL 2841 (register of officers); printed Tanner, *loc. cit.*, pp. 307–435. Updated information in *The Commissioned Sea Officers of the Royal Navy, 1660–1815*, ed. D. Syrett and R.L. DiNardo (NRS Occasional Publications, I, 1994).

15. *Diary*, III, pp. 23–4 & n. 1, 129, 148; V, p. 289 & n. 4; VI, p. 24 & n. 2. PL 2611, p. 127. Tanner, *Naval MSS*, I, pp. 20–3. *Further Corr.*, pp. 253–6. *CSPD 1661–2*, p. 528. B. Pool, *Navy Board Contracts, 1660–1832* (1966), p. 39. *Navy White Book*, p. 389.

16. PL 2611, pp. 208–9 (from 'An excellent and brief Discourse of the well governing of His Majesty's Navy about the year 1649', occupying pp. 192A–211, misbound within the volume).

17. PL 2611, pp. 150–1. *Diary*, II, p. 54; III, pp. 128, 131, 138, 149; IV, pp. 67, 81, 84. *CSPD 1663–4*, p. 77. R.L. Ollard, *Man of War: Sir Robert Holmes and the Restoration Navy* (1969), pp. 78–80. *Navy White Book*, pp. 33–4.

18. *Diary*, III, p. 105, 118–19, 151 (Deane confused as 'Day' in first instance), 159, 161, 169; IV, pp. 103, 176, 189–90, 206, 233, 259–60, 420; V, p. 217. *Further Corr.*, pp. 26–7. *Navy White Book*, pp. 70, 139.

19. *Diary*, IV, p. 420; V, p. 14–15, 55, 72. *Navy White Book*, pp. 67–8, 114–15. R.G. Albion, 'The timber problem of the Royal Navy, 1652–1862', *MM*, XXXVIII (1952), p. 5; *idem, Forests and Sea Power: The Timber Problem of the Royal Navy* (Harvard Economic Studies, XXIX, Cambridge, Mass. 1926), pp. 70–1. Cf. *CSPD 1663–4*, p. 268.

20. *Diary*, V, p. 80; *Navy White Book*, pp. 31–4, 39, 69, 79, 97–100, 108.

21. *Diary*, III, pp. 149, 205. *Navy White Book*, pp. 24, 27–31, 43–4, 48, 72–3. PRO, SP 29/75, no. 121 (*CSPD 1663–4*, p. 181).

22. *Navy White Book*, pp. 25, 38, 145–6, 357. P.G. Rogers, *The Dutch in the Medway* (1970), pp. 57–9.

23. *Diary*, II, pp. 121–2, 192; III, pp. 146, 163, 208; IV, pp. 172, 227, 236, 262–3. Fox, *Great Ships*, pp. 56, 72. H.A. Baldridge, 'Ship models: the collections of Rogers, Sergison and Pepys', *Proceedings of the United States Naval Institute*, LXIV (1938), pp.

1553–66. J. Franklin, *Navy Board Ship Models, 1650–1750* (1989), pp. 179–81. *Further Corr.*, p. 296. PL 2501 (sectional drawings by Deane with calculations of draught). PL 2910; printed *Deane's Doctrine of Naval Architecture, 1670*, ed. B. Lavery (Greenwich, 1981). A.W. Johns, 'Sir Anthony Deane', *MM*, XI (1925), pp. 164–93.

24. *Diary*, V, pp. 108, 109, 143–4, 146–7, 159, 309; IX, p. 5. PL 2820 (Fragments of Ancient English Shipwrightry). *CSPD 1664–5*, p. 386.

25. *Diary*, III, pp. 181, 195; IV, pp. 28, 226; VI, pp 305–6, 315, 321; VII, pp. 1, 2. *Navy White Book*, pp. 66–7. *Further Corr.*, pp. 88, 93–111, 113, 115, 119, 126–30.

26. Aylmer, *Crown's Servants*, p. 47. Collinge, *Navy Board Officials*, pp. 103, 109, 110. *Admiralty Officials 1660–1870*, comp. J.C. Sainty (Office-Holders in Modern Britain, IV, 1975), pp. 130, 131. P. Norman, 'Pepys and Hewer', *Occasional Papers published for members of the Samuel Pepys Club*, ed. Norman, II (1925 for 1917–23), pp. 53–77.

27. *DNB*. Henning, *The Commons 1660–90*, II, pp. 157–63. *Navy White Book*, pp. 221–30. V. Vale, 'Clarendon, Coventry, and the sale of naval offices, 1660–8', *CHJ*, XII (1956), pp.107–25. B. Pool, 'Sir William Coventry: Pepys's mentor', *HT*, XXIV (1974), pp. 104–11.

Chapter Three

1. *Diary*, IX, p. 481.
2. Fox, *Great Ships*, p. 31. Capp, *Cromwell's Navy*, pp. 374–5. Davies, *Gentlemen and Tarpaulins*, p. 128. *Diary*, I, pp. 211, 226 & n. 4, 228, 245 & n. 1, 247, 288 & n. 1, 309 & n. 5; II, pp. 19 & n. 2, 45, 50. PL 2265, nos 8 (estimate of Navy debt to 27 June 1660), 83 (printed copy of 12 Car. II c. 20). *CJ*, VIII, pp. 109, 115, 176, 181, 243–4.
3. K.G. Feiling, *British Foreign Policy, 1660–1672* (1968), pp. 32–4, 36. Pepys had encountered the French envoy, Antoine de Bordeaux, earlier in 1660: *Diary*, I, p. 10.
4. *Diary*, I, pp. 76, 83, 222 & n. 1, 286. O.N. Millar, *The Queen's Pictures* (1977), pp. 78–81 & n. 21 (on pp. 227–8).
5. *Diary*, II, pp. 45–6, 47, 52 & n. 1, 62 & n. 3, 65 & n. 3. Feiling, *Foreign Policy*, pp. 44–9. H.V. Livermore, *A New History of Portugal* (Cambridge, 1969), pp. 190–1. Ollard, *Clarendon's Four Portraits*, p. 103. R. Hutton, *Charles II: King of England, Scotland, and Ireland* (Oxford 1989), pp. 158–60.
6. *Diary*, II, pp. 48, 52 n. 1, 79, 118 & n. 3. Ollard, *Cromwell's Earl*, pp. 98–100. Hutton, *Charles II*, p. 160. Feiling, *Foreign Policy*, p. 48.
7. *Diary*, II, p. 119. PL 2265, no. 7. Pool, *Navy Board Contracts*, pp. 4, 7–8.
8. *Diary*, II, pp. 121. S.R. Hornstein, *The Restoration Navy and English Foreign Trade, 1674–1688: A Study in the Peacetime Use of Sea Power* (Aldershot, 1991), pp. 101–3.
9. *Diary*, II, pp. 33, 184 & n. 2, 185, 186, 189; III, p. 79 & n. 2; VIII, p. 582. PL 754: E. d'Aranda, *The History of Algiers and its Slavery . . . English'd by John Davies of Kidwelly* (1662). HMC, *Hodgkin*, pp. 158–60.
10. *Diary*, II, pp. 189 & n. 2, 202 & n. 1. HMC, *Hodgkin*, pp. 160–1.
11. HMC, *Hodgkin*, pp. 157 (Sandwich to Pepys, 20 Jan. 1662, misdated in calendar 1661), 160–3. *CSPD 1661–2*, p. 191. *Diary*, III, p. 33 & n. 2, 37 & n. 2 (identifying Beckmann's 1662 map as BL, King's Maps, XCVII, 78); V, p. 98 & n. 2. Maps of Tangier retained by Pepys are of later date: PL 1341, pp. 112–13; 2899 (13–15); 2928(2). Ollard, *Cromwell's Earl*, p. 107–8. *Tangier Papers*, pp. xliv, 25 & *passim*. Sandwich, *Journal*, pp. 114–15. E.M.G. Routh, *Tangier: England's Lost Atlantic Outpost* (1912), pp. 9–10.
12. *Diary*, II, pp. 206, 216–17; III, pp. 122–3. Sandwich, *Journal*, pp. 117, 121–2. Ollard, *Cromwell's Earl*, pp. 108–9. J. Childs, *The Army of Charles II* (1976), p. 115. Davies, *Gentlemen and Tarpaulins*, pp. 108–10.

13. *Diary*, III, pp. 34, 61 & n. 2, 68, 72 & nn., 83, 85, 119 & n. 3, 252–3 & n. 1; Latham (p. 72 n. 1) identifies the preacher as Thomas Bragg; but he had been replaced as dockyard preacher in Jan. 1661 by John Meriton: PRO, ADM 2/1732, f. 77; Latham also (p. 72 n. 2) identifies the gift to Catherine as the Seymour salt, now owned by the Goldsmiths' Company. PRO, SP 29/53, no. 31; SP 29/57, no. 98 (*CSPD 1661–2*, pp. 331, 446). Childs, *Army of Charles II*, pp. 163–4

14. *Diary*, III, pp. 88–9 & n. 1, 121–2 & n. 1, 134, 177. Ollard, *Cromwell's Earl*, pp. 112–13, 114–15.

15. *Diary*, I, pp. 205 & n. 3, 213, 253 & n. 1, 316; III, pp. 137 & n. 2, 168; IV, pp. 81–2 & n. 1. PRO, SP 29/46, no. 13; SP 29/70, no. 6 (*CSPD 1661–2*, p. 190); SP 29/70, no. 6 (*CSPD 1663–4*, p. 82; proposal by Pepys for making the Navy Officers J.P.s in London; another copy in *Further Corr.*, pp. 3–5; subsequently enacted as 16 Car. II c. 5). According to Henning, *The Commons 1660–90*, III, p. 226, Pepys was removed from the bench in Middlesex, Essex, Kent and Hampshire 1679–84, but he is on commissions for Kent in 1679 (after his arrest), 1680 and 1681: *Calendar of Assize Records: Kent Indictments, Charles II, 1676–1688*, ed. J.S. Cockburn (1997), nos 438 (p. 87), 667 (p. 126), 693 (p. 134)

16. *Diary*, I, pp. 14, 177 & n. 3, 296 & n. 2; II, p. 4 & n. 2; III, pp. 18, 29 & n. 3, 93; IV, pp. 184–5; V, pp. 172–3; VI, pp. 24–5, 107, 308. HMC, *Hodgkin*, pp. 157–8 (printed copy of the Trinity House oath, with Pepys's note of having taken it; misdated 1661 in calendar). *Further Corr.*, pp. 80–1, 84. *Naval Minutes*, pp. 23, 69, 401–2. *Tangier Papers*, pp. 300, 318. *Navy White Book*, pp. 129, 217. J.R. Tanner, 'Pepys and the Trinity House', *EHR*, XLIV (1929), pp. 573–87.

17. *Diary*, III, pp. 157–8 & n. 1, 170, 171–2, 238 & n. 3, 255, 273, 291, 300 & n. 1; IV, pp. 10, 83 & n. 4, 89; VI, p. 25. Routh, *Tangier*, pp. 12, 31. PRO, SP 29/65, nos 60, 65 (*CSPD 1661–2*, pp. 603, 605).

18. *Diary*, III, p. 177 & n. 1, 291 & n. 6; IV, pp. 17–18; VI, pp. 58–65, 68 & n. 2, 69–71, 215.

19. *Diary*, III, pp. 128, 129, 234 & n. 2, 289 & n. 2; IV, p. 15. *CSPD 1661–2*, p. 550. *Further Corr.*, p. 2.

20. *Diary* IV, pp. 11 & n. 1, 264; V, p. 116 & n. 1. *Further Corr.*, p. 180. *Navy White Book*, p. 140.

21. *Diary*, III, pp. 24, 65 & n. 2, 83, 99–100, 106, 236–7; IV, 60–1 & n. 1, 66, 67, 71, 75, 397–8; VIII, p. 20 & n. 2. PL 2611, p. 150. See generally B. Pool, 'Samuel Pepys and Navy contracts', *HT*, XIII (1963), pp. 633–41, and his *Navy Board Contracts*, pp. x–ii, 1–43.

22. *Diary*, III, pp. 114, 116, 129–30; IV, pp. 49, 194, 364; V, p. 44; VI, p. 40 & n. 2. *CSPD 1663–4*, pp. 186, 324, 327, 395. Cf. *Navy White Book*, pp. 33–5.

23. *Navy White Book*, pp. 44–5, 51–2.

24. *Diary*, IV, pp. 61 & n. 2, 303–4 & n. 1, 314, 421 & n. 3; V, no. 6. PRO, SP 29/80, no 47 (*CSPD 1663–4*, p. 270). *Navy White Book*, pp. 9–12, 35–6, 53–5. *Further Corr.*, pp. 6–10, 20–5. Pool, *Navy Board Contracts*, pp. 26–7.

25. *Diary*, V, pp. 1, 3, 5, 35; XI, p. 55.

26. *Diary*, V, pp. 76, 79 & nn. 2, 3, 262, 269 & n. 2, 280, 293–4, 299–300, 304–5, 315. PRO, SP 29/103, no. 130 (*CSPD 1664–5*, p. 44). J.R. Elder, *The Royal Fishery Companies of the Seventeenth Century* (Glasgow, 1912), pp. 100–3. Callow, *James II*, pp. 257–9.

27. J. Miller, *Charles II* (1991), p. 87. R. Hainsworth and C. Churches, *The Anglo-Dutch Naval Wars, 1652–1674* (Stroud, 1998), pp. 99–101. Henning, *The Commons 1669–90*, II, pp. 224–5. P. Seaward, 'The House of Commons committee of trade and the origins of the second Anglo-Dutch war, 1664' *HJ*, XXX (1987), pp. 438–44. *Diary*, I, p. 258 & n. 2; III, p. 125 & n. 2. Ollard, *Man of War*, pp. 59–74. PL 2698, pp. 11–59 (journal of Holmes aboard the *Henrietta* 1660–1 and related papers).

28. S.C.A. Pincus, 'Popery, trade and universal monarchy: the ideological context of the outbreak of the Second Anglo-Dutch War', *EHR*, CVII (1992), pp. 9–15. *Diary*, V, pp. 105, 107, 113, 115 & n. 1, 129 & n. 2. *CJ*, VIII, p. 548. *CSPD 1663–4*, p. 562.

Chapter Four

1. C. Wilson, *Profit and Power; A Study of England in the Dutch Wars* (Cambridge, 1957). S.C.A. Pincus, *Protestantism and Patriotism: Ideologies and the Making of English Foreign Policy, 1650–1668* (Cambridge, 1996), pp. 195–268. J.R. Jones, *The Anglo-Dutch Wars of the Seventeenth Century* (1996). Hainsworth and Churches, *Anglo-Dutch Wars*, p. 104. *Diary*, IV, pp. 322, 389; V, pp. 59, 111, 121, 212, 353.
2. *Diary*, V, pp. 121–2, 159–60. Seaward, 'Committee of trade', pp. 448-51. Ollard, *Man of War*, pp. 85–94. PL 2698, pp. 73–173 (Holmes's journal aboard the *Jersey*, 1663–5), 175–7, 185–215, 223–41, 243–7.
3. *Diary*, V, pp. 35, 49–50. 108–9. Pincus, 'Popery, trade and universal monarchy', pp. 7–11, 19–20. PL 706: T. Mun, *England's treasure by forraign trade* (1663). Jones, *Anglo-Dutch Wars*, p. 151. A.T. Mahan, *The Influence of Sea Power upon History, 1660–1783* (1965 edn), p. 57.
4. *Diary*, V, pp. 115, 121, 146, 152 & n. 1, 156 & n. 1, 159–60, 162–3, 168, 193, 196, 197. *Navy White Book*, pp. 16, 97, 308. PRO, ADM 106/8, ff. 449, 463; SP 46/136, no. 133 (*CSPD Addenda 1660–85*, p. 102). *CSPD 1663–4*, pp. 472, 562, 578, 607, 623, 626, 633. Ollard, *Cromwell's Earl*, pp. 118–19.
5. *Diary*, V, pp. 175 & n. 3, 181 & n. 3, 258, 264 & n. 4, 286–7 & n. 1, 291, 301. *Further Corr.*, pp. 27–8. *CSPD 1663–4*, pp. 595, 599, 600, 670–1; *1664–5*, pp. 27–9, 38 (quotation from PRO, SP 29/103, no. 39), 67. *Br. Naval Documents*, p. 195. F. E. Kitson, *Prince Rupert: Admiral and General at Sea* (1998), pp. 149–51
6. *Diary*, V, pp. 289 & n. 4, 291, 293, 295, 305–6, 312–14, 317–18, 324; VI, p. 24 & n. 2. *Further Corr.*, p. 29. *CSPD 1664–5*, pp. 68, 327. Pool, *Navy Board Contracts*, p. 39. Fox, *Great Ships*. pp. 73–5. *Shorthand Letters*, pp. 3–4, 7.
7. *Diary*, V, pp. 283 & n. 2, 321 & n. 2, 326 & n. 2, 328, 336, 338, 352–3, 355–7. *Navy White Book*, pp. 338 & n. 2, 360, 366, 372–3. PRO, SP 29/100, no. 58 (*CSPD 1663–4*, p. 640; the phrase 'in the present war' employed by the calendar is not in the MS). *CSPD 1664–5*, p. 82. *Shorthand Letters*, pp. 20–1. *Further Corr.*, pp. 33–4. Callow, *James II*, pp. 265–7.
8. *Diary*, V, pp. 327–30. *CSPD 1664–5*, pp. 88–9. *LJ*, XI, pp. 624–5. *CJ*, VIII, p. 568. *Shorthand Letters*, pp. 20–2, 24. C.D. Chandaman, *The English Public Revenue, 1660–1688* (Oxford, 1975), p. 177. Royal Aid: 16 & 17 Car. II c. 1.
9. *Documents relating to Law and Custom of the Sea*, ed. R.G. Marsden, II, A.D. *1649–1767* (NRS, L, 1946), pp. 48–53. *Diary*, V, pp. 322, 327 & n. 1, 333, 341, 342 & n. 6. *Further Corr.*, p. 31 (summary in *CSPD Addenda 1660–85*, p. 116). *CSPD 1664–5*, p. 122. *Shorthand Letters*, p. 26. *Navy White Book*, pp. 317–23.
10. Marsden, *Law and Custom*, II, p. 52. *CSPD 1664–5*, p. 113. *Diary*, V, p. 329. Evelyn, *Diary*, III, pp. 387–8. J.J.S. Shaw, 'The Commission of Sick and Wounded and Prisoners, 1664–1667', *MM*, XXV (1939), pp. 306–8. H.A. Kaufman, *Conscientious Cavalier: Colonel Bullen Reymes, M.P., F.R.S., 1613–1672* (1962), pp. 199–215. *Part. Friends*, pp. 29–67, 77–89.
11. *Diary*, IV, p. 83; VI, pp. 6, 8 & n. 3, 10, 13–14, 19–20, 56. Ollard, *Man of War*, pp. 79–80, 129–31. Allin, *Journals*, I, pp. xiii–xv, 184–5, 191–3; II, pp. 218–23). *Br. Naval Documents*, p. 195 (Privy Council Committee on Foreign Affairs 16 Oct. 1664, order for Allin to attack Smyrna fleet; presumably the 'letters of concernment' which Allin received at Ibiza on 14 Nov.: *Journals*, I, p. 178). *CSPD 1664–5*, pp. 71, 122. *Further*

Corr., pp. 36–7. Fox, *Great Ships*, p. 176. Cf. *Diary*, III, p. 213 & n. 1; *CSPD 1661–2*, p. 527 (loss of the *Satisfaction*, Capt. Mohun, 1662).

12. *Diary*, VI, pp. 29, 39, 42, 43, 50, 52 & n. 1. Sandwich, *Journal*, pp. 165–6. *CSPD 1664–5*, pp. 210, 214, 232, 236, 249, 252. *Navy White Book*, pp. 110–11. Fox, *Great Ships*, p. 71 (dating accident to *London* 8 Mar., but Pepys's Diary and White Book agree on 7th).

13. Feiling, *Foreign Policy*, pp. 140–3. *Diary*, IV, p. 399 n. 2; VI, pp. 68, 76 & n. 1, 86, 88–9, 91, 93. *Further Corr.*, pp. 43–6. *Shorthand Letters*, p. 39. *Navy White Book*, p. 139. *CSPD 1664–5*, pp. 323, 335, 336. W.G. Bell, *The Great Plague in London* (2nd edn, 1994), pp. 16–24.

14. *Diary*, VI, p. 99, 103, 107, 108, 111, 112. *CSPD 1664–5*, pp. 351, 365, 367, 371, 386, 387, 389, 393. Sandwich, *Journal*, pp. 204–5, 212, 221. W.L. Clowes, *The Royal Navy: A History from the Earliest Times to 1900* (1897–1903), II, p. 258.

15. *CSPD 1664–5*, pp. 402, 403, 405, 406, 408–9, 411. *Diary*, VI, pp. 115, 116, 117–18, 122–3 & n. 1. A.L. Cooke, 'Did Dryden hear the guns ?', *N&Q*, CXCVI (1951), pp. 204–5. Clowes, *Royal Navy*, I, pp. 259–65. Hainsworth and Churches, *Anglo-Dutch Naval Wars*, pp. 120–5. Kitson, *Rupert*, pp. 166–76.

16. *Diary*, VI, pp. 129–30, 131, 130, 135, 138. *CSPD 1664–5*, p. 415. Sandwich, *Journal*, p. 234. Ollard, *Man of War*, pp. 136–7. P. Padfield, *Maritime Supremacy and the Opening of the Western Mind: Naval Campaigns that Shaped the Modern World, 1588–1782* (1999), p. 94.

17. *Diary*, VI, pp. 132 & n. 1, 133 & n. 2, 134–4, 137, 138–9, 141 & n. 2, 146, 147, 148, 151, 184, 186 & n. 1. Sandwich, *Journal*, pp. 236–7. Penn, *Memorials*, II, pp. 361–2. Kitson, *Rupert*, pp. 177–8.

18. *Diary*, VI, pp. 128 & n. 2, 140 & n. 2, 195 & n. 1, 206. *Further Corr.*, p. 49. *CSPD 1664–5*, pp. 449–50, 531, 546; *1665–6*, pp. 3 (printed *Part. Friends*, pp. 38–40), 10, 23, 24, 118, 217, 437, 52; cf. pp. 32, 54. J.F.D. Shrewsbury, *A History of Bubonic Plague in the British Isles* (Cambridge, 1971), pp. 488–9, 493–4.

19. *Diary*, VI, pp. 193, 195–7, 205, 218 & n. 2, 219 & n. 1, 230–1 & n. 1, 297. Bodl. MS Rawlinson A 195a, ff. 218v–221. Sandwich, *Journal*, pp. 251–68. G. Greene, *Lord Rochester's Monkey: Being the Life of John Wilmot, Second Earl of Rochester* (2nd edn, 1976), pp. 51–2.). *CSPD 1664–5*, pp. 520, 537. *Tangier Papers*, pp. 335–7. *Shorthand Letters*, pp. 59–61, 62, 68–9, 72–3. *Further Corr.*, pp. 192–3.

20. *Diary*, VI, pp. 228–9, 253–5 & nn., 271, 279–80, 284, 293–4 & n. 1, 306, 315–16. *CSPD 1664–5*, p. 541–2, 552; *1665–6*, p. 92. *Further Corr.*, pp. 51–3, 63–4 (more fully in *Shorthand Letters*, pp. 70–2), 67–70. PRO, SP 29/134, no. 46 (*CSPD 1665–6*, p. 7); printed from NMM copy in *Further Corr.*, pp. 54–7. *Shorthand Letters*, pp. 56–8, 64–6, 70–2. PRO, ADM 2/1725, ff. 175v–176 (Duke of York's appointment of Pepys as Surveyor-General, 4 Nov.).

21. Additional Aid: 17 Car. II. c. 1. *Diary*, VI, pp. 256, 266–7, 268 & n. 2, 281 & n. 3, 292 & n. 3, 311, 327, 341–2; VII, pp. 87, 88 & n. 3, 90 & n. 1, 242–3, 243–4 & n. 1. *Shorthand Letters*, pp. 67, 74. *Further Corr.*, pp. 70–2, 86–7, 89–91. Chandaman, *Revenue*, pp. 295–300. D.C. Coleman, 'Sir John Banks, financier: an essay on government borrowing under the later Stuarts', in *Essays in the Economic and Social History of Tudor and Stuart England in honour of R.H. Tawney*, ed. F.J. Fisher (Cambridge, 1961), pp. 209–11, 222–3. *CSPD 1665–6*, pp. 16.

Chapter Five

1. *Diary*, VII, pp. 1 & n. 1, 62, 106. *Further Corr.*, pp. 93–111.
2. *Diary*, VII, p. 48 & n. 1, 122 & nn. 1, 3, 205–6 & n. 1. *Further Corr.*, pp. 120–2

(detailing immediate debts of £2,312,876, and alluding to others), 124–5 (calculating the additional debts at £462,768), 133–6. PL 2589, pp. 1–4.

3. Feiling, *Foreign Policy*, pp. 144–50. Hainsworth and Churches, *Anglo-Dutch Wars*, pp. 137–8. *Diary*, VI, p. 323, 342; VII, pp. 24, 40 & n. 2, 108, 109, 117, 123.

4. *Diary*, VII, pp. 124, 138 & n. 1, 139, 140–9,179; VIII, p. 514. R.J.A. Shelley, 'The division of the English fleet in 1666', *MM*, XXV (1939), pp. 179–96. P. Fraser, *The Intelligence of the Secretaries of State & their Monopoly of Licensed News, 1660–1688* (Cambridge, 1956), pp. 78–95. *Rupert and Monck Letter Book*, pp. 55, 201–7. Clowes, *Royal Navy*, II, pp. 267–78. F. L. Fox, *A Distant Storm: The Four Days' Battle of 1666* (Rotherfield, 1996). Hainsworth and Churches, *Anglo-Dutch Wars*, pp. 129–48.

5. *Diary*, VII, pp. 148–58, 159 & n. 4, , 172, 174 & n. 5, 177 & n. 4.

6. *Diary*, VII, pp. 165–6. F.E. Dyer, 'Captain Christopher Myngs in the West Indies', *MM*, XVIII (1932), pp. 168–87. For 'followings' see. N.A.M. Rodger, *The Wooden World: An Anatomy of the Georgian Navy* (2nd edn, 1988), pp. 119–24.

7. *Diary*, VII, pp. 160, 181 (but cf. p. 177 n. 1), 183, 188, 189–91, 193 & n. 5, 215. *Rupert and Monck Letter Book*, p. 87. *Navy White Book*, pp. 118, 140. Fox, *Great Ships*, pp. 75–83. *CSPD 1665–6*, p. 528.

8. *Diary*, VII, pp. 217–18, 221–2, 225–6, 229. Cf. C. Martin and G. Parker, *The Spanish Armada* (1988), p. 65 (giving total of English fleet of 1588 as 197 ships, but of these only 34 were RN). *Further Corr.*, pp. 141–2. Bodl. MS Rawlinson A 195a, ff. 201–5. *Rupert and Monck Letter Book*, pp. 266–79. Clowes, *Royal Navy*, II, pp. 280–3. P. Le Fevre, 'Monck: St James's Day Fight, 1666', in *Great Battles of the Royal Navy*, ed. E. Grove (1994), pp. 48–54. Hainsworth and Churches, *Anglo-Dutch Wars*, pp. 149–54.

9. *Diary*, VII, pp. 247–8 & n. 1 (on p. 247), 252 & n. 1, 259–60 & n. 1 (on p. 259), 263 & n. 2. Ollard, *Man of War*, pp. 148–58. *Rupert and Monck Letter Book*, pp. 137–8. PRO, SP 29/169, no. 34 (*CSPD 1666–7*, p. 71). *Navy White Book*, pp. 128–9.

10. *CJ*, VIII, pp. 628, 635. *Diary*, VII, pp. 286, 292, 294, 295, 298 & n. 2,, 301–2, 308 & n.2, 313, 318 & n. 2, 323. PL 2589, pp. 13–16 (summary in Tanner, *Naval MSS*, I, pp. 102–3), 70–88, 91–2, 98, 124. S. Porter, *The Great Fire of London* (Godalming, 1996), pp. 55, 89.

11. *Diary*, VII, pp. 302, 318, 324–5, 328, 380; VIII, p. 20 & n. 2. PRO, ADM 106/3520, ff. 34v–35v. Penn, *Memorials*, II, pp. 435–6. *Navy White Book*, pp. 148 & n. 2, 176 & n. 1, 192–4. *Further Corr.*, pp. 199–202.

12. *Diary*, VII, pp. 279 & n. 3, 280 & n. 1, 281, 288 & n. 2, 299 & n. 2, 327–8 & n. 1, 350 & n. 1, 373 & n. 2, 374. R.C. Anderson (ed.), 'Naval preparations in the latter part of the year 1666', *The Naval Miscellany*, III, ed. W.G. Perrin (NRS, LXIII, 1928), pp. 32–7. Allin, *Journals*, I, pp. 286–7, 289–92. R. Norrington, *My Dearest Minette: The Letters between Charles II and his sister Henrietta, Duchesse d'Orléans* (1996), p.135. *Further Corr.*, pp. 145–54.

13. *Diary*, VII, pp. 299, 300–1 & n. 1, 316, 338, 418, 424; VIII, pp. 21–4, 123 & n. 1, 130, 134–5, 180, 351–2, 441, 464–5; IX, pp. 29, 99. PL 2871, pp. 665, 667. *Shorthand Letters*, pp. 85–6. *Further Corr.*, pp. 181, 193. *Navy White Book*, p. 245. *CSPD 1666–7*, pp. 24, 288, 373; *1667*, pp. 66, 243, 295. Howarth, p. 39 PL 2836: S. von Pufendorf, *Commentariorum de rebus Suecicis libri XXVI* (Utrecht, 1686), inscribed to 'Pips' by Leijonbergh, 1 Jan. 1687.

14. *Diary*, VII, pp. 380–1, 399–404, 408 & n. 4; VIII, pp. 1, 17, 31 & n. 1, 38, 61–2 & n. 3 (on p. 61), 97–8 & n. 1, 115 & n. 2, 126–7 & n. 1, 140 & n. 4, 149. Chandaman, *Revenue*, pp. 180–1. *Navy White Book*, p. 134.

15. *Diary*, VIII, pp. 125 & n. 2, 186 & n. 5, 254–64. *CSPD 1667*, pp. 166–7; *Addenda 1660–85*, pp. 188, 189–91, 191–2 *Further Corr.*, pp. 176–7. *Shorthand Letters*, pp. 92–3.

16. *Diary*, VIII, pp. 262, 264 & n. 1, 268–9, 309 & nn. 1, 2, 314 & n. 2. *Further Corr.*, pp. 177–8. *Memoirs*, II, Correspondence, p. 12. Rogers, *Dutch in the Medway*, pp. 93–115.

17. *Diary*, VIII, pp. 349–51, 354 & n. 3, 356–60. *Further Corr.*, pp. 178–80.

18. Collinge, *Navy Board Officials*, pp. 2 & n. 6. *Diary*, VIII, pp. 294–5 & n. 3, 334, 462 & n. 3, 582; IX, pp. 244, 305–6 & n. 1, 388 & n. 2, 394–5. *Navy White Book*, pp. 157–8, 172, 185 and *passim*.

19. *Diary*, VII, p. 331; VIII, pp. 8 & n. 3, 414 & n. 2, 419–20, 440; IX, p. 93. *Further Corr.*, p. 155. *Navy White Book*, pp. 216–7, 223.

20. *CJ*, IX, pp. 4, 20. *Diary*, VIII, pp. 484–5 & n. 1, 489–99 & nn., 501–2, 526–7. *Navy White Book*, pp. xxiii–xxiv. Bodl. MS Rawlinson A. 195a, f. 6. Milward, *Diary*, pp. 330–1.

21. *CJ*, IX, pp. 6–7, 49–51, 51–2, 55. *Diary*, VIII, pp. 393 & n. 1, 499 & n. 1, 504, 508–11, 537–8, 540, 545–6 & nn.; IX, pp. 69–70, 103–6. *Naval Minutes*, p. 148. BL, Add. MS 11602, ff. 312–15. Grey, *Debates*, I, pp. 71–4. Milward, *Diary*, pp. 207–9. E.S. de Beer, 'Reports of Pepys's speech in the House of Commons, March 5th, 1668', *MM*, XIV (1928), pp. 55–7 (Grey and Milward texts). B.McL. Ranft, 'The significance of the political career of Samuel Pepys', *Journal of Modern History*, XXIV (1952), pp. 368–9.

22. Act establishing Brooke House Commission: 19 & 20 Car. II c. 1. *Navy White Book*, pp. xxiv–xxx. *Diary*, VIII, pp. 559–60 & n. 1, 599, 601; IX, pp. 43–4, 49–50.

23. *Diary*, VIII, p. 503; IX, pp. 82, 151, 168–9 & n. 2, 254 & n. 2, 267 & n. 1, 282–7, 289–91 & n. 1 (on p. 289), 305 & n. 1, 308 & n. 3, 309–10, 321, 342, 344 & n. 2, 349, 358–9, 360, 474, 482–5, 501, 523, 524–5 & n. 1, 547–8 & n. 1, 555–6 & n. 1, 562 & n.1, 564–5. *Further Corr.*, pp. 192–4, 230–5, 237–8. PL 2242 (papers relating to Pepys's report of 1668); 2867, pp 484–509 (summarised Tanner, *Naval MSS*, I, pp. 28–31). Cf. Aylmer, *Crown's Servants*, pp. 98–9.

24. *Navy White Book*, pp. xxx–xxxv, 334–41. PRO, ADM 106/2886, pt 1. Bodl. MS Rawlinson A.185, ff. 313–14.

25. *Navy White Book*, pp. 271–333, 343, 346, 348, 358, 367, 403, 417. *Diary*, IX, pp. 10, 68.

26. *Ibid.*, pp. 347, 392, 429–32, and *passim*.

Chapter Six

1. *Diary*, IX, pp. 376–7, 385 & n. 1. Ranft, 'Political career of Samuel Pepys', pp. 368–9. Henning, *The Commons 1660–90*, I, pp. 395, 619, 727; III, p. 226. *Further Corr.*, pp. 242–50, 251–3, 256–6. Howarth, pp. 37–8. *Navy White Book*, pp. 334 & n. 4.

2. *Diary*, IX, pp. 374 & n. 1, 474 & n. 1. PL 1788 (Hosier's scheme of storekeepers' accounts). *CSPD 1670*, pp. 112–13. *Navy White Book*, pp. 74, 102, 254–5, 282–91, 396–401. Collinge, *Navy Board Officials*, p. 2 & n. 7

3. *Further Corr.*, pp. 240–2, 268–9. *Navy White Book*, pp. 199–200. Allin, *Journals*, I, p. 258; II, pp. 95, 97, 202, 230–4. Collinge, *Navy Board Officials*, pp. 81, 122. *Diary*, VI, p. 314; IX, p, 274.

4. Collinge, *Navy Board Officials*, pp. 2, 99, 122, 144. *CSPD 1667–8*, p. 258; 1670 (*Addenda 1660–70*), p. 734. Diary, III, p. 70; IX, pp. 100–1 & n. 1 (where for Chatham read Portsmouth), 441 & n. 1. *Navy White Book*, pp. 54, 113, 141, 165, 191–2 & n. 1, 194–7, 212–14, 264. G. Jackson and G.F. Duckett, *Naval Commissioners . . . 1660–1760* (priv. pr. 1889), pp. 24–5. *Further Corr.*, pp. 270–1. Henning, *The Commons 1660–90*, II, pp. 271–4.

5. *Diary*, VI, p. 264; IX, pp. 326, 348 & n. 3, 349–50 & 2, 355, 382, 503, 551. Collinge, *Navy Board Officials*, p. 139. *Navy White Book*, pp. 210–12, 233, 348. Firth, 'Sailors of the Civil War', pp. 258–9.

6. *Diary*, IX, pp. 103, 244, 278, 340–1 & n. 1, 346 & n. 3, 365, 412, 550, 554–5. *Navy White Book*, pp. 158–63, 189–91.

7. *CSPD 1668–9*, p. 118; *1670*, pp. 211, 345, 391, 416, 449; *1671*, pp. 185–6. *Navy White Book*, p. 84, 197. J.D. Davies, 'Wales and Mr. Pepys's Navy', *Cymru a'r môr/Maritime Wales*, XI (1987), pp. 105–6. *Diary*, VI, p. 315 & n. 1.

8. Norrington, *Dearest Minette*, pp. 169–70.

9. *CSPD 1670*, pp. 205–6 (printed from NMM copy in *Further Corr.*, pp. 266–7), 348, 368, 458–9.

10. Fox, *Great Ships*, pp. 95–110. *Diary*, IX, pp. 100–101 & n. 2. *Navy White Book*, pp. 184 & n. 1, 188 & n. 1, 213, 245, 257. *Further Corr.*, pp. 196, 227. PL 2555 (journal of the *Prince*, 1672). Lavery, *Deane's Doctrine*, p. 7.

11. *CSPD 1668–9*, p. 118; *1670*, p. 429. *Navy White Book*, p. 173 & n. 2. PL 2265, no. 36. A. Bryant, *Samuel Pepys: The Years of Peril* (1935), pp. 62–3.

12. *Navy White Book*, pp. 257–8 & nn. 1, 2. *Naval Minutes*, p. 71.

13. Kitson, *Rupert*, pp. 249–50. *CSPD 1672*, p. 429.

14. Clowes, *Royal Navy*, II, pp. 301–8. *Naval Songs and Ballads*, ed. C.H. Firth (NRS, XXXIII, 1908), pp. 82–3. E.R. Cooper, *Memories of Bygone Dunwich* (2nd edn, Southwold, 1948), pp. 33–6. *CSPD 1672*, pp. 83–4 , 102, 191, 256. Sutherland House, Southwold, information leaflet.

15. Bodl. MS Rawlinson A. 174, f. 201r–v (printed *Memoirs*, II, Correspondence, pp. 23–4), 239 (quoted Bryant, *Years of Peril*, pp. 78–9). *Further Corr.*, p. 271 (also Heath, p. 19 & n. 2). *CSPD 1672*, pp. 276–7, 384. Sainty, *Admiralty Officials*, p. 156.

16. *CSPD 1672*, p. 460. Bodl. MS Rawlinson A. 174, f. 442 (printed *Memoirs*, II, Correspondence, p. 24; also Howarth, p. 40); f. 444 (*Memoirs*, II, Correspondence, pp. 26–7). *Further Corr.*, pp. 272–3 (as corrected by Ranft, 'Political career of Samuel Pepys', pp. 369–70 & n. 22).

17. *LJ*, XII, pp. 525–7. Jones, *Anglo-Dutch Wars*, pp. 98–100, 198–201. *CSP Ven. 1673–5*, p. 35. *Letters to Williamson*, I, pp. 54–5.

18. *Ibid.*, pp. 34, 47–8, 75, 80, 84. PL 2870, pp. 401–8 (order of 13 June 1673; other copies PL 2867, pp. 35–8, 149–53; 2902, pp. 10–13; PRO, SP 29/335, no. 303 [*CSPD 1673*, pp. 370–1]). Tanner, *Naval MSS*, I, pp. 36–9; II, pp. 9–10. G.F. James and J.J.S. Shaw, 'Admiralty administration and personnel, 1619–1714', *BIHR*, XIV (1936–7), pp. 178–9 (printing same order from another copy, misdated 23 June). Sainty, *Admiralty Officials*, pp. 18–20. Davies, *Gentlemen and Tarpaulins*, pp. 168–9. N.A.M. Rodger, *The Admiralty* (Lavenham, 1979), pp. 23–4. *CSPD 1673*, pp. 369, 385.

19. PL 2849, p. 1 (Tanner, *Naval MSS*, II, p. 1). Sainty (*Admiralty Officials*, p. 145), dates Pepys's secretaryship from 15 June (the Duke's resignation) on the strength of this entry. Collinge, *Navy Board Officials*, pp. 22, 129. *Memoirs*, p. 27 (also Howarth, pp. 43–4).

20. *Diary*, X, p. 3. Rodger, *Admiralty*, pp. 12–13, 23–4. PL 2879, p. 221 (author's italics). *Letters to Williamson*, I, p. 75 (R. Yard, 27 June: 'hitherto the King has done the businesse himselfe by the hands of Mr. Pepys'). Jones, *Anglo-Dutch Wars*, pp. 203–4. Davies, *Gentlemen and Tarpaulins*, pp. 160–70. Collinge, *Navy Board Officials*, p. 148. PL 2849, pp. 60, 90 (Tanner, *Naval MSS*, II, pp. 22, 35; other instances of James's continuing involvement noted *ibid.*, I, p. 39 nn. 1, 3).

21. Sainty, *Admiralty Officials*, pp. 2, 34–5, 39, 69, 151. *Diary*, I, pp. 174 & n. 4, 183, 204, 226–7, 229, 241. *CSPD 1663–4*, p. 674. Collinge, *Navy Board Officials*, pp. 1–3. W.G. Perrin, 'The Lord High Admiral and the Board of Admiralty', *MM*, XII (1926), pp. 137–8. Aylmer, *Crown's Servants*, p. 87.

22. PL 2849, p. 435. Sainty, *Admiralty Officials*, p. 131. D. Bonner-Smith, 'The Admiralty building', *MM*, IX (1923), p. 272. J.P.W. Ehrman, *The Navy in the War of William III, 1698–1697* (Cambridge, 1953), p. 197.

Notes

23. Bodl. MS Rawlinson A. 172, f. 141v. *Further Corr.*, pp. 272–5, 283–5, 286–7, 330–2. Ranft, 'Political career of Samuel Pepys', pp. 370–1. Henning, *The Commons 1660–90*, III, pp. 226–7.
24. Grey, *Debates*, V, p. 388. *Naval Minutes*, p. 356 and *passim* as used in Ranft, 'Political career of Samuel Pepys', pp. 373–5.

Chapter Seven

1. Evelyn, *Diary*, III, p. 620. C.R. Boxer, 'Some second thoughts on the third Anglo-Dutch War, 1672–1674', *TRHS*, 5th ser. XIX (1969), pp. 78–80, 85–7. PL 1226(1,2): H. Stubbe, *A Justification of the present War against the United Netherlands* (1672), with *A Further Justification of the present War against the United Netherlands* (1673); authorship explicit only in (2). *CSPD 1672*, pp. 319–20. PL 1643: J. Hill, *The Interest of these United Provinces. Being a Defence of the Zeelanders Choice* (Middelburg, 1673). *A History of Magdalene College, Cambridge, 1428–1988*, ed. R. Hyam (Cambridge, 1994), pp. 126, 130. J.R. Tanner, *Mr Pepys* (1925), pp. 5–6. *Diary*, IV, p. 243 & nn. 1, 3. *Naval Minutes*, p. 48 & n. 4.
2. K.H.D. Haley, *William of Orange and the English Opposition, 1672–4* (Oxford, 1953), p. 146. Jones, *Anglo-Dutch Wars*, pp. 214–16.
3. *Navy White Book*, p. 134, 164, 176–82, 207, 232, 248. Tanner, *Naval MSS*, I, p. 190 n. 1; III, pp. xxx–xxxi. G.C. Pitcairn Jones, 'Midshipmen', *MM*, XL (1954), p. 214. Davies, *Gentlemen and Tarpaulins*, pp. 16, 29–32.
4. Tanner, *Naval MSS*, I, pp. 148–9, 214–15; III, pp. 26 (no. 2189), 29 (no. 2200), 336–7 (nos 3536, 3544); IV, pp. liii–lvi, 90, 100–1, 307–8. PL 2867, pp. 217–20. PL 2902, pp. 13–16 (order of 8 May 1676); text as passed to Navy Board 1 July printed by W.G. Perrin in *MM*, VIII (1922), pp. 120–2; as confirmed by James II on 13 April 1686 in PL 2867, pp. 156–61. *Br. Naval Documents*, pp. 293–5 (order of 8 May 1676, from PRO, ADM 1/5138, pp. 488–91). W.E. Mey, 'Midshipmen ordinary and extraordinary', *MM*, LIX (1973), pp. 187–9. Davies, *Gentlemen and Tarpaulins*, p. 52.
5. Davies, *Gentlemen and Tarpaulins*, pp. 40–1.
6. Tanner, *Naval MSS*, IV, pp. lxxxiii–lxxxiv, 86–7, 493–4.
7. PL 2853, ff. 231v–232, 256, pp. [*sic*] 264–5, 303. Tanner, *Naval MSS*, I, pp. 202–5; IV, pp. 535–6, 543–5. PL 2867, pp. 241–5 (order of 18 Dec., passed to Navy Board 22 Dec.), printed *Br. Naval Documents*, pp. 296–9; another copy of the order in PL 2902, pp. 17–18; extract in *Select Naval Documents*, ed. H.W. Hodges and E. A. Hughes (Cambridge, 1922), pp. 72–3. Pepys was elected Master of Trinity House 22 May 1676: Evelyn, *Diary*, IV, p. 91.
8. Tanner, *Naval MSS*, IV, p. 569. PL 2854, ff. 4v, 17v; 2855, p. 207. Bodl. MS Rawlinson A. 179, ff. 14, 70 (printed Smith, *Correspondence*, II, p. 131). *Tangier Papers*, pp. 119, 131–2.
9. PL 2867, pp. 164–7, 222–3, 477–8 (orders of 17 July 1668, 6, 19 May and 26 June 1674; other copies in PL 2902, pp. 22–3, 25–9). Tanner, *Naval MSS*, I, pp. 145–8; IV, pp. lviii–lix, 59, 173. *Br. Naval Documents*, pp. 292–3 (order of 6 May, from PRO, ADM 1/5138, p. 123).
10. *Diary*, IV, p. 7; IX, p. 257 & n. 2. *Further Corr.*, pp. 2–3. *Navy White Book*, pp. 243–4 & n. 1. Tanner, *Naval MSS*, IV, pp. 129, 162–3, 172–7. PL 2867, pp. 167–8 (order of 19 May 1675; another copy in PL 2902, pp. 29–30).
11. *Navy White Book*, pp. 113–14. *CSPD 1663–4*, p. 628; *Addenda 1660–85*, p. 133. PL 2876, p. 476 (order of 20 Jan. 1676; stoppages for neglect of duty were similarly made payable into the Chest). *Naval Minutes*, p. 76. Tanner, *Naval MSS*, I, pp. 205–7; IV, pp. 383, 400–2, 545–6. G.C. Taylor, *The Sea Chaplains: A*

History of the Chaplains of the Royal Navy (Headington, 1978), pp. 67–8, 90–6, 100–1. Davies, *Gentlemen and Tarpaulins*, pp. 20, 105–7.

12. PL 2867, pp. 161–3 (resolutions of 15 Dec. 1677), 258 (form of warrant); printed Taylor, *Sea Chaplains*, pp. 93–6. Other copies of the resolutions in PL 2902, pp. 19–20; PRO, ADM 1/5138, printed *Br. Naval Documents*, pp. 295–6. Taylor, p. 96.

13. Davies, *Gentlemen and Tarpaulins*, pp. 93, 107. Taylor, *Sea Chaplains*, pp. 97–101, 105–7. J.P. Kenyon, *The Popish Plot* (1972), p. 47. R.L. Ollard, *Pepys: A Biography* (1974), pp. 224–5, 240–3. Davies, 'Wales and Mr Pepys's Navy', p. 109.

14. B. Pool, 'Pepys and the thirty ships', *HT*, XX (1970), pp. 489–95. Fox, *Great Ships*, pp. 153–72. PL 2850, p. 155 (Tanner, *Naval MSS*, II, p. 278). Bryant, *Years of Peril*, pp. 143–56. J.D. Davies, 'The Navy, Parliament, and political crisis in the reign of Charles II', *HJ*, XXXVI (1993), pp. 271–3. S.B. Baxter, *The Development of the Treasury, 1660–1702* (1957), pp. 20–2, 27.

15. PL 2265, no. 72 (enquries about shipbuilding, Apr. 1675); cf. nos 63, 65, 66, 68, 71, 87; 2873, pp. 185–98. Chandaman, *Revenue*, pp. 31–2, 151 n. 2. D. Ogg, *England in the Reign of Charles II* (Oxford, 1934), II, pp. 535–6.

16. Ogg, *Reign of Charles II*, II, p. 542. Chandaman, *Revenue*, p. 151. PL 2870, pp. 453–69 (summarised Tanner, *Naval MSS*, I, pp. 48–53). PL 2852, pp. 345–7; printed HMC, *Lindsey* (Supp.), pp. 19–20. PL 2266, nos 109–14 . PL 2852, pp. 345–7, 380–1. PL 2266, nos 109–14 . Statute: 29 Car. II c. 1.

17. Tanner, *Naval MSS*, IV, p. 428. *Naval Minutes*, pp. 13, 318. *Navy White Book*, p. 156. Pool, 'Pepys and the thirty ships', p. 490.

18. 'The management of the royal dockyards, 1672–1678', ed. R.V. Saville, in *The Naval Miscellany*, V, ed. N.A.M. Rodger (NRS, CXXV, 1984), pp. 97–8, 107, 111, 122, 123–4, 130, 131, 136. *Navy White Book*, p. 69. Tanner, *Naval MSS*, IV, pp. xci–xcii, 429–30.

19. PL 2266, no. 116.

20. Fox, *Great Ships*, pp. 160–4, 169–70, 174–5.

21. PL 1338 (*Hampton Court*), 1339 (*Lennox*). Fox, *Great Ships*, pp. 158–9, 175. *Tangier Papers*, pp. 294, 324 and *passim*. National Maritime Museum, *The Art of the Van de Veldes* (1982), p. 114 (where the 3rd-rate in the foreground of the Younger's storm scene, now in the Birmingham City Museums and Art Gallery, is confidently identified as the *Hampton Court*); Fox (p. 164, caption to plate XXXIII opposite) notes that the similar *Captain* 'remains a possibility'. PL 2854, p. 236, cited Davies, *Gentlemen and Tarpaulins*, p. 176.

Chapter Eight

1. Grey, *Debates*, V, pp. 86–7, 91. Henning, *The Commons 1660–90*, III, p. 227. PL 2860, p. 247.

2. HMC, *Ormonde*, IV, p. 431. Tanner, *Naval MSS*, IV, pp. 612–13. J.R. Tanner, 'Pepys and the popish plot', *EHR*, VII (1892), pp. 281–90. PL 2855, p. 265. *Further Corr.*, p. 330. Davies, 'Navy, Parliament and political crisis', pp. 274–5. A. Marshall, *Intelligence and Espionage in the Reign of Charles II, 1660–1685* (Cambridge, 1994), pp. 224, 235–6.

3. *Further Corr.*, pp. 326, 328–9. J.H. Wilson, *The Ordeal of Mr. Pepys's Clerk* ([Columbus,] Ohio, 1972).

4. Henning, *The Commons 1660–90*, III, p. 227. Ogg, *Reign of Charles II*, II, pp. 576–8.

5. *Further Corr.*, pp. 330–54. Ranft, 'Political career of Samuel Pepys', pp. 371–2. Henning, *The Commons 1660–90*, III, p. 227. PL 2250(1, 2).

6. HMC, *Finch*, II, p. 40. Davies, 'Navy, Parliament, and political crisis', pp. 275–6. PL 2856, pp. 243.

7. Ogg, *Reign of Charles II*, II, p. 584–6. Miller, *Charles II*, pp. 304–5, 309. W.A. Aiken, 'The Admiralty in conflict and commission, 1679–1684', in *Conflict in Stuart England: Essays in honour of Wallace Notestein*, ed. Aiken and B.D. Henning (1960), pp. 205–6. J.D. Davies, 'Pepys and the Admiralty Commission of 1679–84', *HR*, LXII (1989), p. 35. PL 2870, pp. 409–11 (warrant for commission, and Pepys's comment on it), 413–16 (commission of 14 May 1679; also in PL 2867, pp. 236–40; 2902, pp. 50–2). Tanner, *Naval MSS*, I, pp. 57–8. *Priv. Corr.* I, pp. 4–10. *Naval Minutes*, p. 181. Sainty, *Admiralty Officials*, pp. 18, 21.

8. PL 2881, pp. 1–13. HMC, *Ormonde*, new ser. IV, pp. 507, 515. Marshall, *Intelligence and Espionage*, pp. 239, 242–3. Pepys's removal was expected in the City by 24 April: *The Letters of William Freeman, London Merchant, 1678–1685*, ed. D. Hancock (London Record Soc. XXXVI, 2002), p. 84.

9. Tanner, *Naval MSS*, II, p. 8 ; IV, pp. 664–5. PL 2856, pp. 275, 279, 282–4. HMC, *Ormonde*, IV, p. 509. Sainty, *Admiralty Officials*, pp. 130.

10. PL 2249–52 (trials); 2350, 2543 (Munden's journal); 2881–2 (Mornamont), esp. 2882, pp. 1165–6.

11. Howarth, pp. 89–90, 98–100, 115–17. Hyam, *History of Magdalene*, pp. 154–7.

12. *Diary*, IV, pp. 375–6 & n. 1; V, pp. 169, 177–8 & n. 1, 328; VII, p. 307 & n. 5; IX, p. 300 ; index (XI, p. 301) incorrectly augments references to the First Dutch War with those relating to the capture of Jamaica (1655). *Navy White Book*, pp. 20 & n. 4, 38, 203, 289–90, 356, 365, 371, 378 & n. 2, 406, 409, 418.

13. *Further Corr.*, pp. 30, 206–7. *Navy White Book*, pp. 221–30, 326.

14. *Diary*, XI, p. 26. *Navy White Book*, pp. 331, 340. J. Yeowell, 'Mr Pepys his queries', *N&Q*, 1st ser. VIII (1853), p. 341; cf. *Naval Minutes*, pp. 125–6, 157, 172 & n. 3, 185 & n. 4, 197, 368 & n. 2. E.C. Teviotdale, 'Some classified catalogues of the Cottonian Library', in *Sir Robert Cotton as Collector: Essays on an Early Stuart Courtier and his Legacy*, ed. C.J. Wright (1997), p. 198. *Further Corr.*, p. 317.

15. Howarth, p. 150. *Part Friends*, pp. 92, 94–6, 99–101, 103–30, 136–40 (also in *Priv. Corr.* I, pp. 14–21; cf. I, p. x). Evelyn, *Diary*, I, pp. 22–3; III, pp. 523 & n. 1, 550 and *passim*; IV, pp. 30, 41 & n. 1. PL 1060: Evelyn, *Navigation and Commerce, their Original and Progress* (1674); esp. pp. 96–100.

16. PL 2873, pp. 56–9, 61–2, 65–89 (printed *Part. Friends*, pp. 100–1, 103–19). A. Ciaccono, *Historia Utriusque Belli Dacici in Columna Trajani expressi* (Rome, 1616) [not PL]; cf. *Naval Minutes*, p. 261. PL 2133 (Fenton), mostly printed in *The Troublesome Voyage of Captain Edward Fenton, 1582–1583*, ed. E.G.R. Taylor (Hakluyt Soc., 2nd ser. CXIII, 1959 for 1957).

17. H. Grotius, *Mare Liberum* (1609) [not PL]. J. Selden, *Mare Clausum* (1635). Pepys retained a copy of this, the Latin first edition of Selden, and of the 1652 English translation; when the latter was reissued in 1663, Pepys was able to buy new preliminary pages with the original dedication to Charles I, substituting them for those which had honoured the Commonwealth: PL 2048, 2131(1). *Diary*, II, pp. 233–4 & n. 1, and *passim*; IV, pp. 105 & n. 2, 107 & n. 3. *Naval Minutes*, pp. 95, 275, 322 & n. 2, 326. *Tangier Papers*, pp. 315, 316. PL 419(1): L. de Baïf, *De Re Navali Libellus* (Lyons, 1537). PL 1763: Baïf, *Annotationes . . . in quibus tractatur de Re Navali* (Paris, 1549), with MS inscription in French on the rarity of this book and its illustrations. PL 2446: C.B. Morisot, *Orbis Maritimi sive Rerum in Mari et Littoribus Gestarum Generalis Historia* (Dijon, 1643); cf. *Naval Minutes*, pp. 67, 363. PL 2678: G. Fournier, *Hydrographie, contenant la Theorie et la Pratique de toutes les parties de Navigation* (2nd edn, Paris, 1667); cf. *Diary*, IX, p. 17 & n. 5; *Naval Minutes*, p. 50 & n. 7, and *passim*; *Tangier Papers*, p. 153 & n. 2. Fournier, *Fortifications, ou Architecture Militaire* (Paris, 1650) [not PL]. PL 1842: (1) F. Dassie, *L'Architecture Navale* (Paris, 1677), bound with (2) *Description d'un Navire Royal* [1667]. PL 2220: N. Witsen, *Aeloude en*

Hedendaegsche Scheeps-bouw en Bestier (Amsterdam, 1671). *Naval Minutes*, pp. 127, 183, 363, 370. The suggested identification of Evelyn's 'de Witesen' as the mathematical author Johann de Wit (*Part. Friends*, p. 95 n. 4) can be discounted. R. Dudley, *Dell'Arcano del Mare* (Florence, 1646–7) [not PL]; cf. *Naval Minutes*, pp. 224 & n. 3, 239, 240, 351, 354, 419; cf. Kaufman, *Conscientious Cavalier*, pp. 116–17. PL 2643, p. 69.

18. *The Anthony Roll of Henry VIII's Navy*, ed. C.S. Knighton and D.M. Loades (Navy Records Society, Occasional Publications, II, 2000). Howarth, p. 102. Matthews, *Charles II's Escape*, p. 80. *Sir Frederic Madden at Cambridge*, ed. T.D. Rogers (Cambridge Bibliographical Soc., Monograph no. 9, 1980), p. 23.

19. *Priv. Corr.* I, pp. 10–14. *CSPD 1679–80*, p. 190. P. Le Fevre, 'John Tyrrell (1646–1692): A Restoration naval captain', *MM*, LXX (1984), p. 151. Howarth, pp. 126–7, 133–7.

20. *Priv. Corr.* I, pp. 139–40. *Part. Friends*, pp. 151–2. *Tangier Papers*; with (pp. 379–449) text of Pepys's Tangier Journal superior to that printed in Howarth. Routh, *Tangier*, pp. 258–9. R. L[uckett], 'A sea-change: Samuel Pepys and the evacuation of Tangier', *Magdalene College Magazine & Record*, XLIII (1998–9), pp. 40–9. J. Carswell, *The Descent on England: A Study of the English Revolution of 1688 and its European Background* (1969), p. 167 & n.

21. P.G. Le Fevre, 'Tangier, the Navy and its connection with the Glorious Revolution of 1688', *MM*, LXXIII (1987), pp. 187–90. Davies, *Gentlemen and Tarpaulins*, pp. 191–6, citing further and unpublished work by Le Fevre, said (p. 195 n. 123) to contain 'important examples of Pepys and his friends manufacturing or distorting evidence'. Davies's own conclusion (p. 195) is that Pepys's Tangier papers are 'emphatically not an accurate account of Arthur Herbert's command'.

Chapter Nine

1. *Tangier Papers*, pp. 216, 218–19, 221–2, 244–5. Davies, *Gentlemen and Tarpaulins*, pp. 191, 196–8. Howarth, pp. 167–9. Bodl. MS Rawlinson A. 190, ff. 113, 115. PL 2867, pp. 40–8; 2879, p. 225.

2. Davies, *Gentlemen and Tarpaulins*, pp. 187–8. *CSPD 1684–5*, p. 41.

3. PL 2857, pp. 1–3, 100–1, 170. *CSPD 1684–5*, p. 34. PL 1490, p. 2; 1534, pp. 8, 12. Hodges and Hughes, *Select Naval Documents*, pp. 81–2 (from Pepys, *Memoires*, pp. 47–9). HMC, *Ormonde*, VII, p. 264.

4. PL 1490, pp. 1–10, 81–121; 1534, p. 51. Tanner, *Naval MSS*, I, pp. 66–75. PL 1490 collects most of the papers relating to the establishment of the 1686 Commission, and (pp. 7–79) Pepys's 'Diary' of its proceedings. PLB 83, pp. 1–53 contains another set of the formal documents, and (pp. 4, 19) two items not in PL 1490; see C.S. Knighton, 'Some Pepysian addenda at Magdalene College, Cambridge', *MM*, LXXXVI (2000), pp. 152–4 (with some corrections to *Modern MSS*, pp. 10–12, 13, but itself vitiated by giving Pepys's budget as '£40,000' for '£400,000').

5. PL 1490, pp. 127–90, 224–6, 351–4; 2867, pp. 64–141. PLB 52; 83, p. 4. In his published account Pepys prints a mere list of shipwrights, which he claims led James to recall Deane: *Memoires*, pp. 52–3 (ed. Tanner, pp. 28–30). The 'characters' (from PL 1490, pp. 145–52) are given in Chappell, *Pepys as a Naval Administrator*, pp. 19–20. HMC, *Downshire*, I, pp. 151, 166–7.

6. *CSPD 1685*, pp. 79 (no. 339), 119 (no. 492), 123 (no. 512). HMC, *Buccleuch*, I, pp. 341–2. Ranft, 'Political career of Samuel Pepys', p. 373. PL 2929: F. Sandford, *The History of the Coronation of . . . James II* (1687), pl. 18.

7. PL 2823 (report of Special Commission 1687). Supply: 1 Jac. II cc. 1, 3–5. Chandaman, *Revenue*, pp. 257, 260. Davies, 'Pepys and the Admiralty Commission', pp. 51–2.

Notes

8. PL 1490, pp. 361–7, 369–82; 2824 (report of Special Commission 1688); abstract (p. 27) compared with that for previous year (PL 2823, p. 43). Pepys, *Memoires*, pp. 206–7 (ed. Tanner, pp. 126–7) (similar abstract 18 Dec. 1688, when of 173 ships, 92 were at or ready for sea, 66 in harbour and repaired, 8 under repair, 3 awaiting repair, and 4 newly come in and awaiting appraisal; these figures apply two months after those at the dissolution of the Commission given by Tanner, *Naval MSS*, I, pp. 94–5). Cf. Ehrman, *Navy in the War of William III*, p. 206 n. 4. Collinge, *Navy Board Officials*, p. 18.
9. PL 1490, pp. 383–6. J.R. Jones, *The Revolution of 1688 in England* (1972), p. 28.
10. PL 1490, pp. 388–413, 415–29, 431–45. Tanner, *Naval MSS*, I, pp. 92–7. Ehrman, *Navy in the War of William III*, pp. 202–10. Davies, 'Pepys and the Admiralty Commission', pp. 37–8.
11. Tanner, *Pepys and the Royal Navy*. Chappell, *Pepys as a Naval Administrator*. Aitken, 'Pepys and the Admiralty Commission', p. 38. Davies, 'Pepys and the Admiralty Commission', esp. pp. 35–8, 41–2, 49, summarised in his *Gentlemen and Tarpaulins*, p. 189.
12. Pepys, *Memoires*, pp. 6, 14 (ed. Tanner, pp. 4, 8). Davies, 'Pepys and the Admiralty Commission', pp. 43–4. Hornstein, *Restoration Navy*, pp. 11–24.
13. PL 2902, pp. 84–7 (prohibition of plate carriage, 15 July 1686; another copy in PL 2867, pp. 245–52; printed Pepys, *Memoires*, pp. 102–26 (ed. Tanner, pp. 55–68). Tanner, *Naval MSS*, I, pp. 210–13. Bodl. MS Rawlinson A. 171, ff. 154–156v. Davies, *Gentlemen and Tarpaulins*, p. 184. N.A.M. Rodger, in the forthcoming second volume of his *Safeguard of the Sea*; I am much obliged to Professor Rodger for sending me a draft section of his text.
14. J.D. Davies, 'James II, William of Orange, and the Admirals', in *By Force or Default: The Revolution of 1688–1689*, ed. E. Cruickshanks (Edinburgh, 1989), p. 102. *Part. Friends*, p. 186. Howarth, pp. 198–9. E.B. Powley, *The English Navy in the Revolution of 1688* (Cambridge 1928), *passim*.
15. Bodl. MS Rawlinson A. 171, f. 143r–v. Powley, *English Navy in the Revolution*, p. 15. Davies, *Gentlemen and Tarpaulins*, pp. 203–6.
16. PL 2861, pp. 304, 350, 368, 386, quoted in J.R. Tanner, 'Naval preparations of James II in 1688', *EHR*, VIII (1893), p. 273, 274–5. Powley, *English Navy in the Revolution*, pp. 21, 28. Jones, *Revolution of 1688*, p. 258. PL 2877, pp. 336–54 (*Modern MSS*, p. 145). Davies, *Gentlemen and Tarpaulins*, p. 205; *idem*, 'James II, William of Orange and the Admirals', pp. 83–5. HMC, *Dartmouth*, I, pp. 139–41. Carswell, *Descent on England*, pp. 181n, 190n. C. Jones, 'The Protestant wind of 1688: myth and reality', *European Studies Review*, III (1973), pp. 209–10. J.L. Anderson, 'Prince William's descent upon Devon, 1688: the environmental constraints', in *Lisbon as a Port Town, the British Seaman, and other maritime themes*, ed. S. Fisher (Exeter, 1988), pp. 40–1.
17. PL 2862, pp. 252, 254 267, 283, 297, 298, quoted in Tanner, 'Naval preparations of James II', p. 278–80. HMC, *Dartmouth*, I, pp. 170–4, 178–80, 181–4. Powley, *English Navy in the Revolution*, pp. 70–3, 78–9, Jones, 'Protestant wind', pp. 210–16.
18. Pl 2862, pp. 311, 312, 315, 319, 337, 344, 347, quoted in Tanner, 'Naval preparations of James II', pp. 280–2. HMC, *Dartmouth*, I, pp. 184–7, 192–8. Carswell, *Descent on England*, p. 190n. The original document presented by Pepys to the King is now in private hands: C. Tomalin, *Samuel Pepys: The Unequalled Self* (2002), p. 348 & n. 32 (on pp. 448–9) and pl. 45. I am grateful to Mrs Tomalin for sharing with me her discovery of the original, though we remain sharply at odds about its interpretation. Cf. *Naval Minutes*, p. 272 & n. 1.
19. PL 2862, pp. 445, 457–8, quoted in Tanner, 'Naval preparations of James II', p. 283. *Part. Friends*, p. 186 n. 3. Powley, *English Navy in the Revolution*, pp. 134–7, 141. Jones, *Revolution of 1688*, p. 305.
20. *CSPD 1687–9*, p.379 (no. 2091). R. Beddard, *A Kingdom without a King* (Oxford, 1988), pp. 68, 76, 170, 178. HMC, *Dartmouth*, I, pp. 226–7, 228–9. Powley, *English Navy in the Revolution*, pp. 142–6, 150. PL 2862, pp. 469, 470, 472. Tanner, 'Naval preparations of James II', p. 283. Carswell, *Descent on England*, p. 218.

Notes

21. J.P.W. Ehrman, 'The official papers transferred by Pepys to the Admiralty by 12 July 1689', *MM*, XXXIV (1948), p. 260.

Chapter Ten

1. D. Bonner-Smith, 'Samuel Pepys and York Buildings', *MM*, XXIV (1938), pp. 230–5. PL 1399(6): *A Second Modest Enquiry into the Causes of the Present Disasters in England* (1690), p. 19. Evelyn, *Diary*, V, pp. 27, 30. *Priv. Corr.*, I, p. 32. HMC, *Finch*, II, p. 333.
2. Ehrman, 'Official papers transferred by Pepys', with (pp. 263–70) inventories. *Priv. Corr.*, I, 168–9, 354. Bodl. MS Rawlinson A. 186; *Catalogi Codicum Manuscriptorum Bibliothecæ Bodleianæ*, comp. G.D. Macray (Oxford, 1862–1900), V, i, pp. 208–16.
3. *Part. Friends*, pp. 216–17, 219. F. Hendriks, 'Samuel Pepys and the reconstruction of the Royal Navy, 1678–88', *N&Q*, 7th ser. VII (1889), pp. 81–2, prompting several comments (pp. 196–7, 274–5, 315–16, 398) about two printings then identified of the *Memoires* of 1690. Pepys's copy (PL 1143) is Wing P1449 (without printer's name); there are two versions with differing full imprints (Wing P1450, 1450A). PL 2643, p. 93. N.M. Plumley, 'The Royal Mathematical School, Christ's Hospital', *HT*, XXIII (1973), pp. 582–3, 587. PL 2612 (Christ's Hospital papers). PL 2140(2): *Copie de las cedulas reales que . . . Don Carlos segundo . . . mando expedir para la fundacion del Colegio, y Seminario . . . en Seuila, para la ensenanca, y erudicion . . . en la arte maritime* (Seville, 1681). *Tangier Papers*, pp. 228, 256–7. Tomalin, *Pepys*, pp. 363–4.
4. PL 2866 (Naval Minutes); ed. Tanner (1926), pp. 58, 88, 105, 147, 153, 231, 418.
5. PL 2643 (Bibliotheca Nautica, and related correspondence). *Maps*, pp. xv, 40. PL 2800: *The Marriners Mirrour . . . by . . . Luke Wagenar . . . for the use of Englishmen by Anthony Ashley* (1588); cf. *Diary*, IV, p. 240 & n. 1; *Naval Minutes*, pp. 347–50. *Priv. Corr.* I, p. 145.
6. *Priv. Corr.* I, pp. 109, 134–5 (also *Part. Friends*, p. 260), 201. Cf. Tomalin, *Pepys*, p. 333.
7. F. Sidgwick, 'General Introduction', in *Bibliotheca Pepysiana*, I, *Printed Books to 1558*, by E.G. Duff (1914), pp i–ix. Missing is PL 825 (list of the fleet during the Third Dutch War): *Modern MSS*, p. 3. Knighton, 'Pepysian addenda', pp. 150–1.
8. *Diary*, VII, pp. 214 & n. 4, 242, 258. Bodl. MS Rawlinson A. 200–7.
9. PL 1: G. Brouscon, [tide tables] (Conquet, 1546); facsimile ed. D. Howse (1980).
10. PL 2797: E. Bernard, *Catalogi Librorum Manuscriptorum Angliæ et Hiberniæ* (Oxford, 1697), II, pp. 207–10. Howarth, pp. 244–6, 251. *Diary*, I, p. lxxiv; the publication history of the Diary follows (pp. lxxv–xcvi). Knighton and Loades, *Anthony Roll*, p. 5.
11. R.W. Ladborough, 'The Library of Samuel Pepys', *HT*, XVII (1967), p. 479. M. Oppenhiem, *A History of the Administration of the Royal Navy . . . 1509 to 1660* (1896, repr. 1988), author's preface, and introduction to the reprint by K.R. Andrews, n.p. *Letters and Papers of Professor Sir John Knox Laughton, 1830–1915*, ed. A.D. Lambert (NRS, CXLIII, 2002), pp. 105, 109 & n. 1; cf. p. 111.
12. PL 2849–62 (Admiralty Letters); Tanner, *Naval MSS*, II (1904), III (1909). Cf. Lambert, *Laughton Papers*, p. 220.
13. PL 2940–1 (Registers of the Royal Navy, and of Sea Officers); Tanner, *Naval MSS*, I (1903), pp. 153–435. Tanner, *Pepys and the Royal Navy* (1920). PL 2865 (Admiralty Journal); Tanner, *Naval MSS*, IV (1923); users should note Tanner's explanation (p. viii) that while much of his edition is transcribed *verbatim*, some routine entries (though he does not say which) are his own abstractions. PL 2866 (Naval Minutes), ed. Tanner (1926). Tanner, *Sea MSS* (1914). Knighton, *Modern MSS* (1981).
14. PL 2502–4 (State Papers): HMC, *Pepys* (1911). PL 2265–6 (Naval Papers collected for Parliament); *Modern MSS*, pp. 41–55.

15. PL 1490 (Diary Naval); 2823–4 (Commission reports); *Modern MSS*, pp. 10–12, 89–90. PL 2242 (Report to the Duke of York, 1668); *Modern MSS*, pp. 38–9. PL 2554 (Pepys's Defence, 1669–70); *Modern MSS*, p. 68. PL 2867 (Precedents); *Modern MSS*, pp. 98–106. PL 2902 (Day Collection); *Modern MSS*, pp. 169–71.

16. PL 1788 (Hosier); *Modern MSS*, pp. 16–17. PL 977 (Battine); *Modern MSS*, pp. 3–4. PL 2910 (Deane); ed. B. Lavery (1981). PL 2899 (Bolland); *Modern MSS*, pp. 168–9. PL 2555–6 (Narbrough); *Modern MSS*, pp. 68–9. PL 2698 (Holmes); *Modern MSS*, pp. 85–6.

17. PL 1461 (Libel); *Cat. PL*, V, *Manuscripts*, i, *Medieval*, comp. R. McKitterick and R. Beadle (Woodbridge, 1992), pp. 15–16; replacing the entry in the earlier catalogue (*Medieval Manuscripts* ed. M.R. James (1923), pp. 12–13). PL 2991 (Anthony Roll); printed Knighton and Loades, *Anthony Roll*; for the binding see *Cat. PL*, VI, *Bindings*, comp. H.M. Nixon (Woodbridge, 1984), pp. xxiii–xxiv, 44, and pl. 22. PL 2820 (Fragments); see M. Blatcher, 'Chatham dockyard and a little-known shipwright, Matthew Baker (1530–1613), *Archaeologia Cantiana*, CVII (1989), pp. 155–72. PL 2269 (*Libro de cargos*); *Modern MSS*, pp. 55–7. PL 2806 (Ubaldini); *Maps*, p. 40 (no. 188); *Modern MSS*, p. 88. Cf. PL 1077(11): P. Ubaldini, *A Discourse concerninge the Spanishe fleete . . . 1588* (1590). PL 2021 (Project for defence, c. 1690); *The Expedition of Sir John Norris and Sir Francis Drake to Spain and Portugal, 1589*, ed. R.B. Wernham (NRS, CXXVII, 1988), pp. 295–6 (extract).

18. PL 2869–80 (Miscellany); *Modern MSS*, pp. 106–59. PL 2869, pp. 51–185 (Pett); *The Autobiography of Phineas Pett*, ed. W.G. Perrin (NRS, LII, 1918). Sainty, *Admiralty Officials*, p. 96.

19. PL 2877, esp. pp. 270A, 285–90, 365–6, 402–36. C.S. Knighton and T.H. Wilson, 'Serjeant Knight's discourse on the cross and flags of St George (1678)', *AntJ*, LXXXI (2001), pp. 351–90.

20. Bodl. MS Smith 53, p. 63. *Letters of Eminent Literary Men of the Sixteenth, Seventeenth, and Eighteenth Centuries*, ed. H. Ellis (Camden Soc. XXIII, 1843), p. 260. S.L. Adams, 'The Armada correspondence in Cotton MSS Otho E VII and E IX', *The Naval Miscellany VI* (NRS, forthcoming), using material from PL 2876 and 2878. I am grateful to Dr Adams for kindly sending me a draft of his reconstruction.

21. PL 1077–80 (Sea Tracts), 32 titles including: M. Cortés, *The Arte of Navigation* (1584); W. Bourne, *A Regiment for the Sea* (1592); T. Hood, *The Marriners Guide* (1592); R. Norman, *The New Attractive* (1585); W. B[orough], *A New Discourse of the Variation of the Compass* (1585); S. Forman, *The Groundes of Longitude* (1591); [R. Kayll], *The Trades Increase* (1615); J. Dee, *A Letter . . . of the Philosophicall Studies* (1599). PL 1477 (Kayll, 'Trade's Decrease'); cf. *Naval Minutes*, p. 424. PL 1399 (Naval Pamphlets), 16 titles, including *The Account . . . of the engagement at Sea . . . June the 30th. 1690* (1691) [Beachy Head]; *An Account of the late great Victory . . . by Admiral Russell* (1692) [La Hogue]; [G. Savile, Marquess of Halifax], *A rough Draught of a new Model at Sea* (1694) [ascribed to Harley in MS contents list supplied by Pepys's clerk]; P. Osborne, Marquess of Carmarthen, *A Journal of the Brest-expedition* (1694).

22. PL 822: N. Butler, *Six Dialogues about Sea-Services* (1685). PL 1365: J. Narbrough, *An Account of Several late Voyages & Discoveries to the South and North* (1694); dedications printed H.B. Wheatley, *Pepysiana* (1899), pp. 59–60, and *Maps*, p. 17; cf. *Part. Friends*, p. 241. Pepys contributed sections on naval dockyards to Edmund Gibson's revision of Camden's *Britannia* (1695: PL 2807), pp. 134, 230, 359; cf. preface (sig. a), repr. in D.C. Douglas, *English Scholars* (1939), p. 335.

23. [In addition to works already cited] *Letters of Samuel Pepys and his Family Circle*, ed. H.T. Heath (1955). C. Marburg, *Mr Pepys and Mr Evelyn* (1935).

24. Lambert, *Laughton Papers*, p. 217 (A.T. Mahan to Laughton). Allin, *Journals*, I, p. 258. J. Collier, *A Supplement . . . to the Dictionary* (1705), quoted *Diary*, I, p. xxxix.

Bibliography

Works are published in London or by issuing societies except where otherwise specified. Printed books mentioned merely as held (or not) in the Pepys Library, are not included; nor are sources for modern quotations heading chapters

(i) *Manuscripts*
Cambridge, Magdalene College, Pepys Library
Library MSS (numbered with printed volumes in a single series)
Unofficial MSS (numbered with other material after prefix PLB)

London, British Library
Additional MSS
Harleian MSS
Sloane MSS

London, Public Record Office
ADM 106 (Navy Board correspondence)
PC 2 (Privy Council Registers)
SP 12 (State Papers Domestic, Elizabeth I)
SP 14 (State Papers Domestic, James I)
SP 29 (State Papers Domestic, Charles II)
SP 46 (State Papers Domestic, Supplementary)

Oxford, Bodleian Library
Rawlinson MSS
Smith MSS

(ii) *Printed primary sources, contemporary works, and catalogues*
Adams. S.L., 'The Armada correspondence in Cotton MSS Otho E VII and E IX', *The Naval Miscellany*, VI (NRS, forthcoming)
Anderson, R.C. (ed.), 'Naval preparations in the latter part of the year 1666', *The Naval Miscellany*, III, ed. W.G. Perrin (NRS, LXIII, 1928), pp. 1–47
—— (ed.), *The Journal of Edward Montagu, First Earl of Sandwich, Admiral and General at Sea, 1659–1665* (NRS, LXIV, 1929)
—— (ed.), *The Journals of Sir Thomas Allin, 1660–1678* (NRS, LXXIX, LXXX, 1939–40)
Aranda, E. d', *The History of Algiers and its Slavery . . . English'd by John Davies of Kidwelly* (1662)
Beddard, R., *A Kingdom without a King* (Oxford, 1988)
Bédoyère, G. de la (ed.), *Particular Friends: The Correspondence of Samuel Pepys and John Evelyn* (Woodbridge, 1997)
Berkeley of Stratton, Lord (J. Berkeley), *Memoirs* (1699)

Bibliography

Bernard, E. (comp.), *Catalogi Librorum Manuscriptorum Angliæ et Hiberniæ* (Oxford, 1697)

Brailsford, M.R., *The Making of William Penn* (1930)

Braybrooke, Lord (R. Neville) (ed.), *Memoirs of Samuel Pepys, esq. F.R.S. . . . comprising his Diary . . . and a Selection of his Private Correspondence* (1825)

Brewer, J., J. Gairdner and R.H. Brodie (ed.), *Letters and Papers, Foreign and Domestic, of the Reign of Henry VIII* (1862–1932)

Calendar of State Papers, Domestic Series

Calendar of State Papers Venetian

Calendar of the Patent Rolls

Chappell, E. (ed.), *Shorthand Letters of Samuel Pepys* (Cambridge, 1933)

—— (ed.), *The Tangier Papers of Samuel Pepys* (NRS, LXXIII, 1936)

Christie, W.D. (ed.), *Letters addressed from London to Sir Joseph Williamson while Plenipotentiary at the Congress of Cologne in the years 1673 and 1674* (Camden Soc., new ser. VIII, IX, 1874)

Cockburn, J.S. (ed.), *Calendar of Assize Records: Kent Indictments, Charles II, 1676–1688* (1997)

Dasent, J.R. (ed.), *Acts of the Privy Council of England*, new ser. (1890–1907)

de Beer, E.S., 'Reports of Pepys's speech in the House of Commons, March 5th, 1668', *MM*, XIV (1928), pp. 55–7

—— (ed.), *The Diary of John Evelyn* (1955)

Dunton, J., *A True Iournall of the Sally Fleet, with the Proceedings of the Voyage* (1637)

Ellis, E., *Original Letters of Eminent Literary Men of the Sixteenth, Seventeenth, and Eighteenth Centuries* (Camden Soc. XXIII, 1843)

Evelyn, J., *Navigation and Commerce, their Original and Progress* (1674)

Firth, C.H. (ed.), *Memoirs of the Life of Colonel Hutchinson . . . by his widow Lucy* (1885)

—— (ed.), *Naval Songs and Ballads* (NRS, XXXIII, 1908)

Grey, A. (ed.), *Debates of the House of Commons, from the year 1667 to the year 1694* (1769)

Hancock, D. (ed.), *The Letters of William Freeman, London Merchant, 1678–1685* (London Record Soc. XXXVI, 2002)

Hattendorf, J.B. *et al.* (ed.), *British Naval Documents, 1204–1960* (NRS, CXXXI, 1993)

Heath, H.T. (ed.), *The Letters of Samuel Pepys and his Family Circle* (Oxford, 1955)

Hill, J., *The Interest of these United Provinces. Being a Defence of the Zeelanders Choice* (Middelburg, 1673).

Historical Manuscripts Commission:

    Calendar of the Manuscripts of the Marquess of Ormonde, K.P., preserved at Kilkenny Castle, new series (1902–20)

    The Manuscripts of J. Eliot Hodgkin, esq., F.S.A., of Richmond, Surrey (1897)

    The Manuscripts of the Earl of Dartmouth (1887–96)

    Report on the Manuscripts of Allan George Finch, esq., of Burley-on-the-Hill, Rutland, (1913–22)

    Report on the Manuscripts of the Duke of Buccleuch and Queensberry, K.G., K.T., preserved at Montagu House, Whitehall (1899–1903)

    Report on the Manuscripts of the Marquis of Downshire, preserved at Easthampstead Park, Berks. (1924–42)

    Report on the Pepys Manuscripts, preserved at Magdalene College, Cambridge, ed. E.K. Purnell (1911)

    Supplementary Report on the Manuscripts of the late Montague Bertie, twelfth Earl of Lindsey, formerly preserved at Uffington House, Stamford, Lincolnshire, A.D. 1660–1702, ed. C.G.O. Bridgeman and J.C. Walker (1942)

Hodges, H.W., and E.A. Hughes (ed.), *Select Naval Documents* (Cambridge, 1922)

Howarth, R.G. (ed.), *Letters and the Second Diary of Samuel Pepys* (1933)

Bibliography

James, M.R. (comp.), *Bibliotheca Pepysiana. A Descriptive Catalogue of the Library of Samuel Pepys*, III, *Medieval Manuscripts* (1923)

Journals of the House of Commons

Journals of the House of Lords

Knighton, C.S. (comp.), *Catalogue of the Pepys Library at Magdalene College, Cambridge*, V, *Manuscripts*, ii, *Modern* (Woodbridge, 1981)

——, 'Some Pepysian addenda at Magdalene College, Cambridge', *MM*, LXXXVI (2000), pp. 148–56

——, and D.M. Loades (ed.), *The Anthony Roll of Henry VIII's Navy* (NRS, Occasional Publications, II, 2000)

——, and T.H. Wilson, 'Serjeant Knight's discourse on the cross and flags of St George (1678)', *AntJ*, LXXXI (2001), pp. 351–90

Lambert, A.D. (ed.), *Letters and Papers of Professor Sir John Knox Laughton, 1830–1915* (NRS, CXLIII, 2002)

Latham, R.C. (ed.), *Catalogue of the Pepys Library at Magdalene College, Cambridge* (Woodbridge and Cambridge, 1978–94)

——, *Samuel Pepys and the Second Dutch War: Pepys's Navy White Book and Brooke House Papers* (NRS, CXXXI, 1995)

——, and W. Matthews (ed.), *The Diary of Samuel Pepys* (1970–83)

Lavery, B. (ed.), *Deane's Doctrine of Naval Architecture, 1670* (Greenwich, 1981)

Lloyd, W., *A Sermon at the Funeral of Sir Edmund Berry-Godfrey* (1678)

Macray, G.D. (comp.), *Catalogi Codicum Manuscriptorum Bibliothecæ Bodleianæ* (Oxford, 1862–1900)

Marburg, C., *Mr Pepys and Mr Evelyn* (Oxford, 1935)

Marsden, G. (ed.), *Documents relating to Law and Custom of the Sea*, II, *A.D. 1649–1767* (NRS, L, 1946)

Matthews, W. (ed.), *Charles II's Escape from Worcester* (1967)

McGowan, A.P. (ed.), *The Jacobean Commissions of Enquiry, 1608 and 1618* (NRS, CXVI, 1971)

McKitterick, R., and R. Beadle (comp.), *Catalogue of the Pepys Library at Magdalene College, Cambridge*, V, *Manuscripts*, i, *Medieval* (Cambridge, 1992)

Mun, T., *England's treasure by forraign trade* (1663)

Norrington, R., *My Dearest Minette: The Letters between Charles II and his sister Henrietta, Duchesse d'Orléans* (1996)

Œconomy of His Majesty's Navy Office, The (1717)

Ollard, R.L. (ed.), *Clarendon's Four Portraits* (1989)

Oppenheim, M. (ed.), *The Naval Tracts of Sir William Monson* (NRS, XXII–III, XLIII–IV, XLVII, 1902–14)

Penn, G., *Memorials of the Professional Life and Times of Sir William Penn* (1833)

Penrose, B. (ed.), *The Barbary Voyage of 1638 . . . from the original Manuscript of Sir George Carteret* (privately printed, Philadelphia, 1929)

Pepys, S., *Memoires relating to the State of the Royal Navy of England, for ten years determin'd December 1688* (1690) [repr. in quasi-facsimile ed. J.R. Tanner (1906), q.v.]

Perrin, W.G., *The Autobiography of Phineas Pett* (NRS, LI, 1918)

——, 'Midshipmen extra and volunteers', *MM*, VIII (1922), pp. 120–2

Powell, J.R., and E.K. Timings (eds), *Documents relating to the Civil War, 1642–1648* (NRS, CV, 1963)

Powell, J.R., and E.K. Timings (eds), *The Rupert and Monck Letter Book 1666* (NRS, CXII, 1969)

Robbins, C. (ed.), *The Diary of John Milward, Esq., Member of Parliament for Derbyshire (September 1666 to May 1668)* (Cambridge, 1938)

Rogers, T.D. (ed.), *Sir Frederic Madden at Cambridge* (Cambridge Bibliographical Soc.

monograph no. 9, 1980)

Rose, S. (ed.), *The Navy of the Lancastrian Kings* (NRS, CXXIII, 1982)

Sandford, F., *The History of the Coronation of . . . James II* (1687)

Saville, R. (ed.), 'The management of the royal dockyards, 1672–1678', in *The Naval Miscellany*, V, ed. N.A.M. Rodger (NRS, CXXV, 1984), pp. 94–142

Second Modest Enquiry into the Causes of the present Disasters in England, A (1690)

Sells, A.L.(ed.), *The Memoirs of King James II: His Campaigns as Duke of York, 1642–1660* (1962)

Smith, J. (ed.), *The Life, Journals, and Correspondence of Samuel Pepys, Esq. F.R.S.* (1841)

Stubbe, H., *A Further Justification of the present War against the United Netherlands* (1673)

——, *A Justification of the present War against the United Netherlands* (1672)

Syrett, D., and R.L. DiNardo (ed.), *The Commissioned Sea Officers of the Royal Navy, 1660–1815* (NRS Occasional Publications, I, 1994)

Tanner, J.R. (ed.), *A Descriptive Catalogue of the Naval Manuscripts in the Pepysian Library at Magdalen College, Cambridge* (NRS, XXVI–VII, XXXVI, LV, 1903–23)

—— (ed.), *Bibliotheca Pepysiana. A Descriptive Catalogue of the Library of Samuel Pepys*, I, *"Sea" Manuscripts* (1914)

—— (ed.), *Further Correspondence of Samuel Pepys, 1662–1679* (1929)

——, *Pepys' Memoires of the Royal Navy, 1679–1688* (Oxford, 1906)

——, *Private Correspondence and Miscellaneous Papers of Samuel Pepys, 1679–1703* (1926)

——, *Samuel Pepys's Naval Minutes* (NRS, LX, 1926)

——, *Two Discourses of the Royal Navy, 1638 and 1659, by John Holland; also, a Discourse of the Navy, 1660, by Sir Robert Slingesbie* (NRS, VII, 1896)

Taylor, E.G.R. (ed.), *The Troublesome Voyage of Captain Edward Fenton, 1582–1583* (Hakluyt Soc., 2nd ser. CXIII, 1959 for 1957)

Tyacke, S. (comp), 'Maps', in *Catalogue of the Pepys Library at Magdalene College, Cambridge*, IV, *Music, Maps and Calligraphy* (Cambridge, 1989), [section ii, separately paginated]

Wernham, R.B. (ed.), *The Expedition of Sir John Norris and Sir Francis Drake to Spain and Portugal, 1589* (NRS, CXXVII, 1988)

Wing, D. (comp.), *Short-Title Catalogue of Books printed in England, 1641–1700*, 2nd edn by J.J. Morrison, C.W. Nelson ad M. Seccombe (New York, 1972–98)

Yeowell, J., 'Mr Pepys his queries', *N&Q*, 1st ser. VIII (1853), p. 341.

(iii) *Secondary works*

Aiken, W.A., 'The Admiralty in conflict and commission, 1679–1684', in *Conflict in Stuart England: Essays in honour of Wallace Notestein*, ed. Aiken and B.D. Henning (1960), pp. 203–25

Albion, R.G., *Forests and Sea Power: The Timber Problem of the Royal Navy* (Harvard Economic Studies, XXXIX, Cambridge, Mass. 1926)

Albion, R.G., 'The timber problem of the Royal Navy, 1652–1862', *MM*, XXXVIII (1952), pp. 4–21

Anderson, J.L., 'Prince William's descent upon Devon, 1688: the environmental constraints', in *Lisbon as a Port Town, the British Seaman, and other maritime themes*, ed. S. Fisher (Exeter, 1988), pp. 37–55

Anderson, R.C., 'The royalists at sea in 1648', *MM, IX* (1923), pp. 34–46

Andrews, K.R., *Ships, Money and Politics: Seafaring and Naval Enterprise in the reign of Charles I* (Cambridge, 1991)

Aylmer, G.E., *The Crown's Servants: Government and Civil Service under Charles II, 1660–1685* (Oxford, 2002)

——, *The King's Servants: The Civil Service of Charles I, 1625–1642* (2nd edn, 1974)

Baldridge, H.A., 'Ship models: the collections of Rogers, Sergison and Pepys', *Proceedings of the*

United States Naval Institute, LXIV (1938), pp. 1553–66

Balleine, G.R., *All for the King: The Life Story of Sir George Carteret (1609–1690)* (St Helier, 1976)

Baumber, M.L., 'Parliamentary naval politics 1641–49', *MM*, LXXXII (1996), pp. 398–408

Baxter, S.B., *The Development of the Treasury, 1660–1702* (1957)

Bell, W.G., *The Great Plague in London* (2nd edn, 1994)

Blatcher, M., 'Chatham dockyard and a little-known shipwright, Matthew Baker (1530–1613), *Archaeologia Cantiana*, CVII (1989), pp. 155–72

Bonner-Smith, D., 'Samuel Pepys and York Buildings', *MM*, XXIV (1938), pp. 226–36

——, 'The Admiralty building', *MM*, IX (1923), pp. 271–82

Boxer, C.R., 'Some second thoughts on the third Anglo-Dutch War' 1672–1674', *TRHS*, 5th ser. XIX (1969), pp. 67–94

Brooks, F.W., 'William de Wrotham and the office of Keeper of the King's Ports and Galleys', *EHR*, XL (1925), pp. 570–9

Bryant, A., *Samuel Pepys: The Man in the Making* (1933)

——, *Samuel Pepys: The Saviour of the Navy* (1938); reissued with epilogue as *Pepys and the Revolution* (1979)

——, *Samuel Pepys: The Years of Peril* (1935)

Callender, G.A.R., 'Sir John Mennes', *MM*, XXVI (1940), pp. 276–85

Callow, J., *The Making of King James II* (Stroud, 2000)

Capp, B.S., *Cromwell's Navy: The Fleet and the English Revolution, 1648–1660* (Oxford, 1989)

——, 'Naval operations', in *The Civil Wars: A Military History of England, Scotland, and Ireland 1638–1660*, ed. J.P. Kenyon and J.H. Ohlmeyer (Oxford, 1998), pp. 156–91

Carswell, J., *The Descent on England: A Study of the English Revolution of 1688 and its European Background* (1969)

Chaplin, W.R., 'The history of Harwich lights and their owners', *The American Neptune*, XI (1951), pp. 5–34

Chappell, E., *Samuel Pepys as a Naval Administrator: A Lecture delivered to the Hull Historical Association on the 29th September 1933* (Cambridge, 1933)

Childs, J., *The Army of Charles II* (1976)

Chandaman, C.D., *The English Public Revenue, 1660–1688* (Oxford, 1975)

Clowes, W.L., *The Royal Navy: A History from the Earliest Times to 1900* (1897–1903)

Coleman, D.C., 'Naval dockyards under the later Stuarts', *Economic History Review*, 2nd ser. VI (1953–4), pp. 134–55

Collinge, J.M. (comp.), *Navy Board Officials, 1660–1832* (Office-Holders in Modern Britain, VII, 1978)

Cooke, A.L., 'Did Dryden hear the guns ?', *N&Q*, CXCVI (1951), pp. 204–5

Cooper, E.R., *Memories of Bygone Dunwich* (2nd edn, Southwold, 1948)

Corbett, J.S., *Drake and the Tudor Navy* (1898)

Davies, C.S.L., 'The administration of the Royal Navy under Henry VIII: the origins of the Navy Board', *EHR*, LXXX (1965), ppp. 268–88

Davies, J.D., *Gentlemen and Tarpaulins: The Officers and Men of the Restoration Navy* (Oxford, 1991)

——, 'James II, William of Orange, and the Admirals', in *By Force or Default: The Revolution of 1688–1689*, ed. E. Cruickshanks (Edinburgh, 1989), pp. 82–108

——, 'Pepys and the Admiralty Commission of 1679–84', *HR*, LXII (1989), pp. 34–53

——, 'The Navy, Parliament and political crisis in the reign of Charles II', *HJ*, XXXVI (1993), pp. 271–88

——, 'Wales and Mr. Pepys's Navy', *Cymru a'r môr/Maritime Wales*, XI (1987), pp. 101–11

Dewar, A.C., 'The naval administration of the interregnum 1641–59', *MM*, XII (1962) pp.

406–30

Dictionary of National Biography Douglas, D.C., *English Scholars* (1939)

Dyer, F.E., 'Captain Christopher Myngs in the West Indies', *MM*, XVIII (1932), pp. 168–87

Ehrman, J.P.W., *The Navy in the War of William III, 1689–1697* (Cambridge, 1953)

——, 'The official papers transferred by Pepys to the Admiralty by 12 July 1689', *MM*, XXXIV (1948), pp. 255–70

Elder, J.R., *The Royal Fishery Companies of the Seventeenth Century* (Glasgow, 1912)

Feiling, K.G., *British Foreign Policy, 1660–1672* (1968)

Firth, C.H., 'Sailors of the Civil War, the Commonwealth and the Protectorate', *MM*, XII (1926), pp. 239–59

Fox, F.L., *A Distant Storm: The Four Days' Battle of 1666* (Rotherfield, 1996)

——, *Great Ships: The Battlefleet of King Charles II* (Greenwich, 1980)

Franklin, J., *Navy Board Ship Models, 1650–1750* (1989)

Fraser, P., *The Intelligence of the Secretaries of State & their Monopoly of Licensed News, 1660–1688* (Cambridge, 1956)

Glasgow, T., jnr, 'Maturing of naval administration, 1556–1564', *MM*, LVI (1970), pp. 3–23

Greene, G., *Lord Rochester's Monkey: Being the Life of John Wilmot, Second Earl of Rochester* (2nd edn, 1976)

Hainsworth, R., and C. Churches, *The Anglo-Dutch Naval Wars, 1652–1674* (Stroud, 1998)

Haley, K.H.D., *William of Orange and the English Opposition, 1672–4* (Oxford, 1953)

Hendriks, 'Samuel Pepys and the reconstruction of the Royal Navy, 1678–88', *N&Q*, 7th ser. VI (1889), pp. 81–2; with responses *ibid.*, pp. 196–7, 274–5, 315–16, 398

Henning, B.D. (ed.), *The House of Commons, 1660–1690* (History of Parliament, 1983)

Hornstein, S.R., *The Restoration Navy and English Foreign Trade, 1674–1688: A Study in the Peacetime Use of Sea Power* (Aldershot, 1991)

Hoskins, S.E., *Charles the Second in the Channel Islands* (1854)

Hutton, R., *Charles II: King of England, Scotland, and Ireland* (Oxford, 1989)

——, *The Restoration: A Political and Religious History of England and Wales, 1658–1667* (Oxford, 1985)

Hyam, R. (ed.), *A History of Magdalene College, Cambridge, 1428–1988* (Cambridge, 1994)

Jackson, G., and G.F. Duckett, *Naval Commissioners: From 12 Charles II. To 1 George III., 1660–1760* (privately printed, 1889)

James, G.F., and J.J.S. Shaw, 'Admiralty administration and personnel, 1619–1714', *BIHR*, XIV (1936–7), pp. 10–24, 166–8

Johns, A.W., 'Sir Anthony Deane', *MM*, XI (1925), pp. 164–93

——, 'The Constant Warwick', *MM*, XVIII (1932), pp. 254–66

——, 'The Principal Officers of the Navy', *MM*, XIV (1928), pp. 33–54

Jones, C., 'The Protestant wind of 1688: myth and reality', *European Studies Review*, III (1973), pp. 201–21

Jones, J.R., *The Anglo-Dutch Naval Wars of the Seventeenth Century* (1996)

——, *The Revolution of 1688 in England* (1972)

Kaufman, H.A., *Conscientious Cavalier: Colonel Bullen Reymes, M.P., F.R.S., 1613–1672* (1962)

Kennedy, D.E., 'Naval captains at the outbreak of the English Civil War', *MM*, XLVI (1960), pp. 181–98

——, 'The English naval revolt of 1648', *EHR*, LXXVII (1962), pp. 247–56

——, 'The establishment and settlement of Parliament's Admiralty, 1642–48', *MM*, XLVIII

(1962), pp. 276–91

Kenyon, J.P., *The Popish Plot* (1972)

Kitson, F.E., *Prince Rupert: Admiral and General at Sea* (1998)

Ladborough, R.W., 'The library of Samuel Pepys', *HT*, XVII (1967), pp. 476–82

Le Fevre, P., 'John Tyrrell (1646–1692): a Restoration naval captain', *MM*, LXX (1984), pp. 149–59

——, 'Monck: St James's Day Fight, 1666', in *Great Battles of the Royal Navy*, ed. E. Grove (1994) pp. 47–54

——, 'Tangier, the Navy and its connection with the Glorious Revolution of 1688', *MM*, LXXIII (1987), pp. 187–90

Livermore, H.V., *A New History of Portugal* (Cambridge, 1969)

Loades, D.M., *The Tudor Navy: An Administrative, Political and Military History* (Aldershot, 1992)

Lockyer, R., *Buckingham: The Life and Political Career of George Villiers, First Duke of Buckingham, 1592–1628* (1981)

Luckett, R., 'A sea-change: Samuel Pepys and the evacuation of Tangier', *Magdalene College Magazine & Record*, XLIII (1998–9), pp. 40–9

Mahan, A.T., *The Influence of Sea Power upon History, 1660–1783* (1965 edn)

Marshall, A., *Intelligence and Espionage in the Reign of Charles II, 1660–1685* (Cambridge, 1994)

Mey, W.E. 'Midshipmen ordinary and extraordinary', *MM*, LIX (1973), pp. 187–92

Martin, C., and G. Parker, *The Spanish Armada* (1988)

Millar, O.N., *The Queen's Pictures* (1977)

Miller, J., *Charles II* (1991)

National Maritime Museum, *The Art of the Van de Veldes: Paintings and Drawings by the great Dutch marine artists and their English followers* (1982)

Norman, P., 'Pepys and Hewer', *Occasional Papers published for members of the Samuel Pepys Club*, ed. Norman, II (1925 for 1917–23), pp. 53–77

Ogg, D., *England in the Reign of Charles II* (Oxford, 1934)

Ollard, R.L., *Cromwell's Earl: A Life of Edward Montagu, 1st Earl of Sandwich* (1994)

——, *Man of War: Sir Robert Holmes and the Restoration Navy* (1969)

——, *Pepys: A Biography* (1974)

Oppenheim, M., *A History of the Administration of the Royal Navy and of Merchant Shipping in relation to the Navy from 1509 to 1660* (1896, repr. with introduction by. K.R. Andrews, Aldershot, 1988)

Padfield, P., *Maritime Supremacy and the Opening of the Western Mind: Naval Campaigns that shaped the Modern World, 1588–1782* (1999)

Perrin, W.G., 'The Lord High Admiral and the Board of Admiralty', *MM*, XII (1926), pp. 117–44

Pincus, S.C.A., 'Popery, trade and universal monarchy: the ideological context of the outbreak of the Second Anglo-Dutch War', *EHR*, CVII (1992), pp. 1–29

——, *Protestantism and Patriotism: Ideologies and the Making of English Foreign Policy, 1650–1668* (Cambridge, 1996)

Pitcairn Jones, C.G., 'Midshipmen', *MM*, XL (1940), pp. 212–19

Plumley, N.M., 'The Royal Mathematical School, Christ's Hospital', *HT*, XXIII (1973), pp. 581–7

Pool, B., *Navy Board Contracts, 1660–1832* (1966)

——, 'Pepys and the thirty ships', *HT*, XX (1970), pp. 489–95

——, 'Samuel Pepys and Navy contracts', *HT*, XIII (1963), pp. 633–41

——, 'Sir William Coventry: Pepys's mentor', *HT*, XXIV (1974), pp. 104–11

Porter, S., *The Great Fire of London* (Stroud, 1996)

Powley, E.B., *The English Navy in the Revolution of 1688* (Cambridge, 1928)

Bibliography

Ranft, B. McL., 'The significance of the political career of Samuel Pepys', *Journal of Modern History*, XXIV (1952), pp. 368–75

Richmond, C.F., 'English naval power in the fifteenth century', *History*, LII (1967), pp. 1–15

Rodger, N.A.M., *The Admiralty* (Lavenham, 1979)

——, *The Safeguard of the Sea: A Naval History of Britain*, I, *660–1649* (1997)

——, *The Wooden World: An Anatomy of the Georgian Navy* (2nd edn, 1988)

Rogers, P.G., *The Dutch in the Medway* (Oxford, 1970)

Routh, E.M.G., *Tangier: England's Lost Atlantic Outpost* (1912)

Sainty, J.C. (comp.), *Admiralty Officials, 1660–1870* (Office-Holders in Modern Britain, IV, 1975)

Seaward, P., 'The House of Commons committee of trade and the origins of the second Anglo-Dutch war', *HJ*, XXX (1987), pp. 437–52

Shaw, J.J.S., 'The Commission of Sick and Wounded and Prisoners, 1664–1667', *MM*, XXV (1939), pp. 306–19

Shelley, R.J.A., 'The division of the English fleet in 1666', *MM*, XXV (1939), pp. 178–96

Shrewsbury, J.F.D., *A History of Bubonic Plague in the British Isles* (Cambridge, 1971)

Sidgwick, F., 'General Introduction', in *Bibliotheca Pepysiana*, II, *Early Printed Books to 1558*, by E.G. Duff (1914), pp. i–ix

Tanner, J.R., *Mr Pepys: An Introduction to the Diary, together with a Sketch of his Later Life* (1925)

——, 'Naval preparations of James II in 1688', *EHR*, VIII (1893), pp. 272–83

——, 'Notes on Pepys's *Admiralty Journal* of 1674–9', *MM*, IX (1923), pp. 110–14

——, 'Pepys and the popish plot', *EHR*, VII (1892), pp. 281–90

——, 'Pepys and the Trinity House', *EHR*, XLIV (1929), pp. 573–87

——, *Samuel Pepys and the Royal Navy* (Cambridge, 1920)

Taylor, G.C., *The Sea Chaplains: A History of the Chaplains of the Royal Navy* (Headington, 1978)

Teviotdale, E.C., 'Some classified catalogues of the Cottonian Library', in *Sir Robert Cotton as Collector: Essays on an Early Stuart Courtier and his Legacy*, ed. C.J. Wright (1997), pp. 194–207

Thompson, G.M., *Sir Francis Drake* (1972)

Tomalin, C., *Samuel Pepys: The unequalled Self* (2002)

Trease, G., *Samuel Pepys and his World* (1972)

Vale, V., 'Clarendon, Coventry, and the sale of naval offices, 1660–8', *CHJ*, XII (1956), pp. 107–25

Wheatley, H.B., *The Diary of Samuel Pepys M.A. F.R.S.*, Supplementary Volume, *Pepysiana* (1899)

Williamson, J.A., *Hawkins of Plymouth* (2nd edn, 1969)

Wilson, C., *Profit and Power: A Study of England and the Dutch Wars* (Cambridge, 1957)

Wilson, J.H., *The Ordeal of Mr. Pepys's Clerk* ([Columbus,] Ohio, 1972)

Young, M.B., *Service and Servility: The Life and Work of Sir John Coke* (Woodbridge, 1986)

Index

Peers, holders of courtesy titles, and bishops are indexed under their family names; titles and offices are as held during the time referred to, except for later attainments by which some individuals are better known

Index

Index